P9-CFI-512

THOSE EXTRAORDINARY BLACKWELLS

ALSO BY ELINOR RICE HAYS

Morning Star: A Biography of Lucy Stone

NOVELS (BY ELINOR RICE)

The Best Butter

Action in Havana

Mirror, Mirror

Take the Cash

ELINOR RICE HAYS

Those Extraordinary Blackwells

THE STORY OF A JOURNEY TO A
BETTER WORLD

Harcourt, Brace & World, Inc., New York

First edition
Library of Congress Catalog Card Number: 67-19200
Printed in the United States of America

To my family:

Jacquie, and Paul W., and Joel, too,

this portrait of a family,

in fulfillment of a promise long delayed

ACKNOWLEDGMENTS

This book would not be complete without an expression of gratitude to the many people who have helped to make it possible, and who have become my friends along the way. Edna Lamprey Stantial, while the Alice Stone Blackwell Archives were in her possession, offered me her hospitality and unlimited access to the manuscripts, including permission to microfilm many of them. My thanks go also to her husband, Guy Stantial, for his inexhaustible patience at my invasion of his home. Miriam Holden has given me the use of her excellent library of books about women, and this has involved my repeated intrusion into her busy life.

The Blackwell descendants have been kind, generous, helpful. I am especially indebted to Lane Blackwell, who from far-off England arranged to have me meet his parents in nearby Massachusetts. The Howard Blackwells received me in their home, and Mr. Blackwell submitted to a two-day interview spoken into a tape recorder thoughtfully provided by his son George Blackwell. During part of this time Mrs. Anna Belden assisted us with her lively recollections. Mrs. Ethel Whidden has sent me invaluable family documents and photographs, and has added her interesting personal memories.

Librarians have a degree of tolerance, intelligence and cooperativeness rarely found in combination in any other segment of the population. I am afraid I have caused many of them endless trouble, and have received in exchange nothing but courteous and competent assistance.

To Diana Trilling, who painstakingly read the manuscript and made invaluable detailed comments, my thanks. To my husband, Paul R. Hays, my sympathy and appreciation for repeated readings throughout the long process, for support in moments of crisis, and for making it possible for me to trace the footsteps of itinerant Blackwells through Europe.

CONTENTS

LIST OF ILLUSTRATIONS

(*Between pages 174 and 175*)

". . . it will be a great good bought at a terrible price,
but progress must always pay a tax to the Devil. . . ."

—Dr. Emily Blackwell, June 11, 1861

FOREWORD

As in the world of science two experimenters often arrive at the same discovery at the same time, so in the social world a climate becomes right for the gestation of a new way of thought or life. In the western world, the nineteenth century had such a climate.

Reform was made newly necessary by the development of machinery, of masses changed almost overnight from hand workers with skills to machine workers who seemed infinitely replaceable, to be worn out quickly and as quickly supplanted. Men—and women and children too—were no more than units for use as parts of machines, and less highly valued than mechanical, and often more expensive, parts.

This necessity for reform gave birth to the revolutions of 1848 in Europe, to the struggle, usually peaceful, for social improvement in England, to the vast surge of radical movements which were, it seemed, indigenous to the United States, and which continued to flourish and expand. Antislavery, woman's rights, moral reform, Utopian colonies had their advocates, dogged, articulate, unafraid. Like William Lloyd Garrison, they said, "I am in earnest. I will not equivocate; I will not excuse; I will not retreat a single inch; and I will be heard."

Women, who had been the silent and suppressed half of the

human race, who were not protected by men's laws or respected in their councils, suddenly awoke and spoke—loud. In the nineteenth century such an evolution was difficult, but it was at least feasible, as it would not have been earlier.

The new climate made possible such rebellious women as Lucy Stone, one of the earliest feminists, Antoinette Brown, the first ordained woman minister, and the five Blackwell sisters. Elizabeth Blackwell was the first woman doctor with a bona fide medical degree, her sister Emily shortly followed her into the medical profession, and the other three were rebels and "new" women. That these seven women should have been found not only in the same group of reformers but, by birth or marriage, in the same family, is certainly curious.

In that family circle, they form, as it were, a microcosm of their time in the world of rebellion and the coming to birth of a new era for women. Perhaps a study of their problems and the resolutions they achieved will cast more general light on the story of the social pioneers of their day, of the gains they made and the price they paid for being innovators. Perhaps it will lend some insight into the problems which modern women have inherited from this breakthrough into freedom.

THOSE EXTRAORDINARY BLACKWELLS

CHAPTER ONE

When Samuel Blackwell and Hannah Lane were married on September 27, 1815, in Bristol, England, Bristol was, as it is today, a flourishing port, where great ships came from the sea, up the wide mouth of the Severn into the center of the city. It must have been a picturesque town before twentieth-century progress and twentieth-century bombings turned it into a place almost wholly new. Of its earlier charm there remain such relics as the ancient cathedral and the Lord Mayor's chapel on College Green, and St. Mary Redcliffe, which Queen Elizabeth I called the loveliest church in England and which, according to tradition, Samuel Blackwell and two friends saved from burning at the hands of rioters in the Corn Law uprisings of 1831.

Because to be legal a marriage had still to be performed by a minister of the Church of England, Hannah and Samuel were married at St. James Church, a venerable structure dating from 1129. But Samuel Blackwell was a Liberal in politics and a Dissenter in religion, and attended chapel, not church, in the very city where John Wesley had established his first chapel less than a hundred years before. And when later Hannah was asked by her brother whether as children they had been baptized, she answered that they could not have been because their mother was a Methodist.

Hannah's family, on her mother's side at least, were well thought of and well-to-do; but Hannah's mother had made an unfortunate marriage, and when Hannah was eight, her father, a watchmaker and jeweler, was convicted of forgery, and sent to Australia instead of to the gallows only because of family influence. After his involuntary departure, Hannah's mother supported her young family by opening a millinery shop, an unusual venture for a lady in those days.

Whether or not it was the influence of her father's disgrace, Hannah Lane Blackwell was the most moral and religious of women. Her none-too-frequent letters to her children after they were grown and away from home were crammed with recommendations for attaining bliss in the life hereafter instead of helpful suggestions about the life of here and now, though they would vastly have preferred the latter and were certainly in greater need of it. No more moral group ever existed than the Blackwell children, and it is hard to imagine how their mother, who had reason enough to worry about their earthly happiness, could possibly have been apprehensive about their salvation.

Hannah and Samuel set up housekeeping at 11 St. James Parade, also known as Kingsdown, next door to Hannah's rich relatives "Uncle and Aunt Browne," who had taken Hannah in after her mother died and who would never, except of necessity, have consented to her church wedding, because they were pillars of the same Bridge Street Chapel which the Blackwell family later attended. Anna, Hannah's eldest child, remembered the Browne home as a place of "handsome and hospitable substantiality, a sort of superior sphere," and Uncle Henry Browne, after whom one of Hannah and Samuel's sons was named, as "one of the last in Bristol to give up the pig-tail." He also "wore breeches, black silk stockings, and silver buckled shoes," and when they later lost their money, Aunt Browne "spent her whole time darning his silk stockings." [1]

The house in which the newly married couple lived still stands, a house with that tan stone front so characteristic of the region of Bristol and nearby Bath. Below it was Mother Pugsley's Field, now reduced to a small square in a busy city, but in those days a "great green expanse sloping down . . . to the beautiful open coun-

[1] **Notes are on pages 311 to 323.**

try beyond,"[2] a favorite spot for Bristol outings. In its center was a well, widely believed to have magical curative powers.

Of the Blackwell home's interior furnishings there remains only the Royal Worcester china which Samuel gave his wife as a wedding gift. It was a tea and coffee service of fifty pieces which the young couple went to Worcester to order. Family tradition states that Samuel wished to have a plain set and Hannah an elegant one, and that the china they bought was a compromise. If so, it is hard to imagine the ornamentation of the set they rejected, for Hannah's delightful choice is edged with gold and covered with a red-and-blue design of a Chinese pagoda and bridge over a pond full of water lilies with birds above and flowers round about. The china seems to have been Hannah's rare protest against a life which, by her own choosing, was otherwise empty of frivolity.

Into this predominantly sober household on June 21, 1816, their first child, Anna, "came poking into this troubled world a month before [she] was due," because Hannah had been hanging curtains "in defiance of prudence."[3] The family grew rapidly. Samuel's parents had had nine children, seven of whom lived to maturity. But Samuel and Hannah outdid them. In sixteen years Hannah gave birth to thirteen children, of whom nine survived.

The nine survivors were Anna, Marianne, later shortened to Marian, Elizabeth, known to the family as Bessie, Samuel, Henry, Emily, Sarah Ellen, who became Ellen, John Howard, called Howic, and George Washington. Whatever profession they later engaged in, and all but two became known far beyond the family circle, they shared a literary bent. They left their history behind. Most, in their early years, kept diaries. Nearly all were prolific letter writers at a time when letters were the sole conveyors of intimate communication, recording vital statistics and minor happenings in those days before the telephone became the most intimate of confessors, and the events of everyday life were spoken and lost. Of the Bristol days there are Elizabeth's published recollections and Anna's volume-long reminiscences written to her brother Henry almost fifty years after they had left the city of their birth.

Samuel Blackwell was a sugar refiner, and for his greater convenience, when Anna was still a tiny girl, the family moved from charming Kingsdown to a house next door to Father's sugar refinery, which backed on the wharves along the "filthy little Frome" river. The street, known as Counterslip, was almost entirely an industrial area. When the Blackwells lived there, countrywomen brought fruit into town in huge baskets which they set down on the pavement's edge. "Two-pence a quart for strawberries in those days." [4] Future moves to Wilson Street and Nelson Street followed Papa's sugar-refining ventures, the move to Nelson Street taking place, in fact, when the Wilson Street factory burned down. In these places their residences were next to, or attached to, the factory buildings. Anna complained that this led them to live in dirty and unhealthy neighborhoods, but that, because of lack of hygienic knowledge, this was not considered important.

"I remember the cries of the watchman on his rounds, crying the hours, with some stereotyped addition of a religious character, and a heavy thump of his cudgel on the pavement, to strike terror into the hearts of malefactors, by showing that he had wherewithal to pound them if they came in his way." She also remembered being "stroked on the head by Mrs. Thrale, Dr. Johnson's friend." [5] And "hearing the proclamation of the coronation of Wm 4th and of seeing the procession." [6]

For the most part though, Anna's recollections were private, and concerned a childhood "most unhappy, uncomfortable, unsympathetic." "I utterly detest everything connected with my constrained, held in, undeveloped girlhood!" she told her brother Henry. With some justification, apparently, for their religious training included stories of the devil waiting to snatch bad children, stories which so frightened her that she used to wake screaming in the night.

There was a far sadder tale of a baby brother, John Howard, born when Anna was just fourteen and whom she adored with adolescent fervor. The baby died one night when he was six months old. Next morning Mamma came in when Anna was still asleep, and awakened her by announcing that it has "pleased God to take our little Howard in the night." Such cruelty in an undoubtedly loving and stricken mother can only be explained by religious beliefs which then and afterward dwelt on the wickedness of this life and the joys of the other. But to Anna, at fourteen, it was bitter treatment indeed, leaving her no confidence in divine love and destroying whatever hope remained of maternal understanding.

Before the funeral, she kept going into the room where the

beautiful little body lay, and could observe, or thought she could, signs of gradual decomposition. The sad story ended when, on the way to the funeral, she and twelve-year-old Marian "held the little coffin between us on our knees in a mourning coach." Or perhaps not quite ended. Less than a year later another John Howard was born, and to him Anna transferred the abundance of her lost love.

The most constant irritant in the Blackwell family, and not only to Anna, was Grandpapa Blackwell. He was an opinionated and cantankerous man who could never hold a job for long, who privately treated his wife and children, as men were able to do in those days, like chattels, and publicly humiliated them. He never, Anna said, spent a cent on "a day's schooling for any of his children," and only their native intelligence and energy provided them with any education.

Grandfather insisted on attending Bridge Street Chapel, apparently to annoy his family. The minister, Mr. Leifchild, wore a sweeping black gown with a snowy band which Grandpapa abhorred as "unscriptural, a relic of the Scarlet Woman." But instead of attending another chapel, the old man hired the front pew, where he would "throw himself back . . . staring right into Mr. Leifchild's face," and make "inaudible snorts . . . looking the very incarnation of hostile and bitter criticism." [7]

Grandfather's one passion was carpentry. Unlike Papa, who "always wore black, with a white cravat . . . of fine muslin, one yard and a half square . . . which was put on clean every day," Grandpapa affected to dress like a common carpenter, humiliating the children by his "dirty appearance, covered with bits of shavings, his white hair full of dust, and his vulgar corduroy breeches." [8]

No one had a lower opinion of Grandpapa Blackwell than his pretty, gentle wife. Anna remembered, too well perhaps, Grandmamma's warnings that girls ought to be careful about listening to men's blandishments, "seeing that all *that* ceases when they'd got a woman to marry them, and then the poor girl found what a dreadful master marriage had given her." [9] Those who remained single were wisest, she said. In Grandmother's terms her female descendants were wise indeed. Only one of her four daughters married, and that one did not surrender until middle life. None of her five granddaughters ever married.

In their youth, however, her daughters were not without marital opportunities. One story illuminates with a single ray their attitude toward marriage and their religious rigidity. It was Samuel's favorite sister, probably Mary, who disagreed with the man she loved on methods of baptism. She believed in sprinkling, he in immersion. So citing the text, "Be ye not unequally yoked together with unbelievers," she unhappily rejected him, and never afterward married.

Anna thought the Blackwells much inferior to the Brownes. "Our Blackwell relations . . ." she told Henry, "were only *not vulgar* because entirely without pretensions. Nature made Papa a gentleman and Aunt Mary a lady; they had nothing but their name in common with the rest of the family."[10] Inevitably Papa had to support the entire family, though his sisters made continuous, rather pathetic efforts to help themselves. Aunt Mary tried for a while to run a boys' school, which of course Samuel and Henry had to attend. Aunt Ann, well-meaning, ignorant and ugly, opened a girls' school in her home—listed in the Bristol Directory for 1825 as 11 Duke Street—and Marian and Anna were "sacrificed to [her] horrid school in which Aunts Barbara and Lucy took part at one time."[11] They were taken out of school when the family moved to Wilson Street and Aunt Barbara became the children's governess.

According to Anna, "Aunt Bar" was a tyrant, ill-tempered, strict, narrow-minded; she adored Marian and Henry, but detested and persecuted the other children, and quarreled constantly with Mamma, who, nevertheless, charitably kept her on. She seems to have loved Henry for his wavy hair, which she curled every morning with such success that passers-by would stop on the street to say he was "a beauty." For such flattery Mamma had a standard answer. "'Yes, Mamma's babies are always pretty; but unfortunately they are like pig's babies, that grow uglier every day!' which was intended to take down any disposition to vanity that might be developed." Mamma herself was exceedingly pretty, but so little was made of the fact that, when a visitor commented that she was the same lovely creature as ever, Anna took his remark as a somewhat unkind joke.

The children's pride was further reduced by allowing Aunt Lucy, "small, kindly and null," to make nearly everything they wore, "sacrificing [them] utterly . . . for the sake of putting a little money into her pocket." The "miserably ugly" and "often shabby" clothes were intended to keep the children "free from vanity and love of finery." [12]

Later Marian and Anna escaped from Aunt Barbara only to be sent to a boarding school in nearby Clevedon, where they learned nothing and were half starved. Papa, who had a reputation as a lay preacher and who liked to go around preaching in out-of-the-way places, had discovered the school one Sunday when he saw before him in the chapel at Clevedon a row of charming schoolgirls and decided, "without any inquiry as to the character of the school," to enroll his two eldest daughters for a twelve-month term. Anna, ingenious for once in her own behalf, managed somehow to get herself removed and poor Bessie "sent down to fill out the rest of the term."

History, public and private, is in the eye of the beholder. In Elizabeth's autobiography—Elizabeth was four years younger than Anna—this same childhood is glowingly described. The large family of children provided "cheerful companionship" under supervision "wise but not too rigid." Aunt Bar was "a somewhat stern though upright ruler," the unhealthy house on Nelson Street "a comfortable family home, made by throwing two houses together . . . our town residence for eight very happy years." [13] But Elizabeth admitted that, like Anna, Marian had so hated her childhood that she refused to try to remember any part of it.[14]

For Marian and Anna there was not even the compensation of an alliance of misery: they fought continuously. Marian, later the family invalid and stay-at-home, was as a child "a perfect ball of quicksilver, always in motion and full of restless activity." Henry, less bitter than Anna, less starry-eyed than Elizabeth, remembered the discipline of those years as "excessively rigorous in some respects . . . extremely lax in others." [15]

Elizabeth speaks of "the dear father, [who] with his warm affection, his sense of fun, and his talent for rhyming, represented a beneficent Providence to me from my earliest recollection." But Henry recalled that Anna was never petted by their father, that being the eldest, responsibility was forced on her long before she was ready for it. Perhaps in these sentences lies the clue to the difference in two so similar childhoods, a clue made clearer by

Anna's pathetic comment: "our excellent, most generous and affectionate Father, whose coldness of manner and austerity of ideas I see, on looking back, had begun rapidly to soften in the latter years of his life." The perception, and perhaps the change, came too late to be useful to Anna.

That their father was an unusual man his children agreed. For one thing, he believed in educating his daughters equally with his sons, an eccentricity almost unheard of, and perhaps in those days no very practical resolution. Their intellectual discipline unfitted the Blackwell girls for the future young ladies were directed to—home and husband—and set them longing to follow paths closed to them by man-made tradition, a tradition men found it highly desirable to maintain.

Yet Samuel Blackwell's political, economic and cultural liberalism was linked to a stern and demanding religion, a religion dissident from the established Church of England and therefore in its way eccentric too. Each morning he assembled the family and servants for a "horrid" reading of chapters, after which they knelt together in lengthy prayer. Anna thought "the infliction was made *before* breakfast." Sundays were spent trudging to and from Bridge Street Chapel for morning and afternoon services, and learning hymns and Bible chapters in between. There were prayer meetings in chapel on several weekday evenings too, but these the Blackwells attended only occasionally. When they went, "Papa was sure to be called upon to pray, which he did very well." Even social events turned into prayer meetings, for when a group of friends spent an evening at the Blackwell home, there usually came a moment when everyone turned to the wall and prayed, kneeling or standing as each preferred.

But Samuel Blackwell was not bigoted. Once he discovered his children reading novels, according to chapel teaching a seduction of the devil. At first he made a dreadful scene; but being induced to read *Scottish Chiefs* and *Ivanhoe,* he was so delighted that he withdrew his objections. He had a beautiful voice, and was almost as fond of reading Mrs. Sherwood's moral tales aloud to his family as he was of preaching and praying. He also liked to compose verses, and made a game of replying to his children's requests in rhyme. On one occasion the three eldest girls wrote a petition asking permission to sleep with a visiting cousin in the huge bed in the best bedroom. Papa had no more read the petition than he wrote:

> If you four little girls were together to lie,
> I fear you'd resemble the pigs in their sty!
> Such groaning! Such grunting!! such sprawling about!!!
> I could not allow such confusion and rout!!!!!
> So this is my judgment: —'tis wisdom you'll own,
> *Two* beds for *four* girls are far better than one! [16]

To all the children, the fondest memories of those early days were family outings. There were day's rambles to green Brandon Hill (still green, but now the very center of Bristol), walks over the downs or to the wild Avon gorge. They made quite a company on these excursions, with five or six adult relatives and a couple of nursemaids, because even the littlest children were always "lugged along." The bigger ones carried baskets of food; but "cake, milk, ginger-beer, etc." were bought on the way. Papa too loved these expeditions and always went along "on the rare occasions when he took a holiday." [17]

Summers were spent at nearby resorts. Sometimes they visited Uncle and Aunt Browne, who in those childhood years moved from Bristol to a beautiful country house in Bourton. Or they rented a house at Weston-super-Mare where the porous rocks along the rugged beach formed natural grottoes, over which Anna and Marian "used to hang a sheet and make their dressing room." It was a dangerous sort of swimming place. Years later Henry found that the "tide . . . came roaring up over the pebbles and seaweed in the old inspiriting way, with the old sound and smell." Yet Anna told Henry that in the early days Papa had "to the terror of the family" swum to Brean Down, "a long green hill which stretches into the channel. . . . He must," Henry commented, "have been a vigorous man and a bold swimmer, for the distance must be nearly or quite a mile." [18] So far and so dangerous it seems incredible we should hear no other examples of Samuel Blackwell's physical prowess.

Other summers they went to Clevedon, which Papa had discovered on his preaching rounds. There they rented a large house called Salt House, on a wooded cliff which stretched beyond it for a hundred yards and ended in a point far above the water. The house still stands, today a public house with remnants of its earlier charm in a lovely divided staircase leading up from the central hall. Henry found the house, when he visited it in 1879, beautifully improved. "I sat on the point and looked out over the Channel just where mother used to comb our hair and sing to us on Saturday afternoon 'Ye gentlemen of England who sit at home at ease—Ah little do ye think upon the dangers of the Seas' . . . The remembrance almost overpowered me." [19]

CHAPTER TWO

More than the children could then know, of course, their lives were bound up with their father's business success or failure, and beyond that with the economic tides that swept across England. Merrie England in the first half of the nineteenth century was not entirely dedicated to merriment. The machine age had brought with it a displacement of enormous sections of the population. Manufacturers were growing suddenly wealthy; the middle class was springing into being and into power. Skilled hand workers and farmers were degraded, when they were lucky enough to work, into tenders of the machinery which usurped their functions, men, women and children drudging from dawn until after dark, from blue Monday to blue Monday. When they were unlucky, they became paupers.

Under the poor laws, thousands of children no more than five or six years old were removed from their parents and sold in gangs to work for any master who would take them, without wages and for pitiful sub-sustenance. Charles Dickens knew from experience what debtors' prisons were; his father had spent a long period inside one. And how a man inside prison could hope to earn the money to pay his debts was one of the mysteries of the transition era.

In this period of economic and social revolution, England's conservative government continued artificially to maintain the price of grain, and as late as 1830 to defeat bills presented to Parliament for reforming the voting system. Up to this time, such popular voting as there was had been in the control of the rich landowners. The burgeoning cities were almost without representation. Indeed, when a reform bill finally passed in 1832, though it removed some representation from the landlord-controlled towns and gave it to the well-to-do middle classes in the cities, the extent of the reform can be judged by the fact that in Manchester 6,726 "ten-pound" householders out of a total of 187,022 persons attained the right to vote.[1] The electorate in England was increased from 478,000 to 814,000, or one-thirtieth of the total population.[2] And electoral remedies proved useless, since any progressive legislation passed by the representative House of Commons was efficiently suppressed in the House of Lords.

Reformers continued to talk of laissez faire, the removal of any government interference in the economy, the working of the natural laws of economics—which were also not to be interfered with by the banding together of workers to attain better pay or shorter hours. Enlightened self-interest was to be the hope of mankind. Meanwhile the self-interest of the middle classes appeared to outrun their enlightenment.

The reformers were much agitated by the existence of Negro slavery in British colonies. The slave trade had been made illegal in 1807, but slaves continued to be a profitable commodity and smuggling them a continuingly profitable business. Even before 1833, when slavery was abolished in the colonies, slaveowners were permitted to work their adult slaves only nine hours a day, and children only six. At home, functioning under the lauded natural law, workers were less fortunate than slaves. In the mines women and girls were harnessed to coal carts and crept on hands and knees along the low passages. There was no limitation on the hours they worked.

The Blackwells, Brownes and Lanes were fortunate in being members of the growing middle class. They had been shopkeepers for several generations at least. Hannah Blackwell's grandfather was a bookseller. Uncle Browne had made his money as a successful jeweler, and only lost it when, at his wife's insistence, he decided to improve his social standing by becoming a banker. Now the Blackwell family were entering into manufacturing, with its many advantages and hazards, Samuel Blackwell into the sugar business, one of Bristol's leading industries, his elder brother into iron smelting.

The fact that they were Dissenters in many respects determined their lives. Into the eighteen-twenties, though the laws against them were not as stringent as in earlier times, when not to conform to the Anglican church was a very real danger, Dissenters could not hold the highest government offices. They were excluded from the professions, and even from a university education. In this situation they developed their own lower schools, where, in fact, a far better education was available than was offered to the Anglican population.

But Samuel Blackwell's disaffection with England had been growing, and in 1832 he decided to begin life again in the New World where, in spite of the existence of slavery, the democratic process was so much further advanced, and opportunity awaited all vigorous men. Certainly Dissenters were not dissenters there, and suffered no liability. His sons, if not his daughters, could receive the benefits of higher education, enter any profession they chose, think as they liked. In later years his children assigned various causes to his decision, but one of these was always his desire to breathe the free air of the United States, his idealistic faith in the land of equality.

For a man of Samuel Blackwell's convictions, the sugar business must have been a source of endless moral questioning. Sugar, though processed by men at least nominally free, was undeniably grown by slaves in colonial regions. Elizabeth records that even in childhood she and her brothers and sisters "voluntarily gave up the use of sugar, as a 'slave product,' "[3] surely a curious protest for a family supported entirely by this same slave product, a protest which must have given their reformist father moments of sober reflection, for Anna remembered his efforts in those early Bristol days to extract sugar from beets in a commercially feasible way.

But the children were the least of their father's problems. There was Grandfather Blackwell, grown more determined in perversity as the years went by. Grandmother Blackwell, that sweet, quiet woman, had died, and without her restraining influence, the old man seemed more than ever determined to harass his son. After his wife's death, Grandfather married again. Anna comments that he began by making a slave of his second wife, an elderly widow, but that she soon betrayed him by becoming rheumatic and bedridden.[4]

Meanwhile Samuel Blackwell had set up a branch sugar house in Dublin, and placed his younger brother James in charge. James was growing increasingly insane, though no one realized it, and when the business unaccountably failed with heavy losses, Samuel believed that his brother had intentionally ruined him and, not unnaturally resentful, refused to have anything more to do with him. At this, James's paranoia directed itself against his brother Samuel and Samuel's children, some of whom he had never seen. In the course of his developing illness James wrote books on obscure doctrinal points, their titles: *A Cry in the Wilderness* and *A Howl in the Desert*. Later he became violent and almost killed his eldest brother, John, who had continued to help him.[5]

But it was not only in Dublin that things were going badly. In England a period of prosperity in the early eighteen-twenties had been followed by overexpansion, business failures and near panic. On the continent a revolutionary situation existed in the late twenties and early thirties, and in England recurrent rioting and disorders were forcibly put down by the military. By the fall of 1831 England was near revolution. One of the worst outbreaks took place in Bristol, where fury was aroused by Sir Charles Wetherell, representative of the corrupt Corporation that ruled the city. Sir Charles not only opposed the popular reform bill, but was vituperative and scornful in his opposition. When, at the end of October 1831, he returned from London to open the Assizes, he was met by mobs of furious men, who for three days overran the city. They released prisoners, burned the jails, the town hall, the bishop's palace. A few were killed and many wounded in battle with the military. St. Mary Redcliffe, according to family tradition, was saved by Samuel Blackwell and two of his friends. Henry, on his return to Bristol in 1879, noted that modern buildings had replaced those burned by "the 'mob' of 3000 men, which I well remember rush howling through Nelson St."[6]

At the time of the riots the family was vacationing in a country house in Olveston, from which each morning Papa used to drive into town in a yellow carriage driven by a grey pony named Bessie Gray in somewhat dubious tribute to daughter Elizabeth. Twice a week Anna, Marian and Elizabeth would ride with him for lessons with masters who, according to Anna, were of no great competence.

One morning when as usual they entered the city on the Gloucester Road, they were told by the keeper of a toll bridge over which they passed that mobs were rioting through Bristol, "that great alarm prevailed, and that Papa would do well to reach Nelson St. by a circuitous route, and get us under cover as quickly as possible. We girls were horribly frightened," Anna says. "I forget how we reached the house; but I remember the strange appearance of the streets, entirely deserted, shops and shutters shut, nobody visible. . . . The rioters were threatening to break into Bridewell, the jail, close by the Nelson St. house, and were in possession of all the adjoining streets." [7] Having deposited the girls behind locked doors at Nelson St., which moments later was swarming with violent mobs, Papa went off to the Guildhall to confer with other leading citizens.

Here family history wavers a bit. Anna says that now Papa and a friend "extinguished with their own hands the fire which the miscreants had commenced for burning down the grand old Cathedral"—not St. Mary Redcliffe—"for which Papa was publicly thanked when the riot was quelled." Contemporary accounts do not speak of any threat to St. Mary Redcliffe. They do say that a group of Dissenters pleaded with the mob against its vandalism, and saved the cathedral. Samuel Blackwell's is not one of the three names usually mentioned as leaders in this action, though he must have been one of the group.

The country's chaotic situation had even more immediate reality for the Blackwell family when, with the failure of two great sugar importers, Samuel lost close to seventy thousand pounds, a fortune at any time, far greater in those days when money was worth so much more. The combination of disasters made him decide that, rather than try to reconstitute his business in so perilous a situation, he would cut his moorings and set sail for the New World.

When the Bristol business community learned it was to lose one of the town's leading citizens, engaged in one of its chief industries, it was much distressed. A "sort of private-public meeting was therefore convened by some of the leading business men of the town," who passed resolutions that "they regarded the loss of such a citizen as a public calamity to the town; . . . and that they consequently pledged themselves, individually and collectively, to furnish him with any amount of capital he should consent to name, as a loan for any number of years at one and a half percent, in order to avoid the threatened loss to the town of so highly respected and useful a member of the community." [8]

In Anna's view her father had everything to gain by staying. He had been spoken of as mayor of Bristol and would probably have been chosen. But he had a "horror of owing anything to others," which had earlier caused him to leave a firm in which he might have made a fortune. He was an exceptional man, self-educated, informed on every subject, bold in the pursuit of his plans, but with an unfortunate defect of character, "an utter inability to brace himself up against unexpected difficulties." And, she comments bitterly, the man who took over the sugar house—he had started as a sugar-boiler for Papa—became a millionaire. "It is difficult . . . to comprehend how so monstrous a piece of folly as this uprooting could ever have been planned and perpetrated by a sensible man." [9]

Before they left England, a special treat was arranged for the two eldest children. Papa's elder brother, "Uncle Blackwell," had just taken a new wife, and the recently married couple were going to London. Anna, aged sixteen, and Marian, fourteen, were to spend a fortnight with them, a plan, one would think, to bring happiness to any girl's heart; but like every project of Anna's girlhood, this brought only disaster. Their strict upbringing had made the girls miserably shy, and in London they were even more unhappily conscious of their dowdy, shabby clothes. They had nothing to wear but "one plain, ugly little pelisse of black silk" each, and were therefore reluctant to go out. They even refused a dinner invitation to the home of Uncle Lowell, the husband of Mamma's only sister. And because they had promised not to sully their souls by entering a theatre, they virtuously refused an invitation to see the famous Edmund Kean in *Hamlet*. After this sad little vacation, they rejoined their family, and set sail from Bristol on the "horrid little boat" *Cosmo*.

It was a large company that boarded the *Cosmo* in August 1832, surrounded by "relations and friends gathered to bid [them] good bye." [10] Besides Papa, a pregnant Mamma and eight children—the ninth was born shortly after they reached the United States—there were three of Father's four sisters, as well as a governess and two servants.

The governess, Elizabeth Major, became an important factor in Blackwell family history, for she later married Hannah's brother Charles Lane. Some years earlier Charles, an army man, had married a rich young woman whose family had promptly disowned her. Their disapproval seemed justified when, after giving her a son and daughter, Charles left her and the children, from whom in any case he had been much separated while with his regiment in India and other far places. As early as Bristol days, and even in England, he passed himself off as a bachelor. Later he followed the Blackwells to America and, "on the mere report that his wife was dead," contracted a bigamous marriage with Elizabeth Major. Amazingly enough, he was encouraged in this dubious enterprise by his sternly religious sister and brother-in-law, who, with a most unworldly innocence, decided that in the eyes of God he was free to remarry because his wife had left him. Later Uncle Charles and Aunt Eliza lived for a long time in France, almost in hiding, for fear he would meet a fellow officer who would realize that he was accompanied by the wrong wife. But on the *Cosmo* in 1832, this bigamous wife was still Elizabeth Major and the children's governess.

In her autobiography, Elizabeth Blackwell says that they left England during a cholera epidemic, and that in the course of the long voyage several steerage passengers died of the disease; but, if so, it is a wonder that the sickness did not spread through the crowded boat, for the trip lasted seven weeks and four days. And at that they were lucky, for another ship which left the same week took twelve weeks to cross the ocean. On the *Cosmo* there were, according to Henry, some two hundred passengers, mostly in steerage, a half dozen in second class, and several family groups traveling first class. There was a cow on board to provide milk, but it died, and the passengers lived on salt beef, pork and hardtack.[11]

In spite of this, Elizabeth says that "ocean life" furnished "delightful experiences to the younger travellers."[12] Nowhere are family differences clearer, for Anna describes these delightful experiences as including "horrid, stinking, filthy" cabins in the stern, where the motion was worst, with windows almost always hatched down because of the rough seas. In the center of the cabin Anna shared with six others was an iron pillar, a drain pipe for sewage which leaked throughout the trip.

Nevertheless, whether with delight or misery, they emerged from their long voyage safely and in good health to begin life anew in a new land.

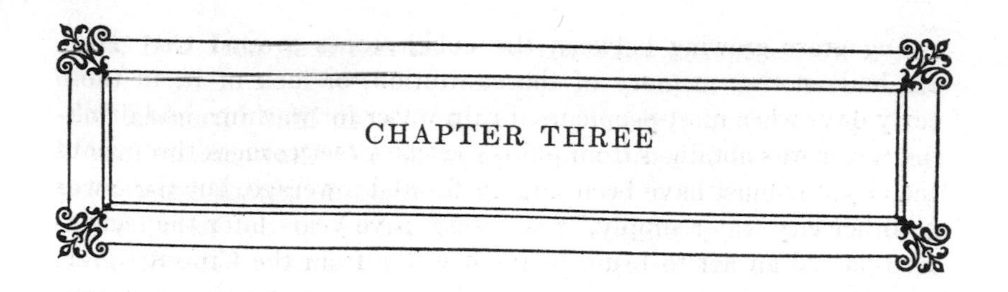

CHAPTER THREE

"Truly thrilling are the emotions with which an English Emigrant approaches these shores . . ." Samuel Blackwell wrote. "The fact that the Land before him *is* America—and . . . all his hopes and fears are about to be brought to the test . . . wonderfully affects him. Upward of two hundred emigrants crowded the sides and shrouds of our Vessel at the welcome sound of 'Land,' but amidst them all scarcely a word was uttered—the fixed and eager eye, and the gushing tear, told their feelings better than words." [1]

A cholera epidemic had afflicted England when they left, and they reached New York to find the city strangely quiet and deserted. The disease had been rampant there too, and everyone who could afford to had fled.

That summer the streets of the city were cleaned in an effort to stem the disease, and for the first time in years enough mud was washed away so that the cobblestones could be seen; but they soon disappeared again under new and unchallenged layers of filth. All American city streets were dirty but, after visiting Boston, Philadelphia and Baltimore, an anonymous gentleman announced that he had seen "nothing in the way of foul streets to compare with New York." [2] The Blackwells must have arrived shortly after the street cleaning, because Henry, who was seven at the time, recalled seeing grass growing between the cobblestones around City Hall. He had another memory of the sanitation, or lack of it, in those early days when most people used rain water for washing, and drinking water was obtained from pumps set at street corners throughout the city. "It must have been largely filtered sewerage, but there was no other city water supply," [3] he wrote. Five years later the legislature passed an act to bring in fresh water from the Croton River; and thereafter it only remained to raise the money for this enormous project.

The children's father was charmed by the natural beauty of the city and its surrounding water and forests. "It is evident at a glance," he wrote, "that Nature has done wonders for New York. If its natural advantages are wisely improved, it must become one of the most airy, healthful, and delightful of all American Cities." [4]

New York was still concentrated in the area south of Washington Square, with the fashionable residential section around the Battery. "Not more than a sixth part of the island is compactly covered with houses, stores, and paved streets," says a contemporary account. "The rest is occupied with farms and gardens. . . . The streets of the ancient parts are narrow, crooked, and irregular. . . . Broadway is a noble street, 80 feet wide and straight as an arrow, extending from the Battery northward nearly two miles." [5] In the next years a few adventurous souls like Mr. Brevoort would begin to build country houses on "the fifth avenue" just above Washington Square.

Henry remembered Papa taking them on a sleigh ride north of the Square, up "what is now Broadway—then called the Bloomingdale road—lined with country seats and villas," and further downtown crowded with pedestrians, carriages and horse-drawn omnibuses. The children must have delighted in the soda-water fountains which had become popular since the first was opened twelve years before. Sam mentions going with Papa to have soda water at "Mr. Hopper's druggist store."

The city was well provided with newspapers. Henry speaks of the *Courier and Enquirer*, the *Journal of Commerce*, and the *Commercial Advertiser*. There were quite a few more. Three years later James Gordon Bennett started a small penny paper without any political principle—without, in fact, much principle of any kind. It was called the New York *Herald*. Besides news, the *Herald* made a specialty of a spicy brand of personal gossip and scandal of a "blackmailing" [6] sort. The talents of its editor, as both a respectable and disreputable reporter, were great, and in circulation the *Herald* soon outdistanced its more conservative and expensive competitors, though it shortly doubled its price to two pennies.

The Blackwell family settled in a house at 39 Thompson Street. In this enterprise they were assisted by Dennis Harris, a Methodist preacher from Bath, by profession a bricklayer, whom they had met on board the *Cosmo,* where he and his wife had traveled steerage. Mr. Harris's "resolute, aggressive Methodism asserted among a crowd of godless passengers" had delighted Samuel Blackwell. Meeting Harris on the street some days later and learning that he was still out of work, Papa gave him a job moving the furniture the family had brought from Bristol. Later he employed the preacher as foreman in the refinery he had by then established for making "molasses sugar." [7]

Shortly after the family moved to Thompson Street, the youngest child, a boy, was born, and was inevitably named George Washington Blackwell. The rest of the family settled into ordinary living. The elder children went to day school, while the younger continued, as in England, to have lessons at home. Their parents joined the Presbyterian church around the corner on Laight Street.

Two years later there was another move, to Long Island, where the Blackwells remained for over a year. From their house three miles from Williamsburg, "between Newton and Flushing," they often drove into the city, and of course Papa continued to work in New York. They had rented "a fine old frame house in an extensive garden full of fruit and bordered by a fine row of cherry trees in full bearing, with a barn and carriage house, an orchard, and one or two clover fields and pastures." [8] Unfortunately, beyond the garden was a marsh which made the place malarious. Father Blackwell did in fact contract malaria and nearly died. He never completely recovered, nor was he ever again the sturdy, vigorous man he had been in England. It was during the Long Island period that Uncle Charles, retired from the army on half pay, arrived in the

United States and fell in love with the governess. Uncle Charles called himself Major Lane; whether the army called him Major or Captain seems to be in doubt.

When Samuel Blackwell left England, he had promised to tell his Bristol friends what the New World was like. Being a conscientious man, he made detailed notes on every aspect of American life: politics, education, newspapers, religious observances and economics from the price of food and lodging to President Jackson's "undignified" battle with the Bank of the United States. At the end of two years he had accumulated so much material that, finding it impossible to transcribe it for his many friends, he decided to revise it and publish it as a book for the aid of emigrants in general. This project he never fulfilled.

His comments, though consciously objective, necessarily reflect his own experiences and emotions. "Nothing can be more injudicious than the indiscriminate rush to America now so much in favor in England," he wrote. Newcomers "must make up their minds to 'rough it,' as the Americans say," and "a true saying" he found it. But he found too that, as a man grows accustomed "to the difficulties of life and sees the independence and comfort to which they lead, he becomes reconciled and gradually feels at home," particularly when he realizes how much better chance his children have in this new land to be educated and to do well in life.

Like every newly arrived foreigner, he found it necessary to explain the national character. "The Americans are . . . a very inquisitive people, asking questions . . . relative to the affairs and intentions of those who settle among them, with a pertinacity and perseverance not easily parried—but there is mixed with it all so much of real kindness, that impressions of an unpleasant kind soon give way." The freedom of manners, it then becomes apparent, are the "wholesome fruits of free institutions." [9]

On December 24, 1835, twelve-year-old Sam Blackwell, his father's namesake, entered the ranks of family diarists. Indeed his are the earliest of the children's contemporary jottings. Sam's highly personal diary begins shortly after they moved from Long Island to Jersey City, not then as accessible from New York as it is today. At the end of January, Sam and Henry went to New York to buy a present for Bessie's fifteenth birthday, but the river was so clogged with ice that, though they reached New York, they could not get home, and spent that night with Papa at the Congress Sugar House. Travel by water was uncertain and dangerous. The diary is full of reports of shipwrecks—in the East River, in the Hudson, along the coast. Off Rockaway, in a "dreadful tempest," "37 souls only were saved out of 123." And a few months later one hundred and eight passengers were frozen to death on a boat shipwrecked close to land.

Sam led the life of a normal adolescent, a blend of work and play. In February he won a French prize at school, and as a reward Papa gave him three dollars. He used it to buy a one-volume edition of Shakespeare, about which Elizabeth commented, "I don't much admire his choice." That summer Sam received another French prize and a prize for classical studies. Papa was invited to attend the oral examinations, at which there was quite a large audience of men and two ladies.[10]

Sam also went with other "Jersey City young gentlemen" to a party where they played kissing games. A young man chased a young lady, and if he caught her, was rewarded with a kiss. And a little later Elizabeth recorded that Mamma, Anna and Marian went to a party and that "all Jersey was there," which Mamma thought "was passing the 'line.'" Family parties were more respectable. The chief entertainment, and one the young people loved, was conundrums, riddles and enigmas. "Why is a tall servant like the marriage ceremony?" "Because she's a high menial."[11]

The family attended a summer concert in Niblo's Garden, at Broadway and Prince Street, a popular amusement center which boasted gardens, a theatre and a refreshment pavilion. A few weeks later, "in the evening," they "went to Peal's Museum to see the Siamese twins." For a while, led by Father's business associate Mr. Gower, the whole family, with varying degrees of seriousness, took up "phrenologizing." Sam reported that he was learning to play the flute. He played chess with Anna. She beat him. Papa beat him too. But Sam could sometimes beat Bessie. On December 24, 1836, he wrote, "On Christmas it is not disgusting to describe the supper, therefore I will write it down. A leg of pork, stewed oysters, turkey, mashed potatoes, mince pies, cranberry tarts, toast and ale, O glorious custom of our immortal forefathers and I suppose of our foremothers also!!!"

Surprisingly, dancing was not taboo, though theatres were. Elizabeth and Marian were to take dancing lessons, and Elizabeth planned to pay for hers with money Papa had given her for her birthday. Mamma was a graceful dancer and encouraged everyone to dance. Even those who didn't know how, she said, could at least hop around.

For more serious entertainment there were antislavery meetings and fairs, at least one of them in Niblo's Garden, for which Mamma and the girls worked. New York was a center of abolitionist activity, and from the time of their arrival, the family, already committed, entered seriously into antislavery work. But the reforming spirit was limited to a small portion of the population, and Papa, who had come to seek the land of liberty, was naïvely disappointed to discover that New York businessmen were peculiarly unaffected by the fate of the slaves. "Were it not for one dark and damning spot, the eye of the Philanthropist would rest upon this land with almost unmixed gratification." But that spot was damning indeed. There was widespread prejudice, widespread belief in the native inferiority of the Negro race, whereas the seeming inferiority was only the result of their unhappy lot. The slightest trace of Negro blood was "instantly detected by the keen, well practiced eye" of prejudice, and effectually excluded "the unfortunate individual from the white man's circle, from his schools, from his churches and from his charities." [12]

This prejudice made it easy for Northerners, with the exception of a dedicated minority, to dismiss slavery as an economic rather than a moral problem, and one which was not their concern. It was up to the South whether it had slaves or not. Even the great majority of Northern churches accepted the institution of slavery as inevitable, and disapproved, often to the point of dismissal, any clergyman's expression of abolitionist opinions. The polite form of objection to slavery was the idea that groups of slaves should be freed and sent to far-off Africa to establish settlements there. In Boston in 1835, William Lloyd Garrison was dragged out of his Anti-Slavery Society office by a mob, and threatened with lynching because of his demands for immediate emancipation; and in New York that same summer mobs attacked and gutted the houses of abolitionists, who fled for their lives. Two brothers, friends of the Blackwells, sought refuge with them in their Long Island home. Henry remembered a meeting the Blackwells attended in New York at which George Thompson, the famous English abolitionist, spoke. Englishmen were still unpopular more than twenty years after the War of 1812 had rearoused anti-British feelings; and an anti-English, antiabolitionist mob disrupted the meeting.[13]

Father Blackwell became friends with the great Garrison, who, on his New York trips, was a frequent visitor at the Blackwell home. Garrison was fond of children, and the young Blackwells were delighted with him, discovering the gaiety and warmth concealed behind his stern, sad face, his long, awkward body, his violent public demeanor and vituperative words. In her diary, Elizabeth describes a meeting in the spring of 1836. "Garrison, Judge Jay and Mr. G[errit] Smith were all there. . . . I think Mr. Smith has the finest countenance I ever saw. To our great joy Mr. Garrison came home and slept at our house . . . he quoted poetry very sweetly." The elder members of the family belonged to an Abolitionist Vigilance Committee the aim of which was to help runaway slaves reach Canada; and a few weeks after the meeting Sam reported that they had an escaped slave staying at their house for several weeks.

The young Blackwells came to know many antislavery leaders. Sam described the Reverend Samuel May as "a short, stout, healthy man and . . . full of little witticisms." The May family came to stay with them, and Marian went to visit them outside of Troy, New York. She was called for there by Mamma, Bessie and Sam, who made a vacation jaunt of the long trip up the Hudson. Theodore Dwight Weld brought the younger children home after a juvenile antislavery meeting, and stopped to visit. "He appears exceedingly pleasant," Elizabeth commented,[14] but "his *gentlemanly* appearance would be greatly increased by the regular use of a toothbrush." A year later Theodore Weld married Angelina Grimké, one of two amazing sisters, who, daughters of a wealthy Southern slave-owning family, freed their slaves, came North, and, in a day when no women spoke in public, faced the verbal onslaught of the church and the often physical violence of their audiences to bring an antislavery message to the world.

Anna, now almost twenty-one, was elected a delegate to a ladies' antislavery convention, and there appointed a member of the central committee. Papa meanwhile was working for abolition in his own way. In July 1837 a volume of *Slavery Hymns* was published anonymously. Anna suspected that Papa had written them, but when she asked, he laughed, looked wise and said nothing. Two days later, however, he presented the children with a copy of the book, which was clearly his work.

Elizabeth's diary gives a more revealing and intimate picture of family life than the younger Sam's. Events were stormy enough at times, with Anna frequently the unhappy center of the storm. Anna and Papa have had a "blowup," which so upset Marian that she burst out crying, while Sam and Elizabeth remained merely amused. On another occasion, Elizabeth mentions, as if it were entirely natural, that Anna has sent her "a most *dignified* and *severe* note of forgiveness for my past conduct, so I suppose our estrangement of more than 3 months is at an end." But surely, although in a large family disagreements are inevitable, three months is a long time for sisters living in the same house to maintain a hostile silence. Even Marian and Elizabeth, usually allies, had their troubles. Papa punished Elizabeth for an argument with Marian about household duties; and though Anna later claimed that the severity which cloaked her girlhood did not envelop Bessie, Elizabeth's punishment on this occasion was startlingly severe. She was to give up her beloved music lessons, a retribution peculiarly unfair since the lessons had been her reward for teaching Howard and Washington, which she had conscientiously done. Elizabeth, in her turn, complained that Mamma let Anna and Henry do anything, but when Elizabeth displeased her, the "strongest punishments [were] resorted to."

Their religious life was as demanding as ever. On Sundays they went to church twice, usually to different churches morning and afternoon. Father gave up morning prayers for a while, then resumed them. On the day after her sixteenth birthday Elizabeth finished reading the Bible, "having been a little more than two years doing it." And six months later she began to read it again.

For a while Anna and Elizabeth were attracted to the Episcopal church and, having argued with Papa about it, were lectured by Mamma on the "'rags of popery' . . . a system of lies and delusions." In spite of Mamma, Uncle Charles became an Episcopalian, largely because he considered it "a much more gentlemanly religion."

Father Blackwell's life was not easy. For a time he had an interest in two sugar refineries in New York, the Congress Sugar House, where Mr. Gower, much admired by young Sam, represented the London firm of Gower, Guppy and Company with which Papa was in partnership, and one on Washington Street where Mr. Harris was foreman. Often, when they lived in New Jersey, Papa could not get home across the river at night and would be away for three or four days at a time. In any case, every third night it was his turn to "sit up and keep watch" at the sugar house "to guard against fire."[15] The two elder boys, who went to school in New York when the river was not icebound, took turns staying with him, and Sam would resort to minor bribery to win Henry's turn. He particularly liked to stay on Friday nights so that he could go with his father to the Saturday morning sugar sales.

By the beginning of 1837 Papa was connected only with the Washington Street enterprise. In spite of precautions, there had been a fire in the underinsured Congress Sugar House, and the English partners had refused to rebuild. Mr. Gower was to return to England. "Oh . . . if I were going to England tomorrow . . ." Sam wrote, "I think I should almost go crazy with joy." And seeing Mr. Gower off, Elizabeth longed to be on her way to "the same beloved land."

On July 24, 1837, Papa brought home the "news of King William's decease." Elizabeth was deeply moved. "How ardently I hope our young queen may prove worthy and capable of governing our flourishing kingdom, and may be an honour to our sex." Aunt and Uncle put on mourning, and Marian and Sam bought black ribbons. But Mamma "delivered quite an oration on our want of respect for America, whilst we were rummaging up all our black trimming." However, that night even Papa, the ardent democrat, came home with crepe on his hat, and on Sunday they "all went to church with black on and made quite a loyal appearance."[16]

The king had died on June 20, more than a month before the news trickled across the ocean to them, and was buried on July 6. "A good while to keep his royal body," Sam commented. "God save our queen." The Victorian era had begun.

Now again, as in England, economic conditions were deeply affecting the family, and another change was in preparation. The depression of 1837 had hit the country. In February Sam told how a mob, "driven by the high price of provisions, attacked 3 flour warehouses," broke the windows and threw the flour out. Papa never talked about his business, but the family knew it was bad. In March Elizabeth wrote, "Papa condescended to inform Mamma yesterday that he had sold his Washington sugar house concern—to Mr. Harris and some other person, what his plans for the future are we do not know." Immediately he hired masons to install a furnace and boiler in the cellar, and began to experiment with methods of sugar making. He particularly hoped to find a profitable way of making sugar out of beets, which could be grown in northern United States. Cuban cane growers had horrified him by explaining, with unabashed frankness, that they found it economical to work their slaves out in seven years and then replace them with a fresh supply from Africa.

Now failure followed failure throughout the country. In April "affairs" were "horrible." On May 4 there was a run on the Mechanic's Bank, and on May 10 Sam reported all banks closed to avert further panic. For the first time there was no servant in the Blackwell home; and the girls took weekly turns "seeing to the meals." Like most sixteen-year-olds, Elizabeth dreaded her turn. By June there was so little money that they had to go to bed in the dark. Uncle Charles and his wife, Eliza, gave up the school they had been trying to run, and came to the Blackwells as boarders at a nominal fee. Later another family took three rooms in the house.

Now too the first separation occurred. Anna, who was considered by the family to be a brilliant pianist, accepted a position teaching vocal and instrumental music in an Episcopalian seminary in Vermont, and left by boat with her employer and his wife. Marian was taking a job teaching arithmetic. Elizabeth had to give up her piano lessons again for lack of money. "I wish I could devise some good way of maintaining myself," she wrote, "but the restrictions which confine my dear sex render all my aspirations useless." She read constantly. She bought Part One of the "papers of the Pickwick Club." She read *Marmion* and the *Bride of Lammermoor,* in which she found "Lucy Ashton's weakness . . . quite provoking. I think if I had been her I should have knocked down my father, overturned my mother, and fled over my elder brother into my lover's arms." [17]

Papa had various schemes which fell through, one of them to move to Philadelphia. It is hard to know whether conditions were such that he was forced to leave New York or whether with patience and stamina he might have weathered the difficulties. Other men, including Dennis Harris in the Washington Street Sugar House, survived. Afterward Henry remembered that when, in the Congress Sugar House, Papa had been in partnership with the London firm, they had used a new vacuum-pan process not yet generally introduced into the United States, which made their profits unusually large. Henry also argued that with the phenomenal growth of the city, which was the center of the sugar-refining industry, his father might have retrieved his fortune had he remained there.

Whatever the facts, Samuel Blackwell followed the pattern which in adversity he had followed before. Discouraged by business conditions and further disheartened by the sugar house fire, he did what he had done in England. Against advice, and certainly against the desires of his family, with a recklessness odd in a family man so stable when things went well, he again decided to turn his back on a life that had grown difficult, and to seek greener pastures. He sold out his remaining New York interests and set off for the comparative primitiveness of the Middle West. He had decided to go to Cincinnati to open the first sugar refinery west of the Alleghenies, and perhaps to make beet sugar there.

When the elder children pleaded to go back to England, he promised that, as soon as he was successful once more, he would put the matter to a family vote, and if the majority still preferred England, they would return.

CHAPTER FOUR

At the end of April 1838 they auctioned the familiar household furniture they had brought from Bristol, and on May 3 left New York by boat. In spite of the advent of George Washington Blackwell, it was a smaller group than had crossed the ocean six years before. Aunt Lucy, Uncle Charles and his so-called wife were returning to England. Marian was remaining temporarily behind because of her teaching job; Aunt Barbara was staying with her; Anna was still in Vermont; and the days when they had traveled with two servants and a governess were long past. Yet there were ten in the party that set out for Cincinnati: seven young Blackwells, their parents and Aunt Mary.

Their first overnight stop was in Philadelphia, which reminded Sam of "'our own our native land.'" Next morning they boarded the railway which would carry them seventy miles to Columbia, Pennsylvania, to one of the canals in a network which then served as water roadways throughout the country. When as an aging woman Elizabeth wrote her autobiography, she recalled that they went by "canal and stage (for it was before the time of railways)." But long memories are faulty, and both Elizabeth and Sam, writing at the time, mentioned their trip by "rail car."

They boarded the canal boat on Friday afternoon and were on

the canal until Monday. Most of their fellow passengers were Irish, Sam reported, "but there were several farmers and mechanics, sensible respectable sort of people beside." [1] Elizabeth described the women's cabin where they spent three nights. "We were in a room about 6 yards by 4 . . . with 16 berths." The floor was covered with beds full of women scolding and dirty children squalling.[2] A broken floodgate made the trip even longer than it ordinarily was, for passengers and cargo had to be unloaded and transferred to another boat which, traveling eastward, had been unable to pass the lock from the other side. For diversion, Bessie, Sam and Henry took a short cut across some hills and met the boat at the next lock. The scenery all along the way was beautiful.

They landed at last at "Hollidaysburgh at the foot of the Allegheny mountain," [3] where they drove to the summit and spent the night in a hotel. "Papa secured a room containing 4 good large beds, which contained all but him and myself," Sam wrote. However, in the middle of the night the hotel owner took pity on the two outcasts and set up a sort of box filled with straw in the barroom, and there they slept until morning.

Next day they left in a heavy snowstorm and went by rail car as far as Johnstown where they again boarded a canal boat. But twelve miles before Pittsburgh there was the now familiar break in the canal, and on Wednesday, in a heavy fog, the passengers had to disembark and wait for a steamboat on the Allegheny River, only a field away from the canal at this point. There was no notice of the arrival of the boat, until around midnight a cry went up, " 'steamboat come,' " at which there was a mad scramble to get themselves and their possessions across the dark, fog-covered field and onto the boat. "I think P. is a horrible place, large, but filthy and disagreeable," [4] Elizabeth recorded.

It was on the evening of May 10 that they boarded a final boat, where they had the luxury of three cabins to themselves; and on Saturday, May 12, they reached their destination. The trip from New York to Cincinnati had taken over nine days. On the boat trip down the Ohio, there was pleasant company. Several young men attached themselves to Emily and Ellen, but as usual Elizabeth was overlooked. She was a pretty girl. "Small, of fair complexion, with clear bluish-grey eyes, light hair remarkably soft and fine, beautiful hands, and a very sweet voice," [5] Anna described her later, but so retiring and silent that she was rarely asked to dance or walk or talk by any young man. Indeed on the boat some of the ladies took the sedate girl for a married woman.[6] It was not without reason that her father had nicknamed her Little Shy.

In Cincinnati they went by invitation to Bellevue House, a hotel owned by a relative of Uncle Browne of Bristol. The cordiality of their reception was heartwarming, and in general their first impressions of Cincinnati were favorable. "It is situated quite high on two rises from the river and an extensive level plain enclosed by mountains," Elizabeth wrote. And Sam thought that "the hills on the Kentucky shore opposite look very beautiful, though in a country cursed by the demon of Opression [*sic*]." They were startled to find trees in bloom after the snow in the Alleghenies. "The land is very rich and vegetation quite rank." [7]

As for the city, Elizabeth admired the handsome houses and well-dressed people, and Sam commented, "They have a good many English customs here. Indeed I believe a third of the inhabitants and more are English, and 5/6th foreigners. . . . Everybody gets rich here somehow." The Blackwells' compatriot Mrs. Trollope, who reached the city ten years earlier, had a less sympathetic view of the same phenomenon.[8] "During nearly two years that I resided in Cincinnati . . . I never saw a beggar, nor a man of sufficient fortune to permit his ceasing his efforts to increase it; thus every bee in the hive is actively employed in search of that honey of Hybla, vulgarly called money; neither art, science, learning, nor pleasure can seduce them from its pursuit. This unity of purpose . . . [is] joined with an acuteness and *total* lack of probity." Mrs. Trollope made a more general social comment on life in America, "where women are guarded by a seven-fold shield of habitual insignificance."

The Blackwells established themselves quickly and in their usual fashion. Elizabeth began at once to teach her younger brothers and sisters, and outside the family to give music lessons for pay. The first Saturday and Sunday they attended Lyman Beecher's church, where they continued for a time to worship. Mr. Beecher, "his sons and daughter," had recently been convicted of heresy by a church synod, and a pamphlet in his defense was handed to the congregation. A few weeks later they heard a Mr. Root, taking Beecher's place, preach an abolition sermon, and saw some twenty parishioners leave in protest. Within a few days of their arrival Papa took a sugar house, and early in July the family moved into their own home, a rented house on Third Street. The transfer to the West had been completed; and they settled down to life as usual, with the hope that it would be more prosperous than it had lately been in Jersey City.

The hope did not last long. At the end of July Papa was taken ill, with repeated fainting spells which terrified the family. He had in fact a recurrence of the malarial fever he had contracted in the East. He grew worse. On August 6 he was in a "torpor," and they sat at his bedside all night. He realized he was dying, and now, too late, advised them to go back to England. Clasping his wife in a last embrace, " 'Dear love,' he said, 'manage your own affairs. There is the house and furniture and nothing to pay till the end of the year. I think it would be better to sell off everything and return to England, if possible. But I am sorry to say that I have no money to leave you.' " [9]

In his notes, he had ascribed much of the gratification of living in America to "a decrease of anxiety in the evening of life and the prospect of competence and repose after so much change and toil." These benefits he was never to enjoy. On August 7, 1838, at ten-ten at night, while Elizabeth was holding his hand, he died peacefully in his sleep. *"He is dead,"* Elizabeth wrote that same night. They were thunderstruck, desolate. In the midst of tears and prayers, "as I gazed at the sky, I wondered if our blessed father had yet reached Heaven." He was laid out "in the back parlour where he had died," and there they each cut a lock of his hair as a keepsake.

The funeral was next day. Before the undertaker sealed the coffin, Elizabeth went to it. "I wiped the forehead, imprinted the parting kiss, the features were awfully changed but still it was part of Papa, and as I gave the last *last* lingering look and turned away for ever I felt as if all hope and joy were gone and nought was left but to die also. We rode to the ground. I hated the light and the beautiful day and the people who stared at us. I seemed alone in the world."

And indeed they were alone and unprotected. The day after the funeral there was only twenty dollars left. Elizabeth returned that very day to giving music lessons; and friends hastened to find such clerking jobs as Sam, almost fifteen, and Henry, thirteen, could do. Henry's first salary was two dollars a week. He later claimed that, before even that salary became available, he acted as family cook, and "concocted savory stews in a broken coffee pot." He boasted that he could make four or five different kinds of bread, all good.[10] Meanwhile Elizabeth and Aunt Mary sent out circulars announcing a school, and by the end of August Aunt Mary was teaching one or two boys in the front room, while Elizabeth taught three girls in the back. Elizabeth continued to give music lessons too. By September 2, "We had considerable additions to our pupils. Mamma had to assist me in the young ladies school." [11]

And still Anna and Marian had not arrived to take their share of the burden. It was not until September 7 that they appeared. Anna, "as lively as ever," brought a breath of the great world with her. In Vermont she had met the celebrated English novelist Captain Marryat, and had "lectured him on his books." Captain Marryat was a Tory and a snob who, though he later wrote about America and Americans with rather less unkindness than most English visitors, managed to make himself hated in the United States by gratuitously entering into a Canadian-United States embroilment on the side of Canada. His antidemocratic views must have shocked Anna, who during her stay in New England had come into contact with many radical ideas, and was beginning to express herself in writing. She and Elizabeth discussed "ultra abolition, women's preaching etc. Anna lent me her drama to read." According to Sam's later account, Anna, the drab, disconsolate girl, had by some alchemy of living been transformed into "the brilliant social member of the family." However, on her arrival from the East, she was assigned the unbrilliant task of keeping house. With the school sufficiently established to require large meals and extra help, they hired two servants and bought a "cooking stove."

Yet fate seemed to have turned against them. At the end of September Aunt Mary was taken ill, and within a week the grim scene of the bedside vigil was repeated, with the same sorry ending.

Aunt Mary died less than two months after her brother; she had been forty-six, he forty-eight. At Aunt Mary's funeral, which took place on the day she died, Elizabeth felt herself to be without emotion. "Now it seemed as if whatever arrived I should never feel again." For none of them was there time for grieving.

The school continued and flourished. In October they had to shift their bedroom arrangements to make room for new boarders. By November life was again moving smoothly enough so that they were paying visits to friends; and Elizabeth reported that "Mr. Smith went with Anna and me to see the Giraffe, tis just like the pictures of him I've seen."

Two days later there was another blow. From the East came news that Aunt Barbara too was dead. The death of a brother and two sisters within three months from unrelated causes was astonishing even in those days of early deaths from lack of sanitation and primitive medical skills. But the necessary work of life went on. They acquired two new boarding and two new day pupils; and immediately the servants left without notice.

Schoolteaching might be the only career a girl could hope for, but for boys the possibilities were of course far wider. Henry decided to become a lawyer, and by the summer of 1840, his family were managing among them to earn enough so that he could go to college. In September he set off for Kemper in St. Louis, a new college of which Dr. Crane, a family friend and Anna's employer in Vermont, had recently become president.

Again the trip into the undeveloped West was long and hazardous. Because of "the low state of the River,"[12] the trip from Cincinnati took two weeks instead of the five days Henry had expected. And when he reached his destination, he found "the state of things . . . quite curious. Here is St. Louis with about 25,000 inhabitants, and one hundred miles west you may hunt buffaloes and hardly see a trace of a settler. Indeed in the winter there is first rate deer hunting within three miles of the College." He was living with the Cranes, whose beautiful daughter his brothers and sisters assumed would win his heart, though there is no evidence that she did.

Henry's success meant a great deal to them all, and since they were of a moral bent, letters from home contained, along with news, banter and affection, exhortations to work, to be serious, not to disappoint their hopes. Henry was the gayest of the lot, the one most given to pranks, practical jokes and merriment. They had invested in his future, but they were not convinced of the seriousness of his purpose. He had no more left home than Anna wrote, affectionately enough, but hoping he would return "a sober learned respectable and delightful *gentleman* in place of the thoughtless ignorant (*or what is worse* only *half-knowing*) impertinent little loafer we have just bid adieu to!"

Marian urged him, with more piety than literacy, to work "dilligently" and to "throw away then all folly, indolence, and 'childish things' and endeavour in thought and action to become what 'the spirit of truth' within you, and above you, will approve." [13] Anna and Elizabeth worried about his acquiring low Western manners and "Missouri slang." This flood of epistolary morality had its source in Hannah Blackwell, whose infrequent letters to her children were prolonged groans over the state of their souls. Her first letter to Henry told him how as he left he had pained her "very Soul by the words [he] so wickedly uttered." For when she asked "When shall I see you again?" he had jestingly replied, "'In the Judgement Day! and on the left hand side of the Cross!'" How, she lamented, could he so blaspheme when his own dear father was "at this moment singing anthems of praise." [14]

Many years later Henry admitted that in St. Louis he succumbed to an evil against which none of the family would have thought to warn him. He made friends with the sons of slaveholding families, became interested in the Democratic Party, and as late as 1844 was in favor of Polk and the annexation of Texas. As he recalled it forty years after, it was only in 1846, when he heard the abolitionist Stephen Foster and his wife, Abby Kelley, speak, that he became, as he ever afterward remained, an ardent abolitionist. But perhaps the passage of time had prolonged in memory the period of his defection. It is hard to imagine how in that avidly abolitionist and verbal family he could have clung to reactionary views for over five years.[15]

In his mother's November letter there was an unusually large admixture of news. The family was busy. They had three boarding pupils, and the girls also have had a "large accession to their music and French pupils—so that Anna and Elizabeth are teaching by 7 in the morning— (with scarcely allowing themselves time to take their meals) til 7 at night." Marian is teaching classes as well as giving music and drawing lessons. Mamma misses Henry very much, but knows that he will benefit from his college education. He must never forget that he is the child of "a long line of eminently pious ancestry—better this than the short lived Titles or riches of earth, which so quickly pass away."

Though Henry seems to have survived this barrage of morality, he had more practical problems. He was growing disaffected with the idea of studying law, chiefly because he found it so hard to make a decent "offhand" speech, and was considering civil engineering as a profession. His mother was sympathetic to the change: law, though a noble profession, also offered more temptations to deviate from the "rule of right." Yet it soon became apparent that he was to follow neither profession. Affairs were again going badly at home. By spring there was only one boarder and far fewer French and music students. Henry kept offering to leave college and come home to work, and at the end of the school year he did just that. He did it with great good will, but it was the end of a dream for them all.

Sam too had given up a cherished hope. Eager to leave the clerking job which, though his duties had expanded, was still dull and beneath his growing abilities, Sam hoped to follow in his father's footsteps as a sugar manufacturer. He had been corresponding with Dennis Harris, his father's former assistant, now a successful sugar refiner in New York, and Mr. Harris had offered to teach him the business. But after much soul searching, Sam decided that, though there was no clear principle to be adduced on the use of slave products, he preferred to remain as free as possible "from participation in the sins of the wicked." He therefore determined not to manufacture sugar for the time being, but to investigate the possibility of importing the raw material from the "free West India Islands."

Elizabeth too had for some time been contemplating her future, and without enthusiasm. At New Year's 1839 she had assessed her situation. The school was successful enough to support them, but she hated teaching. She felt "too young and inexperienced. . . .

The elder girls were very wild Western young women," whom she controlled by a quiet, reserved manner which they took to be sternness but which was really fear. Their establishment in Cincinnati was accomplished, but Elizabeth hated America, hated it so much that when Mamma advised her "to set her wig at Mr. S. G.," the brother of Sam's boss, Elizabeth considered her distaste for living in the United States an insuperable obstacle to marrying an American.

Meanwhile candidates for a husband of whatever nationality were woefully absent. Elizabeth mourned again her inability to talk even to family friends. She wrote to Henry that she didn't enjoy parties, though her sisters did, "because I'm such an unsociable being, and have so little small talk." [16] She brooded over the obliviousness of young men to her presence, but knew that it resulted from an embarrassment in their company so deep that on one occasion Marian rebuked her for rudeness.

Anna's view of life was different. She told Elizabeth that she intended to marry, intended indeed "*courting some body* if a better does not turn up." Yet that spring it was not Anna but Marian who had a suitor, brother of the Mr. Smith who had taken her sisters to see the giraffe. As for Elizabeth, she was driven to tears thinking of her situation and "of the long dreary years in prospect." She knew she should be grateful for what she had, but as Anna had so cogently put it, it's "very hard to be thankful for being a schoolmistress." And with the limitations placed on ladies by age-old tradition, what else could any of the sisters hope to be? The future looked drab indeed.

CHAPTER FIVE

In the young Blackwells the search for righteousness was from their earliest days linked to religion and reform. This was an inheritance—or contagion—from both parents, with their father placing more emphasis on making a better world here and now, their mother on preparing for the next. As Dissenters and abolitionists, the children had been taught to question prevalent ideas and institutions, which for them implied a constant reappraisal of their own religious principles as well. With their father no longer present to assert his authority, the elder girls were once more drawn to the Episcopal church, and it was not many months after his death that they began to go to services at the cathedral. In those long intellectual discussions which so absorbed Anna and Elizabeth after Anna's return from the East, Anna had told Elizabeth that she did not "care a straw" what church she attended as far as sermons were concerned. She "could almost always make better ones herself so she never [attempted] to listen to them." [1] But listening or not, she accompanied her sisters to St. Paul's Cathedral when the Bishop preached, and there Elizabeth, and shortly afterward Marian, decided to be confirmed. Elizabeth could not find the courage to tell her pious mother of her dissent from Dissent, until one day when the minister unexpectedly called on her at home, and the awful truth was revealed. An unhappy scene followed, with Hannah crying and bewailing Elizabeth's lost soul. Nevertheless the three girls took a pew at the large cost of forty-eight dollars a year, and instantly had cause for complaint, because the Bishop made "unjust and quite uncalled for remarks on the inferiority of women." Yet Elizabeth and Marian persisted in their plans for confirmation, and on the day they took their vows, Anna, Sam, Emily and Ellen were present, though Mamma showed her disapproval by remaining away.

Sam was not led by these defections to abandon the tenets of his childhood. Two years later he was still accompanying his mother to prayer meetings on Wednesday and Friday evenings, besides attending chapel twice on Sundays and teaching Sunday-school classes. At seventeen the most innocent and conscientious of mortals, working by day to help support his family, finding his simple recreations in walking, playing ball, visiting the neighbors, gazing at the heavens through a friend's telescope, he was yet overwhelmed by a sense of sin. "My soul sickens at the sight of her own depravity; would to God I could remember and feel and see my vileness more as it is." And among the many such exclamations with which he studded his diaries: "How numberless are the means of grace which I enjoy. Alas! How little have I improved them. Weather very warm." [2] Yet there is no doubt about his sincerity, the intensity of his adolescent fervor.

By the time he wrote these words, there had been dramatic shifts in the religious adherence of his brothers and sisters. "I suppose you are aware," Henry wrote from college to an English cousin, "of the Sisters having joined the Unitarian church. There are now, therefore, three different parties in our family. Anna, Marian and Elizabeth are Unitarians; Mamma and Sam stanch Presbyterians; Emily and myself, Episcopalians."

In the two years since their venture into Episcopalianism, the elder girls had come under the powerful influence of William Henry Channing, a nephew of the great William Ellery Channing and like him an idealist, an abolitionist and a Unitarian minister. Before moving to Cincinnati to spread the Unitarian gospel in the West, William Henry had been associated in Boston with the group known as the Transcendental Club, though there was never any such organized club or any such established title.

It was after his departure, in April 1841 to be exact, that the Transcendentalists established the Brook Farm Colony, an attempt at achieving a perfect, if limited, society on earth. These intellectuals turned farmers conceived one of the basic necessities of Utopia to be earning a living, not by the work of other men's hands and the sweat of their brows, but by one's own. Brook Farm was one of the many Utopian colonies that sprang up and withered in the United States, and indeed in Europe as well, in the mid-nineteenth century. Brook Farm, which lasted as a functioning community for some eight years, was longer-lived than most. It had a school and a magazine and a group of gifted and dedicated supporters who were not dedicated only to hard work and philosophic discussion. There was gaiety too, dancing, boating, pageants, charades, love. The community's decline began when Albert Brisbane imported the restrictive organization of those phalanxes created by the French Utopian philosopher François Fourier, whose influence on reform groups in the United States was enormous and whose followers Anna, Marian, Elizabeth and Emily for a while became.

Long- or short-lived, the Utopian communities scattered across the country—there were more than forty Fourierist phalanxes in the United States in the eighteen-forties—were monuments to the reforming spirit of the age, the belief in man's—and woman's—ultimate perfectibility in a perfect society. In the United States, which had cast aside the bondage of an alien government and where a new society was in the making, reform seemed more possible and Utopia more imminent than in Europe. Americans knew the continent was theirs for the taking. They had only to create a free society which in turn would spread freedom, virtue, happiness. "In the history of the world," Emerson said, "the doctrine of Reform had never such scope as at the present hour. . . . [N]ow . . . all things . . . . hear the trumpet, and must rush to judgment—Christianity, the laws, commerce, schools, the farm, the laboratory; and not a kingdom, town, statute, rite, calling, man or woman, but is threatened by the new spirit." [3]

In this general atmosphere of optimism it was easy to believe that the millennium was at hand. Religious groups predicted the Second Coming of the Lord, not in some distant era but at once. The Millerites were so sure of the date that they sat, dressed in white muslin, so many pre-angels, on housetops and hills, presumably so as not to waste a moment of eternity when it came. Even the fact that their leader William Miller several times changed his appointment with salvation did not at first discourage them.

The imminence of glory was everywhere. To Henry at Kemper his mother wrote that she had talked to a rabbi, and was struck anew by the realization that all sects and religions agreed that the Second Coming of Christ would occur "during the present generation," the farthest date she had heard mentioned being 1865. Such an eminent preacher as Lyman Beecher believed that the Second Coming might take place at any instant, and so in more moderate fashion did William Henry Channing.

Not that Channing was a moderate man. It is easy to understand how, in conviction, temperament and appearance, he would have seemed to the Blackwell sisters the incarnation of an ideal. He was a reformer, he was a minister, he was an impassioned and eloquent speaker. Singularly handsome, with dark eyes, complexion and hair, "elegant; expressive in countenance and manner," he stood "radiant and enchanting on reform platforms, and fascinated all hearers by his ringing voice, his buoyant mien, his rapt countenance, and his glowing appeals." [4]

He was, like the Blackwells themselves, highly sensitive and torn by very human doubts. And, in addition, he held a belief in the potentialities of women unusual in those days. His mother, descendant of Cabots, Clevelands, Lowells, was a woman of extraordinary force and intelligence. Margaret Fuller, darling of the Transcendentalists, famous for her "conversations," intellectual companion of the great men of her time, was his good friend. Nowhere could the Blackwell sisters have found stronger support for their discontent with woman's lot, their ambition to spend their lives at some profession other than schoolteaching. They quickly became his parishioners, and grew friendly with him and his wife. Anna wrote to Henry that Mr. Channing had raised her opinion of human nature;[5] and Sam's diary in 1841 is full of notations that Mr. Channing called, or that Anna, Marian and Elizabeth were at Mr. Channing's or had gone to hear him lecture. In April Sam himself went to hear Mr. Channing, "as I was anxious to hear him once before he goes."[6] Mr. Channing was returning East; but William Ellery Channing, namesake of their common uncle, was coming to Cincinnati to preach, and incidentally to take up his cousin's friendship with the Blackwell family.

One day that spring, Emily, now fourteen, came to Sam "suddenly in her blunt way" and said, " 'Sam, how do you know the Bible is inspired? The epistles of Paul for instance.' " And Sam, who by his own report—he was seventeen—had only recently begun again to feel the power of God after remaining obdurately cold to Him for some time, had several long talks with Emily, hoping to save her from the skepticism of their elder sisters. But the very atmosphere of religious zeal combined with so much earthly and celestial questioning was fertile soil for doubt. When young Henry returned from Kemper, "grown amazingly, voice changed," Sam hoped that Henry's soul might also "prosper and be in health." But in Sam's view, it did not, for a year later he was grieved "to hear Henry avow his unbelief of a future punishment," and shocked by his brother's "habitual desecration of the Sabbath" in such pagan delights as walking, swimming, riding. "The Lord save him, man cannot."

Whatever religious and social doubts they passed through, one unchanging conviction held them all. The present world was far from perfect, and until the millennium arrived, though it should be tomorrow, it was the duty of good and honest people to fight against slavery, against inequality, social, moral and economic. If Sam went to prayer meetings twice weekly, and at certain intense periods almost daily, his sisters and he too went to antislavery meetings, to lectures, to classes; and these meetings and lectures were as often as not addressed by the same ministers who guided their religious lives: one of the Channings, Mr. Beecher, Mr. Blanchard, Mr. Brisbane.

In a city within view of the Kentucky border, antislavery was no mere theoretical problem; it was a burning issue. Slaves were constantly smuggled across the border, and all too frequently

Negroes were captured and returned, sometimes after years as freedmen, on the "suspicion of their being slaves." [7] In the fall of 1841, when economic conditions were becoming steadily worse and fear of competition from freed Negroes increased, there were anti-Negro riots in Cincinnati. Negroes were kidnapped back into slavery: abolitionist offices and presses were attacked by mobs. On at least one occasion Sam and Henry joined the companies of citizen militia patrolling the streets. In the spring of 1842 anti-abolitionist papers published lists of abolitionists' names, and a friend whose name appeared told Sam that copies were posted in Southern towns, so that if the people listed were ever foolish enough to go South, they would be identified and killed.

The keynote of the Blackwells' lives was seriousness. Not that they did not play. There were frequent gatherings of young people, country excursions, evening singing, parties. But that life was purposeful they never questioned. Those who were old enough worked by day to improve the family fortunes, and rose at dawn and sat late at night reading and studying to improve their minds. Emily, at fourteen, was learning Latin and planning to learn Greek. Sam reported at various periods that he was studying Shakespeare, mathematics, Latin, chemistry, physics. Besides these, he was learning bookkeeping to improve his earning power.

Through the Channings, through Anna too, they were kept in touch with the most advanced thought of their day. With fascination they followed the Brook Farm experiment in association. They read its paper, *The Harbinger,* and they read about it in the *Democratic Review*. When Anna became a Swedenborgian, Sam dutifully, though skeptically, read Swedenborg. He even read the Millerite paper to see what those prophets of the Second Coming had in store for him.

Meanwhile there was hard work to be done to keep the family solvent. The years 1841 and 1842 were critical. The country was in the throes of a deepening financial crisis, and again the fortunes of the Blackwells suffered with the general welfare. The falling off of pupils in their school, which caused Henry's withdrawal from college, continued, but at first his return did the family little good. For several months he had no job, and that autumn decided to work part time with Sam until he could find full-time employment. Finally, late in November he took a position with a Mr. Ellis, owner of a flour mill. Sam was in an unfortunate situation too. He had tried in vain to find another position. Now his employer was in financial difficulty and could not pay his salary, nor did there seem any immediate prospect of his being able to.

The most dependable part of the family income came from taking boarders. They moved several times, once at the end of June 1841 and again a year later, to houses more suitable to their lowered circumstances and to their need for rooms for paying guests. In 1841 Ellery Channing and his bride were among the first boarders in their new home; but when the Channings took their own house, the Blackwells had no trouble replacing them with tenants from the church and reform circles in which they moved. To find employment was another matter. The first break in the family ranks occurred when Anna went to Dayton to live with friends and look for work there.

On January 11, 1842, Sam wrote, "The Bank of Cincinnati broke today, and a mob collected and burst open and tore down it and the Miami Express Gu[arantee] Co. They afterwards in their frenzy destroyed the Exchange Bank. . . . I think I read in the . . . disregard of law, first in the swindlers, then in the mob, the knell of this Country's liberties." Two days later the newspapers reported that a mob had torn up a bank in Louisville, Kentucky.

Sam, who worked at the courthouse, continued to be paid irregularly or not at all. Part of his job was "dunning poor creatures for cost bills," [8] and his salary may have depended on these collections, for he complained that his time was spent trying to get his salary "or some part thereof." That spring a wealthy cousin sent the family one hundred and fifty dollars from England to tide them over the crisis, but late in that same October Sam described their jumping and cutting capers around the parlor "in the absence of fuel to raise caloric"; and it was not until four days later that they bought coal, which he and Henry shoveled in.

Neither Sam nor Henry was happy with his work or with the limited possibilities life seemed to offer two intelligent, self-educated young men with no training for any profession and no time or money to acquire one. Henry went so far as to try to get into West Point, unlikely as an army career might seem for a young man of his upbringing and convictions. Sam tried to arrange for a job in New York. He had vague dreams of becoming a doctor, but his ambition never moved further from the realm of fantasy than in home study of chemistry and physics.

Yet gradually the family fortunes improved. Anna was working in Dayton, then reluctantly, just as she was beginning to find an interesting circle there, moved to Columbus, where a better position was offered her. She had been writing, and from time to time articles of hers appeared in papers or magazines. In November 1843 the long-awaited opportunity to change his job came to Sam too. He was to be a bookkeeper in a situation which he described as "involving great assiduity and occupation of time." This was an understatement. For eight weeks he spent from thirteen to fourteen hours a day working, and the work continued at such a pace that, instead of writing daily in his diary, he now wrote only on Sundays, and often missed several weeks at a time. A year later he was keeping the books of three mills. "I abominate . . . business distorted from the means to the end of life," he noted bitterly; but of necessity, this continued to be his pattern of living.

By the end of February 1844, Anna was in New York teaching, and Elizabeth had accepted an offer inviting any one of the three eldest girls to come to Henderson, Kentucky, as governess-teacher. "Beyond the verge of civilization," Sam said of the slave state. A month later the rest of the family made a move they had long dreamed of. They took a house in the country, in Walnut Hills, then a suburb of Cincinnati. The young people would have more freedom there to wander over the countryside, as they loved to do, and more companionship too. Walnut Hills was the home of Lane Theological Seminary, of which the leading spirits were the exuberant, controversial Beechers and morose Calvin Stowe. Dr. Stowe had married Lyman Beecher's daughter Harriet, though what romantic young Harriet found of romance in her unlikely mate, except perhaps his grief at the death of his beautiful first wife, is hard to imagine. The Beechers and Stowes were friends of the Blackwells, and Henry and Sam became friendly too with many of the seminary students, who shared their combined devotion to religion and reform. Next year they were members of a seminary debating club, and later, when a new home they bought was overcrowded with family and paying guests, Henry lived at the seminary.

The improvement in their finances was such that they had a man to tend the grounds and do the heavy work, and that they bought a horse and carriage, and kept a cow. Yet when Anna's employer offered Emily free schooling at his fashionable seminary, there was much doubt about her accepting. The family still needed the money she brought in by giving lessons, and Marian needed help with the boarders. In the end, though, Emily went, and plans were made for Ellen to go later. Little Sarah Ellen had begun to paint, and hoped to be an artist.

The Blackwells were growing up. The diverse interests, necessities and emotional pressures which were to drive them to various careers in different parts of the world had begun to express themselves. For all but the two youngest boys, their childhood, short and burdened as it had been, might be declared officially over. They had maintained their home under extraordinary difficulties in the years after their father's death. Now they were turning from whatever security family life had given them, to cope with a wider world.

CHAPTER SIX

That world was much changed since they had made the long trip West seven years before. "One day is usually . . . almost" the same as another; but this "is less true of the life of this generation in this country than of almost any other period or place in this world or its history," Sam wrote toward the end of 1845. "How singular is the triumph over distance and separation which commercial enterprise has effected . . . annihilating space; news . . . sweeps a continent in a few days." As long ago as 1841 he had "read the substance of Pres. Tyler's message," and noted with astonishment that "the message came by Express in 60 hours from Wash. here." And in 1844 "Marianne rec'd a letter . . . containing an impression made by the new electric telegraph," which was beginning to reduce the time that news took to travel across the country from days to hours or minutes.

In the New York of their childhood clear, healthy water had now been available for more than three years. "The water is let into New York by the Croton waterworks amid 10000s of spectators," Sam noted in 1842. "The work has cost the city $12,000,000."

The great country they had crossed in 1838 was growing larger. In 1846, to Sam's disgust, the American army invaded Texas. In May General Zachary Taylor, in three successive, decisive victories, drove "the poor Mexicans" beyond the Rio Grande; and a week later, "Our army has invaded Mexico. Shameful!" In 1845, when the House of Representatives passed a "rash" bill for the annexation of Oregon, Sam worried that it would result in war with his beloved England, and was much relieved a year later when an agreement was reached and the Oregon treaty confirmed by the Senate.

The changes in their own lives had been drastic too, for growing up is always drastic. What were these young men and women like? How did they seem and look to their contemporaries? It is impossible to view people clearly through the haze of time, no matter how many diaries they write or how many daguerreotypes they leave behind. It is surprising to learn that the family's friend, Harriet Beecher Stowe, thought Henry a "wild boy," or that later Elizabeth, consoling Marian for her lack of purpose, wrote, "beauty is strength, and you are to me the most beautiful woman I've ever known." And, though the Blackwells were all of less than average height, it is amazing that, when Sam entered his twentieth year and took out his first papers in preparation for becoming an American citizen, he described himself as weighing "114½ lbs . . . a gain of 14½ since the setting in of cold weather." Yet no one thought of him as puny or unhealthy or unable to do a man's work.

In the years just after their father's death, the main burden of family support had fallen on the three eldest girls. Now, as Henry and Sam reached an age at which they could earn a living, they were not unnaturally expected to take over the obligation. The climate of rebellion in which the young Blackwells were nurtured, combined with the conventional idea that the work of the world was done by men, operated to release the Blackwell girls while it chained their brothers. Indeed it was almost at the moment when Sam gave up his dream of being a physician and Henry his of being an engineer that Elizabeth conceived of the possibility of overthrowing the barriers of prejudice and becoming a doctor.

It is impossible now to imagine the outrageous courage of such a project in a day when any girl's determination to embark on a career would have horrified any average parent, and when there were no accredited women physicians. There was only one respectable career for a woman: matrimony. The unfortunate girl who did not acquire some sort of husband might perhaps teach school, but she would be far more likely to end up as unpaid housekeeper and pensioner in the home of a married brother or sister. The Blackwells grew up in just those years when it became possible for a few rare, vigorous, dedicated women to be more than this; and the intellectual background, the liberal associations of their family made the choice less incredible for them than for other girls of their time.

Not that the possibility of marriage was entirely lacking. The first recorded opportunity came, surprisingly, to their mother. She had been a pretty girl, and at fifty was a handsome woman. In 1842 Hannah began receiving letters from a Mr. Howells, a friend whose second wife had recently died, saying that he was considering marrying again. She gave Sam one to read. "It certainly amounts almost to an offer, but she says her only motive in such a union would be the obtaining of a home for the 4 youngest children and to leave them would at once settle the question in the negative." [1] A few days later she wrote a definite no to Mr. Howells, who, far from inconsolable, a month later found another, more amenable lady.

Of Anna, who believed that everything and everyone was against her, and who throughout her life was embroiled in conflict with family, friends and associates, Sam wrote that when she came home on visits the house was full of guests. Life was a continuous party. "She seems a universal favorite." Her superficial gaiety of manner belied the turmoil underneath.

Indeed in Columbus Anna found a suitor, and became engaged. On June 30, 1843, Sam recorded: "The die is cast! The fascinating, handsome, amiable, learned, wealthy John Murdock Esq., Mayor of Springfield, urged anew his claim, and she 'gave a pledge she must one day redeem at the Altar'!" Mr. Murdock was a part-time mayor, who also kept a "country store, a sort of shop universal, in Springfield."

Two weeks after the pledge was given, "Mr. J. M." visited the Blackwells in Cincinnati. If he had hoped to cement his relation with his fiancée, he must have been disappointed. The family had seen him only a few times when they closed ranks against him, and "all wrote to Anna pretty strongly dissuasive letters," by which she must, Sam thought, have "been fairly puzzled." Puzzled seems a significant word, for if such a barrage of family objections was based on any reality greater than a reluctance to have Anna married and separated from them, it might have been expected to dismay rather than puzzle Anna.

Poor Anna. At first her "decision" continued "firm." She came home to buy her trousseau and plan her wedding, but family solidarity had done its work, and soon her feelings were "none of the liveliest in anticipation of the union." She wrote asking Mr. Murdock to postpone the wedding. In answer he came to see her and "left her a letter full of manly kindness releasing her from all engagements, 'restoring the plighted faith and the accepted hand.'" Yet this "manly kindness" was not enough to convert the Blackwell clan from their unstated objections.

So the romance ended. It is the most precise record of any of the girls' love affairs. Later Marian fell in love with a missionary going to the Far East, presumably Henry and Sam's seminary friend Jones, "a noble fellow," [2] who on his way to India wrote a letter to Sam enclosing one for Marian. But noble fellow though he might be, Elizabeth urged Marian, the sister to whom she felt closest, to give up a union that involved going to India. "Oh the idea of going to India, it seems to me so terrible, that I would charge you never to entertain it. To have loved and been loved is a blessed thing, you can never regret it, whatever the issue—the idea of your union seems to me now utterly impossible, the gulf between you too broad ever to be passed." [3] That gulf seems to have been between her lover's undeviating missionary spirit and Marian's religious doubts, for she could not "reconcile Fourierism with Christianity, nor believe in either." [4] Her struggles were long. Over a year before she wrote this letter, Elizabeth had offered consolation for Marian's romantic difficulties by suggesting that sometime in the future she herself would need a friend and adviser, and if Marian could put up with the company of a "rather queer being," they could live together, and "perhaps some phalanxes may be in grand operation then, and we may lead out a missionary colony . . . to far away India," [5] no less! Apparently India with a sister and Fourier was less terrible to contemplate than India with a husband and Christ.

Of them all, Elizabeth seems to have been most opposed to marriage, though in later years she believed she had sacrificed to medicine the hope of love to which her heart was drawn. But the fantasy was more alluring than any earthly manifestation. And in 1844 when Emily was in New York and her family were urging her return to Cincinnati, Elizabeth told them she had written "urging her by all means to go home at once, promising her eight and forty students to drive out any presumptuous coat and pants that may perchance have found their way to her heart, as my letter contained a touch of the sweet, a twinge of the bitter, a dash of the heroic, and a sparkle of the satirical, it must certainly affect some change in the strange composition of her unknown heart."[6] Unknown, anonymous, but a possible husband and therefore to be decried.

She had already warned Henry against his current lady love who, though beautiful and interesting-looking, was too fashionable, and had a frivolous and somewhat coarse mother. Elizabeth knew Henry must share her "dread of the weary horrors of an unhappy marriage." And then, rather pathetically, in case Henry were not persuaded by such logic, Elizabeth added the hope that his "Miss G." might turn out to be the friend she so longed for.[7]

In general, though, the family seems to have accepted the boys' adventures in romance more readily than the girls'; Henry and Sam were constantly in love. They were teased a little, lectured a little, but perhaps because the outcome was never serious, and because, various as their lady loves might be, they shared always the high-minded virtue of the Blackwells themselves, there was no serious effort to dissuade them. In 1845 Sam had been for nearly a year in love with Gabriella, and "fully expressed both my love and my apprehension of her inability to return it. She told me freely, noble girl! that she had considered herself too young to think of loving anyone but members of her own family, and that she had regarded me more with respect than affection."[8] But whether it was Sam and Gabriella, or Henry and Appoline Guilford, who had "one of the loveliest faces and noblest minds that God almighty ever put on this glorious earth,"[9] or Kate Vail, whose family shared a house with the Blackwells and with whom both Sam and Henry fell in love, the course of their romances was much the same.

Like Marian's attachment, Henry's feeling for Kate coincided with a religious crisis. To his mother's and Sam's dismay, Henry had for some time been an agnostic. Now Kate too enlisted in defense of his soul. At twenty, having temporarily become a diarist too, Henry wrote, "I am sick of the selfishness and coldness of the world. I have tried the pleasure of its dissipations and found it bitterness. . . . I have weighed all my old idols and found them wanting." He tried to recover his belief, but without result. He had public help from old Dr. Beecher, who preached a sermon on faith, directed, as they all knew, at Henry; and Henry was "perhaps from nervousness—perhaps from a higher cause—" deeply affected. Later that day, while he was in his room praying, "a dear, sweet voice" asked permission to enter, and Kate came in, burst into tears, and exclaimed, "Oh, dear Henry, do be a Christian!" [10] He promised to try; but the alternation between moments of faith induced by prayer, by reading the Bible as Dr. Beecher recommended, by talks with friends "on the blinding power of sin, and of [his] present dark condition," and more extended periods of doubt continued for months. In the end, when at last he felt ready "thoroughly" to consecrate himself to Him, when he had "resigned forever . . . those temptations which once were irresistible," just then he lost Kate, whose influence in the battle for his soul had been so great.

While the boys struggled at home with the vicissitudes of love and the complexities of finance, the girls, except for Marian, were, strangely enough, seeking their fortunes farther afield. It was a time when women did not customarily travel unescorted, and even the Blackwells attempted always to find a family friend to watch over their wandering girls. Yet when none was available, the girls went alone, and with amazing fortitude took trains and coaches and boats of doubtful safety into unknown and possibly perilous situations.

Anna's ventures always began in glory and ended in disaster. Perhaps because she had found her own small world so unhappy, she was overcredulous of the world outside, a credulity which extended to ideas as well as people. In Dayton she had attended lectures on animal magnetism, and became a firm believer in its curative powers, even attempting to cure people by hypnosis. A few months later she was "fully possessed" with the idea that she had seen a "spectre." [11] She was becoming an established writer, and, on each topic which caught her easily won conviction, she contributed articles to newspapers and magazines.

With each new teaching job, Anna had found the ideal position. Each ended with an embroilment, often with some established family friend. As early as 1840 there had been a tripartite misunderstanding among Anna and two families who were close friends of the Blackwells, ending in a breach with one of the families. In 1844 there was unpleasantness between Anna and Dr. Cox, who had befriended and employed her. "Extraordinary," said Sam, "were not Anna the actress." From the family's point of view, the most disastrous of these feuds occurred at the school to which Anna took Emily and where she planned to take Ellen.

In March 1844 Anna was in excellent spirits because of her new position at St. Ann's, a female seminary in a New York suburb. It was, she reported, a splendid school, more like a luxurious home than an institution. Her employer, Dr. Schroeder, was a noble, generous man. That fall Emily went East to St. Ann's and, to Sam's intense envy, studied ten hours a day. She completed a full academic year before the family learned that, because of Dr. Schroeder's "extraordinary and absurd" behavior, Anna was leaving the school. This came as an "utter surprise, for hitherto we had received no hint of anything but perfect satisfaction." [12] Anna told Henry that the formerly generous Dr. Schroeder had begun to think of her as "his secret foe," and that when she left he cheated her of eighty dollars of her salary.

On leaving St. Ann's, Anna went to Brook Farm. Like all the young Blackwells, she was drawn to the ideal of association. A year earlier Marian, Sam, Emily, Howard and little George Washington had gone to visit the new Clermont Phalanx thirty-eight miles up the river from Cincinnati, but Anna was the first to join a Utopian colony. That summer and fall of 1845 she was at Brook Farm, and later spent short periods at other phalanxes. Of the Brook Farm days she said long afterward, "Those days were the happiest of my life. . . . Everyone was so genial, so happy. . . . A good deal of love-making went on, and nothing delighted the rest so much as when it ended, as happened several times, in marriage. . . . Ah! it was a happy time. Nothing ever grieved me more than the failure of the scheme." But that was in memory. Life was never so glamorous to Anna in the living.

In the next year or two Anna deviated, at least philosophically, even further from her family's stern morality. She came to know Albert Brisbane, leading exponent of Fourierism in America, whom, according to Elizabeth, she worshipped and called her dearest friend. Under his highly personal influence, Anna became an advocate of free love and unlimited association. Perhaps in support of Mr. Brisbane, who had recently been involved in a much publicized marital scandal, she went so far as to laugh at constancy and advocate "a continual change of lovers." She said Elizabeth knew nothing of life, "that there was scarcely one married woman that had not had a dozen lovers beside her husband" and that the evil was in maintaining a union "instead of reserving her body to go with her soul." Yet this defense of sexual freedom seems to have been largely theoretical, for at the same time Anna expressed a wistful regret that she herself "was not of a passionate nature and that all the women in our family were so deficient in that way." [13] It is significant that this information about Anna, along with an estimate of monogamy as a dull and demeaning institution, was transmitted by Elizabeth in the letter to Marian in which she attempted to dissuade her from marrying and going to India.

Anna did not even momentarily persuade Sam. Early in 1847 there was published Anna's translation of George Sand's *Jacques*, a feeling and perceptive translation of a romantic-philosophic novel. But its plot, a complexity of loves and kinds of love inside and outside marriage, shocked Sam, who found it the "production of a noble but misdirected and unhappy mind . . . exceedingly injurious to most minds particularly young ones." The theory "of conjugal relationships of which this book is a . . . brilliant special advocate is false and of the most evil tendency. Dear Anna! I fear she has thoughtlessly exposed herself to an odium much greater than she deserves or anticipates." [14]

What was to become of them? What did the future hold? It was a problem which in one way or another constantly concerned them. A year earlier, in the spring of 1846, when Emily had finally responded to her family's appeals to leave New York and the possibilities of her "unknown heart" and return to the known safety of home, she and Sam speculated one day on where they would all be ten years later. "Anna and Marianne," Sam recorded, "were both to be in Phalanxes, or with Hy. or me in case we had households and were in business. Emily in a phalanx or married—Ellen married. Henry preaching either as a missionary, or in the West somewhere, not yet settled. Sam doubtful in business in Cinti. or preaching somewhere. Howy civil engineering or in business in the West. Washy also in business. Harry probably married!" About Elizabeth they apparently hesitated to speculate.

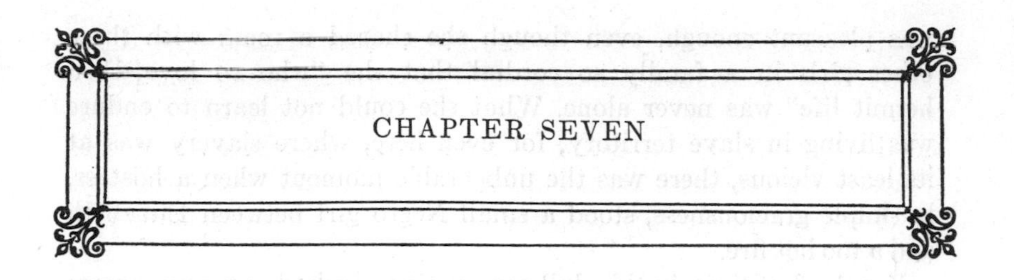

CHAPTER SEVEN

It was in 1844, just after her twenty-third birthday, that Elizabeth had left home to teach in Henderson, Kentucky. Henderson was "beyond the verge of civilization" in more ways than the keeping of slaves. Yet in those days of protected womanhood, the shy girl, frightened in a group of her contemporaries, was able to travel into the wilderness, and her family permitted her to do so. They did find a family friend who happened to be going that way and, accompanied by "Mr. S.," Elizabeth set off on the long boat trip down the Ohio. It was not until the fourth morning that a turn in the river revealed her destination, of which she could see nothing but "three dirty old frame buildings, a steep bank covered with mud, some negroes and dirty white people at the foot." The boat stopped. She and her trunks were unceremoniously dumped into the mud, and she was left there alone, watching the boat bear away her last connection with home.

The next few hours, agonizing in their uncertainty, were also full of seemingly insurmountable problems. The building where the school was to be set up was dirty, the plaster crumbling, the rooms filthy, the windows broken. Yet the following days proved Henderson, though a dull country town, not so hopeless as her first discouraging sight of it had indicated. The house where she lodged was pleasant enough, even though she shared a room with three other girls in a family so cordial that she "who so love[d] a hermit life" was never alone. What she could not learn to endure was living in slave territory, for even here, where slavery was at its least vicious, there was the unbearable moment when a hostess, in simple graciousness, stood a small Negro girl between Elizabeth and a too hot fire.

For the first time, in this dull community, she had as many escorts as she could desire and went several times with the town's young people to a place along the river which was a center for Sunday strolling and flirtation. Then one Sunday she was suddenly so "dreadfully tired of it" that without a word to her companions she "started off on a good brisk walk home." When the others returned and asked "in some consternation" why she had vanished, she replied by laughing "at them and their sentimental doings"—which effectively ended her popularity. She wrote home that she could see, in the dim future, her mother visiting in "my beautiful residence near Boston, where I shall present to you my adorable husband, my 3 daughters, Faith, Hope, and Charity, and 4 sons, Sounding Brass, Tinkling Cymbal, Gabriel, and Beelzebub." But in the clearer present, far from pursuing this dream, she admitted that she liked to make her contemporaries "a *little* afraid" [1] of her.

At the close of the school year she gave up her position and returned to Walnut Hills, where her family were then sharing a house with the Vails, and where Elizabeth found associations that were an intellectual treat after the deprivations of Henderson. But the companionship, the musical evenings when she and her brothers and sisters played and sang, the study of German and metaphysics were not enough to occupy her, and left her restlessly contemplating an uncertain future.

It was shortly after her return that a woman friend, dying of cancer, suggested that Elizabeth, with her love of study, ought to become a doctor. "If I could have been treated by a lady doctor," she said with Victorian modesty and a far from Victorian view of the role of women, "my worst sufferings would have been spared me."

Since Elizabeth had always "hated everything connected with the body" and been "foolishly ashamed of any form of illness," once even shutting herself in a closet so her family would not discover how sick she was, she not unnaturally rejected the idea of becoming a doctor; but in spite of herself it continued to plague her. One of its strongest appeals was a strange one, for, though there is little indication of such emotion in family letters or journals, including her own, Elizabeth says that from earliest years she had fallen constantly in love, but that, whenever she learned to know the object of her affection well enough "to realise what a life association might mean, [she] shrank from the prospect, disappointed or repelled." Now she began to see the study of medicine as an insuperable barrier against marriage, against love, a way to engross her thoughts, to "fill this vacuum and prevent this sad wearing away of the heart." [2]

She made inquiries about the possibility of a woman studying medicine, and received almost everywhere the reply that, though the idea might be excellent, its achievement was impossible. Impossible? The word was a challenge, canceling out her antagonism to the human body. Another spur was the realization that—insupportable insult to her sex—the term *female physician* referred only to women abortionists. "The study and practice of medicine," she said later, "is in my thought but one means to . . . the true ennoblement of woman, the full harmonious development of her unknown nature, and the consequent redemption of the whole human race." [3]

Little rays of encouragement came from Mrs. Vail and from Mr. Perkins, another family friend, but the outlook was gloomy. For one thing, even if an education could be arranged, she would need more money than she had; for another, she still felt that her "natural inclinations" led her away from such a career. At this point an opportunity presented itself to teach music at a school in Asheville, North Carolina, with the special inducement that the school's head, the Reverend John Dickson, was a former physician who was willing to help her study, an important factor, since medical students generally received a major part of their training in private study with practicing physicians.

It had been no light matter to travel to Henderson. The trip from Cincinnati to Asheville was longer and far more hazardous. So it was decided that Sam, with fourteen-year-old Howie for company, would drive her there. They set out on June 16, 1845, and spent almost eleven days in hard, uncertain driving, like the evening when they expected to lodge on the near bank of the Cumberland but at nightfall found themselves "at the foot of the wildest hills, on the wildest road amid the wildest forests and our way completely obstructed by a river ¼ mile broad, with a swift current."[4] Seeing a house on the other side, they "halloed" until a boy on a nag was sent over to guide them across shallows to the farmhouse, where they spent the night.

The first sight of Asheville, set on a mountain-rimmed plateau, was very different from Henderson, as was the school, the doctor's house, and Elizabeth's airy, unshared room. The boys stayed several days at a nearby tavern, and Sam approved of Dr. Dickson, an intelligent man and "right" on the slavery issue. But in spite of the pleasant surroundings, on the morning her brothers were to leave for the long journey home, Elizabeth found herself overwhelmed by despair at the lonely course she had chosen. Terrified, she called on Jesus to guide her. Suddenly, a "glorious presence, as of brilliant light, flooded my soul. There was nothing visible to the physical sense; but . . . all hesitation as to the rightfulness of my purpose left me, and never in after-life returned." It was "the most direct personal communication from the Unseen" she ever had.

She passed a pleasant winter in Asheville, teaching, studying medicine under Dr. Dickson's guidance, reading the *Harbinger* which confirmed her faith in association, becoming friends with nice little Mrs. Dickson, the doctor and their son, Flinn. Her greatest disappointment was that she was unable to hold classes for the Negro children. North Carolina law forbade their being taught to read. She did manage to organize a Negro Sunday school with four local ladies and one gentleman as coteachers, only to find that the ladies' sense of virtue at teaching their slaves the Scriptures was almost worse than refusal. However, she stifled her emotions, knowing that any display of anger would arm them in their prejudices and destroy even so slight an effort in the Negro's behalf.

The Asheville episode did not last long. At the end of the year, Dr. Dickson, ill and overburdened, decided to close his school. Instead of returning home, Elizabeth accepted an invitation from the doctor's brother, Dr. Samuel Dickson, to visit his family in Charleston, and on January 13, 1846, she, Mrs. John Dickson and Flinn set off by stage on a beautiful journey from the inland mountains to the low-lying rice fields and moss-hung trees of the coast.

In Charleston Dr. Dickson, a distinguished professor at the medical college, arranged for Elizabeth to teach music at a fashionable boarding school nearby, and in her free hours directed her medical reading. It was a busy, attractive life, which lasted for a year and a half, with a summer interval when Elizabeth moved with the school to Aiken, a healthier and cooler summer spot than Charleston.

She had been in correspondence with Emma Willard, whose academy in Troy, New York, was one of the earliest attempts in modern times to give women more than a rudimentary education. Mrs. Willard, who, to assemble a staff, had had to teach her teachers before they could instruct in any but the most elementary subjects, reassured the public that she was not going to turn out college-bred or aggressive females, nor undermine the institution of matrimony or male supremacy. Yet Mrs. Willard was not shocked at Elizabeth's desire to enter a masculine profession, and suggested her writing for advice to Dr. Warrington, a liberal Quaker physician in Philadelphia.

Dr. Warrington's reply was not encouraging. If the divine will was in favor of her project, he assured Elizabeth, it would prosper. As to mere human cooperation, his inquiries among both men and women showed them to be opposed to her course. The good old doctor himself believed woman had been designed as man's helpmeet; therefore man should be the physician, woman the nurse. But as Elizabeth had told Marian, opposition only made her firmer; so, in the spring of 1847, she went by sailing vessel to Philadelphia, then the chief center of medical learning. There she boarded with another liberal Quaker, Dr. William Elder, and his wife. The Elders became her close friends and the doctor one of her firmest supporters.

Once settled, she began anatomical studies at a private school run by a Dr. Allen, who with great tact gave her as her first lesson "a demonstration of the human wrist" whose structural beauty she could admire without embarrassment. Meanwhile she applied without success for admission to the four medical schools in Philadelphia. In discouragement she decided to try her luck in France, but was told that life for a decent woman alone in immoral Paris was impossible, and if she went, she must go disguised as a boy.

Anna, in Philadelphia to take the popular water cure, newly imported from Europe, also lived with the Elders, who were ardent associationists. Sam felt relieved that Elizabeth, with her "cool, unimpassioned judgment," was near Anna. Yet it was here that Anna initiated her younger sister into her views of association; for though Elizabeth had read and applauded Fourier, she had instinctively retreated from the sexual implications of his free association. At first she was shocked by Anna's acceptance of these views, but after meeting Anna's dear—and persuasive—friend Albert Brisbane, Elizabeth too was caught for a time by his radical Fourierist philosophy, so alien to her usual way of thought. To Marian she wrote, "I began to understand how rich life might be, where these free beautiful relations prevailed, how ever varying the enjoyment, how grand the knowledge to be gained—the isolated household seemed a prison, marriage a hopeless slavery." Plans for a new association were being developed in Philadelphia, and Elizabeth sent young Emily the "constitution of our Union."[5]

It was not in fact so long before Elizabeth's medical dreams met with success. After being rejected by the Philadelphia schools, she applied to twelve of the most prominent smaller colleges around the country. Rejections were immediate, among the stated reasons being not only the inappropriateness of a woman's studying medicine but the fear that women would be so popular as physicians that they would drive men from the field!

Then at the end of October came a letter from the Medical Institution of Geneva College (later Hobart College) on beautiful Seneca Lake in northern New York State, telling her she had been admitted there. Her acceptance had come about in a curious way, for the faculty had consented to take her only if her classmates voted without a single objection for her admission. One of these classmates said later that the faculty were obviously shunning responsibility on the assumption that the students would reject her application, but it is possible that they believed a hostile class could make life unbearable for her. In any case, when the Dean told the students of "the most extraordinary request which had ever been made to the faculty" and asked their opinion, the vote delivered with handkerchiefs waving and hats thrown in the air was an astonishing "Yes," except for a lone student who attempted to vote "No," and who was riotously and forcibly suppressed.[6]

At the time the study of medicine required so little effort that boys who could not hope to qualify for such serious professions as law or the ministry became doctors. Indeed there was a saying that a boy who was unfit for anything else must be a doctor; and a physician arguing in 1859 for the admission of women into the profession found it necessary to indicate at some length that medicine was an honorable profession, and doctors generally moral.[7] Medical students were notoriously rowdy and uncouth—those in Geneva so objectionable that the town residents tried to have the college declared a public nuisance—and it is likely that these boisterous young men conceived of admitting a woman to their group as a kind of practical joke. Whatever their reason, Elizabeth was to study medicine.

Requirements for a medical degree were not what they are today. They were in fact dangerously inadequate. To earn a degree at Geneva, candidates needed only to study for three years under the supervision of a physician, as Elizabeth had already done, and then to attend two sixteen-week sessions at the college and pass the required examinations. In medical schools the courses given in the first session, usually clinical surgery, medicine, therapeutics, materia medica, obstetrics and diseases of women, were repeated without the addition of new material in the second session, so that a student might have the chance of learning in the second year anything he had been too dull or careless to catch the first time. It was not until 1859 that a graded course was introduced in the medical department of Lind University in Chicago, with Harvard offering graded courses two years later. Harvard's initial efforts failed because the graded courses were optional, and students did not care to venture into unknown fields. Most medical schools had no hospital connections, and a physician could enter practice without ever having seen a patient, unless he had happened to encounter one in his years of private study with a doctor.

The state of medical education was appropriate, if not adequate, to the primitive state of medicine, which was just beginning to move from a philosophical study to an experimental science. There had been a great advance in the first half of the century in diagnosis and description of disease, but no comparable advance in treatment. The great cure of the famous Dr. Rush, who died in 1813, was to bleed and purge fever patients to the point of faintness. But he did concern himself with mental disease and even went so far as to advocate humane treatment for the insane.

Only four years before Elizabeth entered medical school young Dr. Oliver Wendell Holmes had suggested that puerperal fever, which caused the death of so large a proportion of women at childbirth, was spread by physicians moving from patient to patient without even washing their hands. He was furiously attacked by leading obstetricians. And it was in 1847, the year Elizabeth went to Geneva, that Dr. Semmelweis in Vienna, in the first known application of antisepsis, forced hospital attendants to wash their hands in a solution of calcium chloride before examining a patient. Anesthesia was equally new. Ether was first used in 1842 in minor surgery, in a major operation in the United States in 1846, and in Europe late in 1847. It was more than fifteen years later that Pasteur, a chemist, not a physician, promulgated the germ theory of disease, and was immediately and vigorously attacked as a charlatan by doctors everywhere. And Lister's papers of 1867 describing the excellent results of his use of antisepsis in surgery created a storm of protest in the medical profession.

It was into this profession that Elizabeth was determined to enter. Delighted by her acceptance at Geneva, she left Philadelphia at once, arriving in Geneva on November 6, 1847, a month after classes had started. There were one hundred and twenty-nine medical students enrolled that year.

For her first appearance at a lecture, Elizabeth entered the room accompanied by the professor. "She was quite small of stature"—in fact, a passport description in 1850 gives her height as only one and a half inches over five feet—"plainly dressed, appeared diffident and retiring, but [with] a firm and determined expression of face. Her entrance into that Bedlam . . . acted like magic upon every student. Each hurriedly sought his seat, and the most absolute silence prevailed. For the first time a lecture was given without the slightest interruption. . . . The sudden transformation . . . from a band of lawless desperadoes to gentlemen . . . proved to be permanent." [8]

Not only did the faculty benefit because their lectures could for the first time be heard, but their own manners were improved. When one of them, famous for his bluntness and for the vulgarity of his humor, told Elizabeth that she might be excused from his lecture on the reproductive organs, she replied that she was enrolled as a student and would attend every class. She offered, if her presence embarrassed him, to sit in the back of the room. The professor reported this encounter to the class, which when Elizabeth entered the room for the offending lecture, applauded vigorously; and with his humor curbed, the professor gave the best course of his career.

The situation was far from simple for Elizabeth, and required her full determination. At first, she almost starved herself, in the belief that if she were undernourished and pale, she would be less likely to blush when embarrassing subjects were discussed.[9] But this frailty of appearance, her clear grey eyes, her innate modesty of manner, the almost Quakerish style of her dress, did not spare her from community gossip. The women refused to talk to her, even the wife of a professor who lived at her boarding house. When they passed her on the street they drew away, clear of contamination, but stood and stared at her in shocked surprise. They were convinced she was either wicked or insane, and were looking for signs of one or both disorders. It was a lonely life.

When the first short session ended late in January, Elizabeth returned to Philadelphia, where she again stayed with the Elders, and tried to augment her small capital by giving music lessons. During that summer she "was admitted to reside in the [Blockley] Hospital and Alms House as a medical student," [10] and given a room in the women's syphilitic department in the hope that her presence there would subdue the unruly inmates. To these women she was as much a mystery as she had been to the matrons of Geneva. She could hear them in the evening stealthily approaching to peek through her keyhole, so she obligingly moved her desk into line with the keyhole so they could satisfy their curiosity about a woman involved in respectable work. As for Elizabeth, these patients were a revelation to her too, and her future opposition to legalized prostitution, her determination to "wage a war of extermination" on "licentiousness," dated from the days at Blockley.

The miserable atmosphere of the almshouse was intensified that summer of 1848 by Irish immigrants fleeing the famine in their homeland but bringing the famine fever with them. They fell sick on board ship, and were brought to Blockley in such numbers that there were not beds enough to hold them. Elizabeth used her experience with these poor dying immigrants as the basis of her Geneva graduation thesis. Written in forthright style, quite unlike the usual ornate medical writings of the time, the thesis was accepted and published as a leading article by the Buffalo *Medical Journal.* It described with remarkably advanced psychological insight how the poor peasants, seeking to escape "the evils of famine and pestilence," were crowded into "ill-ventilated steerages . . . filled to overflowing," where because they were "deprived of all excitement, without employment or exercise . . . fear, sorrow, anxiety, joined with the physical evils of their condition, tended to depress their vital energy, and the seeds of diseases . . . were thus nourished into life." [11]

She returned to Geneva in the fall for her second and final session. The students continued friendly and encouraging; yet of necessity she spent most of her time alone and lonely. In November she had a short visit from seventeen-year-old Howie, whom she had last seen in 1845 when he drove with her to Asheville. Howard was on his way to England. Their English cousin Kenyon had come to the United States to induce Henry to return with him and help Kenyon's brother, the English Sam Blackwell, in the management of their iron foundry. Henry was not interested, so Howie, young though he was, had been invited in his stead. With him went Anna, who had lavished on him her vast love for the little lost Howard of her childhood. Anna, who had been living in New York, was to visit Cousin Sam and rest up before undertaking a translation of Fourier for which she had been offered five hundred dollars a year and her travel expenses to Europe. At her departure her mother made one of those small, portentous comments which momentarily illuminate a secret side of life rarely revealed even in the Blackwells' most intimate journals. "Dear precious girl," her mother said, "she little knows how tenderly I feel towards her." [12] With Anna's departure Elizabeth's isolation in the East was greater than ever.

She passed her examinations brilliantly and on January 23, 1849, was graduated at the head of her class. Of the family, only Henry, then working in New York, attended the exercises at the Presbyterian church. It was a winter day unusual for cold Geneva, full of "sunshine and almost the warmth of summer." [13] The formerly hostile community turned out in force, and a Geneva lady described the difficulty even an hour before the ceremony of finding a seat in the gallery, where there was nothing to be seen "but a vast expanse of woman's bonnets and curious eyes." [14]

Elizabeth had refused to march in the class procession, for despite her determinedly unladylike revolt, she was enough the daughter of her age to strain at this gnat of rebellion. Instead she entered the church demurely on Henry's arm. She was "without hat or shawl. She wore a black dress—and cape—lace collar and cuffs and her *reddishly inclined* hair was very nicely braided." "I could not avoid the expense," Elizabeth explained about the new dress. "I can neither disgrace womankind, the college, nor the Blackwells by presenting myself in a shabby gown." Last of the students, she ascended the platform alone, a small, blonde, female David who had slain a giant. "The President [Dr. Hale] touched his cap and rose. You might have heard a pin drop. . . . She seemed embarrassed and after an effort, said to the Dr.—'I thank you, Sir. It shall be the effort of my life, by God's blessing to shed honor on this Diploma'—then bowed, blushed scarlet, left the stage and took her seat in the front pew among the Graduates, amid the Enthusiastic applause of all present." [15] That afternoon the Geneva ladies, who for over a year had made her life so difficult by refusing to acknowledge her presence, came belatedly to call.

Elizabeth has traditionally been called the first accredited woman doctor, but in her application to Castleton Medical College she attributed that honor to another. "I find," she wrote, "that in Berlin, the daughter of Professor Sebold had passed through the regular courses, obtained a Degree in Medicine, and is practicing successfully in Berlin." In fact, however, Dr. Sebold's stepdaughter, though she passed the university examinations in obstetrics, was no more than a midwife.

The day after she received her degree, Elizabeth returned to Philadelphia to continue her education at the hospitals there. She was received in a far friendlier spirit than before, and permitted to attend lectures. A letter to her mother shows changes in her own way of thought too, and another, unrecorded kind of education. Now she again believes in the "Divine marriage institution, and shall always support it by precept, and as soon as I get the chance by example too, and all those who upset it I consider fools and infidels." The *Harbinger* does much mischief. Fourier is twaddle, associationists often "a poor set of people" who ought to begin by reforming themselves.[16]

It was over five years since she had left home. Now Cousin Kenyon, returning to England after more than a year in the United States, asked her to go with him to explore the possibilities of European study before starting practice in America. Having decided to accept, she went to Cincinnati to say good-bye to her family. When she left, all the family still at home came to see her off, "mother leaning on S., the three sisters on one side, H. and G. on the other, all hearts in sympathy. I could not keep down the tears as I caught the last glimpse of those dear, true ones."

CHAPTER EIGHT

During these years when the close-knit family was beginning to disperse, they kept in touch not only by letters and visits but by a Christmas Annual, a volume to which each contributed, and of which copies, laboriously written out by home members, were sent away to the travelers. The contributions were thinly pseudonymous, their authors soon identified. There were stories, poems, essays, some of them decorated with charming pen-and-ink drawings of humorous little figures.

In 1844 Henry contributed a letter from Mr. Destiny to his female friends, the Misses Fates, describing a family persecuted by "a fiend entitled 'Pecuniary Embarrassment.' " The head of this family, Mrs. Melodious Songster, is "a lady equally conspicuous for the extreme strictness of her religious faith . . . and her genuine goodness of heart and sweetness of temper" who victimizes "her children under a small iron car of Juggernaut, entitled 'Family Prayers' which four times a day she tries to drag them to." These children are Miss Changeable Earnest (Anna), Miss Peptic Painter (Marian), with "a passion for milk and novels, both of which she imbibes in large quantities," Miss Transcendental Nightingale (Elizabeth), "the Lion of the Family . . . a desperate and energetic sort of female," Sacred Awe (Sam), "a fellow of decidedly reverential and orthodox character," Voracious Noodle (Henry himself), "fond of lying, in joke, and no less so of lying—in bed of a morning, very loud of voice, and with something of the asinine about him," Lymphatic Carrot (Emily), Dumpling Snub (Ellen), "a little girl equally remarkable for the vivacity of her temper, and the vinegar of her disposition, the shortness of her figure, and the length of her nails," Lumpy Crackabout (Howard), whose "favorite passions are eating and flying kites," and Idle Ichabod (George Washington).

In the years when the Lion of the Family was achieving her astonishing success, her brothers Sacred Awe and Voracious Noodle were struggling with the disheartening problem of supporting the family. For several years their efforts were like a sad little ballet of hope and failure. In the fall of 1845 Sam and a Mr. Denning bought a broken-down flour mill, and Sam, full of optimism, began traveling on buying expeditions to Madison, Wisconsin, and other wheat markets; but by spring, when the repaired mills were ready to grind, the price of flour had slid rapidly, and it was obvious they would lose money on their first operations. Henry continued discontentedly in his bookkeeping job, while searching for more interesting and profitable work, even if it meant leaving Cincinnati. Within a year he too was involved in Sam's enterprise and, like Sam, busy on wheat-buying expeditions.

Travel was still slow and dangerous, and once Sam was on a river boat which in the middle of the night was rammed by another vessel. "I woke with the sound of a tremendous crash and leaping from my berth, found the boat's head turned up stream and sinking. I . . . slipped on my coat and one boot when the water began to seep through the floor. I seized my clothes and ran out to the guards, the water by this time drenching me up to my pockets. I clambered on to the hurricane deck, over the chimneys which had fallen down and up on the pilot house. The boat sank to the hurricane deck and then grounded," whereupon the boat which had rammed it came up and took off all "except 5 or 6 of the poor fellows on deck who were drowned." [1]

By early 1847 business had improved enough for them to pay off a thousand-dollar note on the mill. A little later, by an exchange of services with a millwright and foundry concern, they were able to acquire an interest in that business too, but this proved a burden weighing down their entire enterprise, and too late they tried to rid themselves of it.

That summer, undaunted by his shipwreck, Sam set off with his mother and Marian for a trip East. Elizabeth, who had recently come to Philadelphia from Asheville, was surprised and delighted by their visit. She found her mother and sister looking much as always, only better dressed, "quite stylish" in fact. Anna was in the country—she spent part of that summer at the North American Phalanx in Red Bank, New Jersey—but returned in time to see them.

Sam went on to New York to visit Dennis Harris. Mr. Harris had recently bought the Congress Sugar House, vacant for eight years after the fire which had gutted it in Father Blackwell's time, and he was prospering. Sam found his father's friend one of those "lowly, earnest, cheerful, practical, Xians . . . who keep the bright earth around them greener for their presence." [2] Mr. Harris offered to take Sam into his home and to teach him sugar refining, a business which he believed was easy to learn and could be started in a small way. Sam declined, but when, back in Cincinnati, he told Henry of Mr. Harris's proposition, Henry set off at once to take advantage of the opportunity.

His letters from New York were hopeful. He planned to come home in December to start a refinery; meanwhile Sam was to search for a suitable building. Henry had barely returned when Sam's mill failed, and though Sam consoled himself with the thought that with God's help he had naught to fear, such consolation, in that uncertain world, was necessary. The necessity increased when Henry's first attempts with his "pans" were unsuccessful. Nevertheless, in April 1848, Sam "started bed, board and business quite literally" [3] with Henry. Soon they had news that Mr. Harris's refinery had burned, with heavy loss to him. A few weeks later their own affairs took another bad turn, and in the middle of May Henry's sugar house burned down too, "the end of 8 months of more effort and anxiety than he ever felt or made before."

Now both brothers were out of work. Henry returned to New York to look for opportunities there, and even considered the possibility—almost surely shut off from him by the need to earn a living—of studying medicine with Elizabeth, a possibility for which, in her loneliness at medical school, Elizabeth longed. Sam stayed in Cincinnati to close up the business and find a job; and it was at this moment that he had the opportunity to buy a share in a friend's wholesale and retail hardware store. From New York Henry wrote, offering Sam his small capital. Sam was overwhelmed by a generosity which meant that Henry himself must give up hope of going into business. Yet the proposition seemed sound and, with three partners to share the burden, he decided to take the chance. Henry was working and even living in the refinery which Mr. Harris had rebuilt on an immense scale. New York was to be his home, and Cousin Kenyon, who had come to the United States to persuade him to return to England and the family foundry, was unable to do so.

Yet even so absorbing a preoccupation with ways and means did not divert the brothers from their concern with world betterment. Sam continued to teach Sunday school, attend antislavery and temperance meetings, and to debate, when he was in the milling business, whether he ought to have dealings with distillers in their nefarious trade. From New York Henry visited the North American Phalanx in New Jersey, and became an ever more convinced associationist, with the result that Sam was finally persuaded that his worrisome younger brother was "a noble soul, and the Lord will have him—not Satan." And Henry told a friend that, though he was now comfortably situated, he felt he must, with Fourier's guidance, aid in solving the " 'problem of Human destiny,' " and that, though considered a heretic, he wished "to practice the precepts of Christ." [4]

These personal events were played out against the background of a world in crisis. The ferment of the nineteenth century, which, as in a reducing mirror, could be viewed in the Blackwell family, culminated in 1848 in revolutions throughout Europe. The old order everywhere was crumbling, and even the triumphant bourgeoisie felt the pressure from beneath of the overworked yet starving lower classes. Machine methods had congregated the new middle class and the new factory workers in cities, where contact was closer and rebellion spread far more rapidly than in feudal lands. Telegraph, travel, printing presses sped news now from country to country, and the February revolution in Paris, which deposed Louis

Philippe, had repercussions throughout discontented Europe. Frightened rulers hastened to grant small reforms, but they were not enough. Uprisings with democratic demands occurred in Vienna, Berlin, Milan, Venice and other cities across the continent.

Sam noted with delight that "Hardly a blow has been struck for the preservation of hereditary privilege—hardly a popular demand but has been at once conceded and that with a sort of trembling haste as tho. the echoes of the savage vengeance of the French Revolution still lingered with a nightmare spell in the ears of Europe's frightened Sovereigns." [5] But by mid-year his tone had changed. "Another insurrection in Paris, and again subdued by the Natl. Guards"; and a month later, in France "15,000 are said to have fallen by brothers' hands in the sanguinary 3 days war."

The forces of rebellion had begun to founder. The demand for constitutions was inevitably linked to a demand for the federation of cities and small separate states into larger entities, so that just as the democratic movement seemed to be succeeding, nationalistic upsurgings confused the issue and gave repressive powers a chance to restore their governments and clamp down on their discordant populations. In the loud clamor of revolution and repression, the publication early that year of a small volume by Karl Marx and Friedrich Engels, the *Communist Manifesto,* went largely unnoticed.

In the United States the great news of 1848 was the increasing rumor of vast deposits of gold in California. By the year's end the gold fever had seized the nation and "multitudes . . . flocked to the El Dorado." [6] Among the infected was Henry, who alarmed the family by leaving his job with Mr. Harris and deciding to head for California. They commissioned Cousin Kenyon, who was then visiting them, to go East and cure the "yellow fever" victim. As Marian wrote to Henry on Christmas day, "Nothing but a feeling like life or Death" would have persuaded them to part with Kenyon. She warned Henry that Sam would probably be ruined too if he had to return the money Henry had lent him. In the same letter young Ellen added her plea: "Harry how could you think of setting off so hastily on a journey of six or seven thousand miles away from us all on such a wild goose chase . . . the papers you have sent us are so full of discrepancies, and bear such evident marks of wild exageration [*sic*] that . . . you must be very credulous to risk everything on their statements."

Yet for all their logic, the folks back home were not performing so logically, for in July, Howard, the least communicative member of the family, had broken his silence to report to Henry that "Mother is *wild* for speculating in real estate and in case of selling the homestead wants to buy all kinds of lots and put up impossible buildings, consisting of 2 rooms and 2 over, that are to serve as back buildings to magnificent edifices after a while." [7] Her plan included borrowing enough from friends so that she would not need cash for a year. It was hard for people who had labored so long and conscientiously with so little success to resist the epidemic of speculation fever and the lure of quick riches.

Young Ellen too had been bitten by the real-estate bug, and hoped her small savings would buy some lots. At twenty Ellen had taken her place in the ranks of gifted Blackwells. She was to be a painter. Now, having taught in the Vails' school, she was resigning to give private music and painting lessons instead.

Henry had actually put money into the California scheme in partnership with two other men when the cumulative family pressure descended on him. Sam, urging against "these desperate leaps for instant fortunes . . . not to be depended on," pointed out that Henry was taking the entire risk, that his partners had neither capital nor reputation.

Perhaps, as in the case of Anna's marriage, family argument prevailed. Perhaps it was because Sam believed there would soon be an opening for Henry in his successful hardware venture, and Kenyon documented this possibility by arranging a loan of one thousand dollars from the English Blackwells. In any case, Henry headed not for California but for home, and on March 8, 1849, "Coombs, Ryland and Blackwells unfurled their flag and launched the firm ship." In May the money arrived from England, and they also sold their house to add to the firm's capital.

In July, when they were moving into a new home, there was a cholera epidemic so severe that President Zachary Taylor, hero of the Mexican War, declared a national fast day. Sam, still indignant about the war, referred to Taylor as the Robber President. News from the family travelers reported that, after a month in

England, Elizabeth had gone on to Paris, where she had been joined by Anna. She, Anna and Howard had been visiting the English cousins at Portway Hall, their home outside the town of Dudley, in the mining district near Birmingham. Kenyon had contracted rheumatism on the sea voyage and was very ill.

Howard continued to live with their English cousin Sam, whose wife had recently died. The iron trade had suffered from the unsettled conditions throughout Europe. Prices were low, and wages little more than half what they had been two years before. Howard, at eighteen, was too young and inexperienced for the responsibilities heaped upon him. Yet he envisioned an exciting, profitable future in a giant manufacturing enterprise. Cousin Sam's ironworks were already too small for his ambition.[8] Meanwhile he was further burdened by separation from the kind of companionship he was accustomed to, since he now spent most of his time with colliers and "navvies." The Blackwell aunts had visited Portway Hall, and in one of his rare letters home Howard described poor Aunt Ann, who had had a long, solitary, hard-working life, as an exceedingly stiff old lady "with a cap a foot and a half high—who utters commonplace observations in a very slow voice." [9] Aunt Lucy, the only aunt who had married, he thought a gentle and pleasant person.

Elizabeth and Anna had left before the aunts came. Elizabeth had in fact stayed only a few weeks at Dudley. From there, through the efforts of Charles Plevin, a young friend of Cousin Sam's, she was able to visit the leading Birmingham hospitals under the guidance of important doctors on their staffs; everywhere she was treated with courtesy mixed with that curiosity to which she was growing accustomed. She found Cousin Sam and his friend Charles the kind of idealistic young men she had known at home. They longed for a better world, and took Fichte, Carlyle, Emerson and Channing as their teachers; but Elizabeth regretted that they still did not know Fourier and Swedenborg, and so could not work with true insight and practical efficiency.

Charles was going to London and offered to escort Elizabeth there; and another friend of Cousin Sam's gained her admittance to various hospitals and introductions to leading physicians. It was very different from the trip her elder sisters had taken to London before leaving England. She spent a happy week seeing the sights, and attended some gay parties, at one of which she was induced to drink a glass of wine, the first she had ever tasted. She had then gone on to Paris to see whether she could enter a hospital there, and also to visit Alphonse de Lamartine, poet, historian, politician and associationist, to present officially to him the proceedings of the Philadelphia Association, entrusted to her for this purpose. She was much struck by his home, which was large and elegant, and by Lamartine, whose "exterior harmonised perfectly with his poetry," [10] for his every movement was music, his voice clear and melodious.

In Cincinnati, her brothers, having finally established themselves in a stable business, were able to indulge more than before in the cultural activities they so enjoyed. They had already organized a debating club. Now, with his neighbor and friend Ainsworth Spofford, later Librarian of the Library of Congress, Henry helped to form a literary club, which continued for many years and had among its members Rutherford B. Hayes and, later, William Howard Taft. The family and their neighbors started a group for reading new books aloud. They read Charlotte Brontë's *Shirley,* published under the pseudonym Currer Bell, a name she had originally taken because the idea that a nice English girl should write novels was too shocking to be admitted. They read *David Copperfield* as it appeared periodically, and Harriet Martineau's *The Hour and the Man: A Historical Romance* dealing with the slave rebellion in Santo Domingo and its great leader, Toussaint L'Ouverture. In May 1850 Emerson gave a series of lectures in Cincinnati to which they all went. Henry met him several times, and was one of a party which accompanied him on a day's excursion.

A year later they went to hear Jenny Lind, so popular that tickets to her concert brought from two to twenty dollars or even thirty dollars. Sam found her "very graceful and apparently artless in her movements. Her voice did not seem to me equal throughout its Compass. . . . But there was a range of high notes, not the highest, which seemed to me perfect, as clear as the clearest bell and as sweet as the sweetest flute. . . . Barnum, who accompanied her, is a most adroit manager and is said to have netted some **$70,000** in Cincinnati alone, to be divided between her and himself." That summer Sam read aloud to the family their friend

"Mrs. Stowe's capital little story 'Uncle Tom's Cabin'" which was appearing serially in the newspaper.

The working members of the family had been increased by George Washington, who had insisted on leaving school to get a job. Sam saw God's constant beneficence to them in the fact that Washy quickly found just the right job. Washy's first act as a businessman was to insist on being called George.

For a time now there were no sisters at home. In January 1850 Emily was offered Elizabeth's old job in Henderson, Kentucky. She had opened her own school, which was doing fairly well, but the offer of five hundred and twenty-five dollars a year and board was better than she could hope to earn in Cincinnati, and she accepted, making the difficult trip with the same unconcern her sister had. She came home that summer and went back next fall, but found the "total isolation unspeakably monotonous and wearisome," and at the end of her year returned to take a teaching job in Cincinnati.

Not long after Emily's first departure for Henderson, Marian and Ellen were invited by a family friend, Mrs. Alofsen, to visit her in the East, and at the end of April 1850 they set off. They stopped to see the sights at Niagara and Albany, then spent three weeks with the Alofsens in Jersey City. Marian had planned to go on to Boston alone, but at the last moment Ellen, apparently afraid of being left without a member of her family, decided to accompany her. On their way they visited Marian's old mentor, William Henry Channing.

In Boston they moved at once into the most advanced intellectual circles, boarding with Elizabeth Peabody, whose home was a meeting place for the Transcendentalists. She was the lady of whom Henry James later made rather cruel use in *The Bostonians*. At the time, Channing warned the sisters, "You must not be frightened by her rough manners . . . or hair not so smooth as might be—but if you can get beyond that she is an angel—and I sometimes think how people will wonder when they see her in the other world with her wings on."[11] In this world, Marian found her "a short dumpy fair complexioned lady with gray hair." One of her sisters had married Horace Mann, the other, Nathaniel Hawthorne. Elizabeth was not married then or later.

In June, when Marian left with her new friend Anna Parsons to take the currently popular water cure at Brattleboro, Vermont, Ellen found the courage to return to the Alofsens, where she could continue her art studies. Although she stayed with them for some months, she was rarely free of the sense that they did not like her, that everyone was relieved when she retired to her room after dinner. "It seemed to me," she confided to her inevitable diary, "I need never expect much real, lasting friendship out of our own family." Yet the Alofsens continued to urge her to stay, and Augustus, a young man who also lived there and was a more advanced student of art than she, helped her in friendly enough fashion with her painting.

From the amount of thought she gave him, Ellen must have been unconsciously in love with Augustus. Yet her Blackwellian demands for him were lofty and uncompromising. "I have sought to find some traces of generous unselfish feeling, some high aim for the future, but I cannot see a sign of anything of the kind," she pronounced; while of herself she inexorably asked, "What can I do to grow wise and perfectly unselfish?" Like most young people, she felt misunderstood. She had no more decided that for once Mrs. Alofsen looked on her with "some of that true friendship" for which she longed than, in the course of an intellectual discussion, her hostess revealed that she found Ellen cold-hearted and self-satisfied, interested only in intellectual pleasures. "I am surprised how little people can judge my character," said Ellen.

With the Alofsens' encouragement she began to attend social gatherings. She went several times to the opera, where she "longed to live the music, and come to a tragic end, to be an opera singer, or at least a gentleman, that I might go every night to the opera, and do a thousand wild independent things. . . . I feel as if I had hardly commenced to live, as if there was a deep wild life somewhere that I long to taste." [12] Yet the little she was permitted to taste was too much for her. The parties she attended seemed too uproarious, and she blamed herself for being too gay. She believed a certain restraint should be maintained among a group of young people, that too much freedom was undignified. She went to the ballet and was virtuously shocked. The dresses were "insufficient," the story mean and low. Impossible to imagine decent people enjoying such spectacles! Yet, in spite of this respectability, Ellen found it necessary to reassure her mother that, though she had tempted her soul with such traps of Satan, she still "usually" went to church, and that the devil had "not got her yet."

Meanwhile Marian was not faring well. She had chosen Brattleboro for her cure because there she could continue the intellectual companionship of Boston. The antislavery writer and preacher Thomas Wentworth Higginson was there with his wife, the sister of William Ellery Channing and Higginson's own cousin, and so was one of Miss Peabody's sisters. Like Anna, at first contact with a new environment Marian was incredibly optimistic. She wrote home that she had reached "journey's end at last—the paradise towards which I have for the last three years been turning such longing eyes—is gained." She was ecstatic about the chief doctor, an old man who reminded her of her father, except that he was an agnostic, a fact which amazed her, for she had believed doubts to be the exclusive property of the young.

Then, as Anna's always did, her mood veered. She was taking a water cure; drinking water in quantity, soaking in sitz baths, going for long, prescribed walks. The doctor disapproved of her habit of sitting in her room writing endless letters. She suffered from headaches, and he recommended fresh air and company. She tried to mingle, but "most of the ladies except a few dreary old folks like myself—are so gay that I feel quite out of my element among them and feel happier alone." [13] She was not yet thirty-two. "How is it," she wrote later that summer, "that all girls but those of our own family seem to be so full of spirits and fun?" [14]

She had always been afflicted by what she called fits of laziness, but now her lethargy had grown so that it was "too much trouble to open my mouth and make myself agreeable . . . can scarcely rouse . . . to brush my hair . . . or walk down to my meals." By August she had had enough and, after considerable indecision, departed for Marblehead, Massachusetts, because she felt that the ocean and the remoteness would cure her.

Her family might well have been more disturbed by her account of the energy which now possessed her than by her earlier lethargy. She arrived at a seaside resort in August after dark, knowing no one and with no place to stay. She accepted advice from a stranger on where to get off the train, and once off, applied for information to "a decent looking young woman carrying a bundle. . . . She took me to the most dismal old house I ever saw kept by a good old soul with a nutcracker face." Into this strange house Marian unquestioningly entered, and the good old soul took her in and lent her night clothes. Next day, while looking for permanent quarters, she lost her way in a fog, was caught in drenching rain, went into a bog up to her ankles. It is impossible to convey the sense of incompetence, confusion and unnecessary risk, or to imagine a sick woman surviving the physical exertions Marian describes.

Marian and Ellen stayed in the East. In September Ellen enrolled in a small art class in New York, and enjoyed the first lessons. Then suddenly she was seized by a conviction that studying art and music was not what she wished to do; but she could not think of a substitute. She began to be overwhelmed by "downright dreadful blue fits" in which she again believed no one cared for her.[15] She decided she must join Marian.

They met in October 1850 at Worcester, Massachusetts, where the First National Woman's Rights Convention was being held. Woman's rights had become an organized cause only two years before, when the quiet-mannered Quaker Lucretia Mott and pretty, rebellious Elizabeth Cady Stanton, with a few friends, had arranged the first Woman's Rights Convention in the small town of Seneca Falls in upper New York State. At the Seneca Falls meeting the right to vote was hardly mentioned. It was too daring a demand. The first considerations were the disabilities of women before the law, for in most states of the Union a married woman had no property rights, not even the right to be guardian of her own children, and her husband was her absolute ruler.

Even before the Seneca Falls convention, a few free and determined spirits had taken up the cudgels for the oppressed half of the human race. Foremost among them was Lucy Stone, who, alone and unknown, had decided to dedicate her life to preaching woman's rights. Henry Blackwell had met the courageous little woman one day in the summer of 1850 when, on her way through Cincinnati, she had come to the hardware store to cash an Anti-Slavery

Society draft on its former owner, Frank Donaldson, an ardent abolitionist. Dismayed at not finding Mr. Donaldson, she had confided her problem to Henry, who not only offered to cash the draft but, finding "something beautiful in her expression and wonderfully eloquent in her voice and manner,"[16] decided she would be an ideal wife, not for him, but for Sam. Sam, meeting her next day, did not share Henry's conviction.

Now, in the East, Marian and Ellen heard Lucy Stone and others speak at the convention. The press, with few exceptions, was wildly derisive. The New York *Herald* headlined the convention as an "Awful Combination of Socialism, Abolition and Infidelity," and characterized its members, male and female, young and old, as "crazy old women." But the Blackwell sisters were delighted by the "talent and grace of the speakers." They had never felt more at home. They were officially listed as members of the convention from Ohio, and were both appointed to committees. They had found a new form of association.

CHAPTER NINE

A year and a half before, Elizabeth had gone from England to Paris to continue her training and to add surgery to her other qualifications. In the United States, enchanted then as always by the idea that European culture was far in advance of American, she had been assured that in Paris she could pursue her medical education without difficulty. But this proved to be part of the continental delusion, and after the disappointing discovery that she could not attend public classes or arrange for private instruction,[1] in the early summer of 1849 she had entered La Maternité, hoping to become an accomplished obstetrician instead. Even here her status was that of the young uneducated girls who came to study midwifery.

La Maternité was an odd place for a forward-looking young woman to find herself. Originally a private estate, the site had been enlarged in the early seventeenth century and converted into the convent of Port-Royal. It accumulated its share of legends and miracles, was turned into a prison during the Revolution, and after the guillotine had reduced the need for prison space was made a maternity hospital. In Elizabeth's day high convent-prison walls, now almost gone, still enclosed the ancient buildings and the old cloisters and gardens. In appearance and regulations it seemed a convent still, if not a prison.

It was hard for Elizabeth to turn her back on an exciting and turbulent city, where that June of 1849 she and Anna had even witnessed an insurrection and its suppression. Now, though stirring political events continued in nearby streets, the inhabitants of La Maternité were unaware of their existence. The famous hospital was a training center for the *sages-femmes* of France, and the rosy-cheeked *élèves* came from the provinces to learn their profession. They lived frugal, rigidly supervised lives, worked throughout the day when not attending lectures, and were on duty as often as every fourth or fifth night, losing a whole night's sleep. They slept, when there was time, in dormitories, bathed in tubs ranged side by side the length of a single room, and did not go outside the high walls of the institution for months on end, though at specified hours they could welcome visitors in a parlor "filled with wooden benches where all manner of rough looking people . . . assembled to visit the *élèves*." Elizabeth received no dispensation for her special status, but shared every aspect of the lives of the young students. She liked the warm-hearted, boisterous girls, and they liked her, once they had recovered from their disappointment at her appearance. They had believed all Americans were black.

Elizabeth's closest friend at the hospital was the chief intern, Monsieur Hippolyte Blot, "a very handsome, somewhat dignified physician, with, I fancy, a rather cross temper." When Monsieur Blot overcame his first shyness in Elizabeth's presence, he asked her to teach him English, a pleasant relaxation for her, since she found communicating entirely in French a considerable burden.

So rigid were the rules that it was nearly four months before Elizabeth walked for the first time out of the gateway in the high walls, and then Anna was required to call for her at nine in the morning, and to bring her back not a moment later than eight o'clock in the evening. Close outside the walls were the Observatory, the narrow streets, the formal flower beds of the Luxembourg gardens, the sound of wooden shoes clattering along the pavements, the limitless charms of Paris. "How gay and free and delightful the city seemed, after my four months imprisonment."

They went to the Louvre, where the works of art "seemed more beautiful than ever." For Elizabeth's further entertainment, Anna had chosen a magnetic séance, but unfortunately none of the reported miracles, in which Anna was a firm believer, occurred that day. Elizabeth's comment on the séance, like her comments on so much of life where personal emotions did not enter, was perspicacious. "There is an odd side to all reformers," she said, "to all who are pursuing a new idea earnestly, that is very whimsical." Did she include herself and Anna in this estimate?

She was so pleased with the wide experience in obstetrics the hospital provided that she decided to stay on. She had originally planned to leave after three months, and it would have been well if she had done so, because on November 4 she noted in her diary that "in the dark early morning, whilst syringing the eye of one of my tiny patients for purulent ophthalmia, some of the water had spurted in my own eye. It was much swollen at night, and in the morning the lids were closely adherent from suppuration."

She asked permission to leave until the infection was cured, and when this was refused, went in alarm to Monsieur Blot. He examined the eye and, equally alarmed at its condition, obtained permission to devote the next days to caring for Elizabeth. During that painful period her friend Mademoiselle Mallet, first assistant *sage-femme,* and Monsieur Blot came day and night at alternate hours to treat her eye. "The sympathy was universal and deep, the *élèves* asking after me with tears. An unheard-of permission was granted to Anna to visit me three times a day." [2] And three times a day "in rain and snow" Anna trudged to and from the hospital to give Elizabeth magnetic treatments.

Anna had seized on animal magnetism, as on most new ideas, more enthusiastically than judiciously; the hospital authorities were either tolerant or shared her faith. Mesmer's animal magnetism, later recognized as a form of hypnotism, consisted in part of the healer passing his hands over the afflicted areas of the patient's body. It had for some time been a rage in Paris, and was now linked to a passion for spiritualism and spirit rappings. Anna's hands may have gently hypnotized Elizabeth or only soothed her. In any case they had little relevance to the progress of her disease.

"For three weeks I lay in bed with both eyes closed, then the right eye began to open gradually." At last she was given her *congé*. With eyes bandaged and a veil over her face, she was led to a carriage, and went to live with Anna in her apartment on the Rue Fleurus opposite the Luxembourg gardens. There Anna too was defying the tradition of women in her time by trying to support herself as European correspondent to American newspapers. Sam, as her agent, noted that summer that the "Pittsburgh Com. Journal wrote accepting Anna as a correspondent at $5 pr. letter once a fortnight. . . . The Columbian has not yet paid the amt due to her." She was also to write for the Methodist literary monthly, *Ladies' Repository,* and later she made a "fresh arrangement with Greeley to correspond occasionally with the Tribune." A nearby neighbor and frequent visitor was handsome Monsieur Blot, who had by now left the hospital to enter private practice.

There have been attempts to construct a romance between Monsieur Blot and Elizabeth, and fragments of evidence tend to suggest such a possibility. "I shall miss him exceedingly when I leave [Paris]," Elizabeth wrote to Emily, "for there is a most affectionate sympathy between us—but—a reformer's life is not a garden of roses." [3] Then, without apparent emotion, she told Marian, her closest confidant, that Anna had fallen in love with the doctor, and, weaned from "ultra Fourierism" and a former undesirable attachment (perhaps to Albert Brisbane), was now a "firm supporter of marriage." But, said Elizabeth, Anna—who was thirty-four—knew that a young man of twenty-seven with a tendency to consumption, starting practice without fortune or resources, was no fit husband for her. Elizabeth's own friendship with Monsieur Blot was "beautiful," though they were not "elective affinities." She would welcome him as a brother, but in matters of the heart feared "disappointment and suffering."

Yet shortly afterward, when she had left Paris, she confided to her even more intimate diary, "I wrote to him—how strongly my life turns to him, and yet that terrible suffering has put a distance between us that nothing can remove." If this was not Monsieur Blot, it is difficult to imagine who it could have been. And several days later there was another notation: "A letter from Anna much affected me—ah I cannot view the past with calmness, and for her I grieve deeply." Again Elizabeth's fantasy of love seems to have been at variance with her response when it came close. The beautiful dream in human, male attire turned always into a threat of disappointment and suffering.

The family in America knew nothing of Elizabeth's accident until they received a letter written by Anna just before Elizabeth went home with her, when she was able to tell them that Elizabeth's right eye at least had been saved. But having spared them the uncertainty of the first terrible weeks, she spared them nothing now. She began by describing Elizabeth's misery and her own—"For the first few days after her illness began I wept almost the whole time" [4]—before giving them the least clue as to the nature of the illness. Finally she told them the whole sad story, and two weeks later reported that it seemed certain Elizabeth had lost the sight of her left eye. The right had now opened enough for her to read her letters, but she could not yet write.

Later Elizabeth wrote to her ex-army-uncle, Charles, and Aunt Eliza that "a brave soldier's niece . . . will be proud of the wounds gained in a great cause and resolved more strongly than ever to 'conquer or die.'" She rejoiced that her disfigurement was not striking, but "then happily I never had any beauty to boast of." She had rarely, she said, wavered in her conviction that she would see again, and that she would be a physician. Nor was her "faith shaken in Providence in the least." Yet the months after she left La Maternité were bitterer than she would admit, and seemed endless, since she had no occupation except suffering with which to fill them; she could not work or study or even read.

In June 1850 she decided to go to Gräfenberg, Germany, for a water cure. "Travelling rapidly through France, Germany, and Prussia, in five days [she] reached the famous water-cure region." [5] The sanitarium had been established by an Austrian peasant named Priessnitz, who, in spite of the fact that he was not a doctor, was making a fortune out of hydrotherapy. Elizabeth, so insistent on a proper degree for herself, nevertheless seemed content to accept Priessnitz as an authority. She liked his appearance, which was "honest and good," and relied on his assurance that he could make her strong again without injury to her eye. And indeed almost immediately the fresh air, the milk, bread and fruit diet, the mountain walks, and the water inside and out renewed her energy.

She was astonished to find that she had come to a fashionable resort crammed with European nobility, including a Princess Oblenska, who asked her to pay a professional visit for which Elizabeth collected her first fee. She was at Gräfenberg at almost the moment her sister Marian was undergoing similar treatment at Brattleboro; but in spite of Elizabeth's sad disease and her "not very striking disfigurement," her determination to continue her career, her witty estimate of her fashionable copatients and their fashionable clothes, which showed up the poverty of her own simple wardrobe, stand in dramatic contrast to Marian's lethargy, despair and the hysteria which almost caused her to leave immediately after her arrival because one of the lady guests, who tried to be her friend, was an antiabolitionist, and Marian "could not bear" such people.

Unfortunately for Elizabeth and her optimistic belief that her eye would recover, the new way of life caused a serious inflammation in the afflicted eye. She hurried back to Paris, where she suffered the further misery of having the sick eye removed and replaced by a glass one. With it went her hopes of becoming a surgeon, and perhaps other more fanciful hopes, but not the determination to pursue her career.

In England, meanwhile, faithful Cousin Kenyon had been trying to arrange a hospital connection for her; and in May 1850 St. Bartholomew's Hospital, after meetings of its Medical Council and its Board of Governors, had duly recorded in the great handwritten journals which contained the minutes of the period: ". . . it was agreed 'that it appeared desirable that the Treasurer should grant permission to Miss Blackwell to attend the Hospital as requested.' " She was to "visit at the Wards appropriated to females, during the attendance of the Physicians and Surgeons," and male wards, "excepting the Syphilitic Wards, as the Physicians and Surgeons may from time to time deem advisable." She would dissect in a room "separate from the general dissecting rooms," and attend lectures by any "Lecturers who are willing to grant admission."

In fact, every department was cordially opened to her except the department of female diseases, whose director did not approve of women doctors.

She could have had no better connection. St. Bartholomew's was an admirable and ancient institution. Founded as a charity hospital in 1123, it was the only medieval hospital in London which still occupied the site—much enlarged—on which it had been built. Its impressive main building had a staircase decorated with murals by Hogarth and a banqueting hall lined with portraits of the hospital's famous doctors painted by the great English portrait painters. Among them today is Sir James Paget, whose long, serious, reformer's face must in his lifetime have smiled on Elizabeth, for he was largely responsible for her admission to St. Bartholomew's, and while she was there invited her to his home and introduced her to "distinguished scientific men."

Elizabeth went back to England early in October and settled in rooms in Thavies Inn, only a five-minute walk from St. Bartholomew's, even though she used a roundabout route to avoid the horrendous smells and sounds of the huge Smithfield Cattle Market across the square from the hospital. Her return to London opened up a fuller and more exciting life, not only professionally. She had become famous enough so that *Punch* had published a long, cordial poem on her graduation from medical school. One of the verses read:

> Young ladies all, of every clime,
> Especially of Britain,
> Who wholly occupy your time
> In novels or in knitting,
> Whose highest skill is but to play,
> Sing, dance, or French to clack well,
> Reflect on the example, pray,
> Of excellent Miss Blackwell!

One day, shortly after her arrival, when London seemed drab and cold and dull, she had three unexpected visitors, rebellious modern girls like herself, who had heard of her and come to make her welcome. One was Barbara Leigh Smith, intelligent, handsome, a talented painter, whose rich, enlightened father, unlike most fathers of the time, believed in the right of women to be people.

With her were her sister Anna and her friend Bessie Rayner Parkes, who, herself a poet, was to become the mother of two extraordinary children, Hilaire Belloc and Mrs. Belloc Lowndes.

Barbara Leigh Smith was to lead a distinguished and varied life too. Five years later she took the initiative in forming the first feminist committee in England. More romantically, she became George Eliot's model for Romola, a girl with hair of "reddish gold colour" and with "an expression of proud tenacity and latent impetuousness" which might "inspire love or only that unwilling admiration which is mixed with dread."

Barbara Leigh Smith's appearance in Elizabeth's lodging house was the beginning of a lifelong friendship. It was also the beginning of a new world for Elizabeth. Not only did her new friends decorate her drab rooms with charming paintings and bowls of flowers, but they invited her into their homes and social circle. She was soon part of a group which included the astronomer John Herschel, the physicist Michael Faraday, "Mrs. Jameson," the gifted writer and interpreter of early Christian art, and Lady Noel Byron, who was still making a career of the destruction of her long-dead husband's reputation. Elizabeth never questioned the moral rightness of the "rather small but venerable looking lady of 60," who had "never recovered from the blow caused by the conduct of her husband, whom she had worshipped with real idolatry." [6]

In March 1851 she spent three days at Brighton visiting Lady Byron whose "rare intelligence" she much admired, and when she left in a second-class coach, "Lady Byron, in a purple velvet mantle lined with white silk, a rich dress, and a purple satin bonnet trimmed with black lace," [7] escorted her to the train. The two women met and corresponded over the years, their subjects ranging from love and magnetism to woman's rights and the establishment of a hospital for Elizabeth to direct. "I should also want in my hospital," Elizabeth wrote, with a perceptiveness well in advance of her time, "to cure my patients spiritually as well as physically, and what innumerable aids that would necessitate! I must have the church, the school, the workshop . . . to cure my patients—a whole society, in fact."

In April she went for a visit to Barbara Leigh Smith's cousin, Florence Nightingale. The Nightingales were uncorrupted by such ultramodern notions as Mr. Leigh Smith's, and at Embley, the luxurious family estate, their thirty-year-old daughter was virtually a prisoner of her family's conventions and their understandable horror at her determination to become a nurse. Nursing was a degraded and degrading profession, its members drunken and immoral; most hospitals were filthy, smelly, indecent and full of infection.

On the surface Florence Nightingale was a pretty, popular young woman, fond of dancing and brilliant in social conversation. Except that beneath this gay exterior was the fact that at seventeen she had had a vision of God calling her to his service, and had since seen and talked to Him on several occasions. Except that more and more she sank into trancelike states in which the real world disappeared for hours on end. When Elizabeth met her, Miss Nightingale had known for five years that she wished to reform the system of hospitals, of nursing, of sanitation. For this dedication—or so she believed—she had given up a brilliant marriage. For this she was more and more sinking into brooding despair in a world where she had no means of expressing the cool intelligence and the passionate, sick energy caged within her. As they walked on the grounds of her beautiful home, she said to Elizabeth, "'Do you know what I always think when I look at that row of windows? I think how I should turn it into a hospital ward, and just how I should place the beds!'" In that less self-conscious age, she could add that she would be perfectly happy working with Elizabeth; she would want no other husband.[8]

How much Elizabeth's achievements influenced her new friend cannot be known, but shortly after Elizabeth's visit, Florence Nightingale found the courage to break through her family's resistance and went to Germany for a three months' nursing course. She obtained their grudging consent only because she announced that she would go with or without it, and then only on the promise of absolute secrecy. To have it known that their daughter was studying nursing would have been an unendurable social blow. But if Florence was influenced by Elizabeth, Elizabeth was also influenced by her, and from that time was dedicated to the belief that sanitation was the supreme goal of medicine.

The moment had come for Elizabeth to choose whether she

would practice in England or go back to America. A decisive influence was the fact that Emily too was now determined to become a physician. Elizabeth decided to return, so that when Emily was graduated they could practice together. St. Bartholomew's great book of minutes records that on July 22, 1851, Elizabeth came before the Board of Governors to thank them for their permission to use the hospital facilities and for the help she had received there. The Board in turn resolved "That the result of such permission had been most satisfactory."

CHAPTER TEN

In August 1850 while Elizabeth was in Paris for her eye operation, Emily was at home on vacation from Kentucky. She had left the loneliness of Henderson for a new kind of loneliness; her sisters were away, her brothers at work. For company, Emily started a diary.

"I have broken somewhat through the indolence and dejection that oppressed me so painfully on my return home," she wrote. Now she was able to take up again the studies which had filled her dreary hours in Kentucky. Of these studies, Anna said that Emily learned Latin, French and German, and acquired a fair knowledge of Greek and mathematics, for she could memorize anything at one reading, and never forgot what she had learned.

Like Elizabeth, she had now firmly decided to become a doctor; but unlike her elder sister, Emily, bigger, sturdier, in appearance so much more determined and invulnerable, was full of "terrible self-doubt." She decried "something sprawling in [her] character and way of doing things," believed her aspirations checked by a "fatality" that attended all her "practical undertakings." Like Ellen, she was convinced she had made no friends and would never make any, that her family were her only friends. She wandered through the empty house, which "brought up so many old

Sunday afternoons" and filled her with "a quiet deep feeling, half longing, half remembrance, it is no clear remembrance, no definite desire, but a thrill of old childish feeling . . . an intense objectless longing."[1]

Sam was involved in one of his unsuccessful love affairs, and Henry often away on business, but George was growing up, and that summer, in her loneliness, she reached out to a new friendship with him. He had arrived at an age of inquiry and doubt, and they had a long philosophical discussion which must have astonished her, for alone among the Blackwells, George's doubts were not of right and wrong and God. Instead he attempted to convince her that expediency was the basic rule of life. Such an attempt was doomed to failure, but she and George found a community of interest, if not in moral problems, in the study of astronomy and botany.

At the end of a month she returned reluctantly to Henderson, where the spring before she had felt herself so unsatisfactory a teacher. She spent her twenty-fourth birthday there alone. She tried to study. She tried her hand at poetry, at a novel. She communed with nature. She went through a period of dedicated religious feeling, all earlier doubts resolved, and her fervor, as she called on God, almost matched Sam's. Her moods rose and dipped from bright visions to despair. Any contact with her brothers and sisters, a letter, a message, strengthened her. Family life was the happy life.

In November Henry wrote that she had been offered a teaching job in Cincinnati at three hundred dollars a year. Her younger brother at fourteen had earned twice as much, but then he was a male.[2] She decided to accept. Her exile was over; and now, too late, she learned that she had not been a failure, that the people of Henderson regretted her departure.

In January 1851 she began teaching at Mr. Hurd's school and spent weekends at home conscientiously studying medicine. She made arrangements to practice dissecting. She also found time to write three articles for a literary contest sponsored by *Sartain's Union Magazine of Literature and Art.* But in March her mother was ill with suppurating boils, a common disease in those days of inadequate sanitation, and Emily had to stay home from work to nurse her. The family wrote to Ellen, now in Boston with Marian, that she must give up her art studies and come home, so that Emily could return to work. Meanwhile Emily indicated in her diary another reason for wishing to be relieved of her nursing duties. While taking care of her mother, she had realized, evidently not for the first time, how "far apart" they were. She had tried to be patient and gentle, but "could not lay aside her strong natural repugnance toward those to whom [she was] not drawn." An odd reaction in a future doctor, an odd emotion in a daughter about her mother.

Two weeks after the appeal to Ellen, Marian, not Ellen, appeared. The two young women had spent a successful winter in Boston, where they had joined a union of associationists and attended Sunday "Conversations" at Bronson Alcott's. The summer before, Marian had announced that she would not return while the family continued to take boarders; but they still had boarders, even at the cost of the Blackwell boys' sleeping in the seminary dormitories to make room. By returning, Marian fortified the tradition that, although she was considered one of the most gifted of the family, she was doomed by illness or hypochondria to fill the daughterly role while her sisters pursued their careers. Ironically, on her return she found her mother almost recovered, so Ellen, who had been prepared to come home if necessary, went instead to Philadelphia to enter the new School of Design there. She boarded with Elizabeth's old friends Dr. and Mrs. Elder.

Life in Cincinnati was not entirely grim. There were diversions too. Henry and his friend Ainsworth Spofford attended a spirit-rapping séance. Emily did not believe the rappings were true communications from the spirit world, though she saw in magnetism and clairvoyance signs of an approaching time when the human race would attain a point where it could communicate with the other world.

Along with spirit rappings went character analysis through handwriting, mystically accomplished by holding a sample of writing on the interpreter's forehead. Inevitably this game led Emily to complain that she was misunderstood even by her brothers and sisters, who could not sense the tumult beneath her apparent calm.

Not only misunderstood but unappreciated. She felt she had met few who were her intellectual equals, yet most surpassed her in achievement. In five years of teaching, a "most detestable occupation," Emily had been able to save only five hundred dollars, a pittance on which to start her medical studies. She was envious of young Ellen, who, had Emily but known, was suffering comparable doubts herself. Ellen had executed several orders for lithography, had sold some short stories, and had won a prize in the very magazine contest Emily had unsuccessfully entered. For that matter, three of the sisters, Ellen, Marian and Elizabeth, who had submitted a story written for the Christmas Annual years before, had won a hundred dollars apiece in the contest, to the dismay of the *Sartain* editors who asked them to use assumed names for fear their readers would suspect collusion. Only Ellen's entry appeared under her own name. It was a moral, sentimental story about an artist who saw immortality in beauty while his more spiritual friend the monk was misled by the surface miseries of mortality.

That summer of 1851 Marian and her mother, entirely recovered, went East to see Ellen and to meet Elizabeth on her return from England. Ellen joined Marian for a short stay at the North American Phalanx in New Jersey, then went with her to New York to welcome Elizabeth. Mother Blackwell meanwhile boarded in New York.

In October, still teaching, Emily applied to medical schools in Cincinnati, Cleveland, Columbus. She was given hope; she was refused. "I am twenty-five. I can no longer class myself among young women." She applied to college after college. Other women had received medical degrees of sorts since Elizabeth had attained hers; female medical schools, in fact, had been opened in Philadelphia and Boston; but they were inadequate even by the standards of the time. Elizabeth urged her to go to England, but Emily was determined that, like Elizabeth, she would get her medical education in the United States and at a bona fide school, not a college of homeopathy or some other variant where she could easily have been accepted. Emily felt increasingly that her desire for achievement was not only for herself but to raise women, "not in position only, but in nature—to inspire them with . . . loftier aspirations, to teach them that there is a strength of woman as well as of man."

Mother returned to Cincinnati in early November, carrying a reluctant Ellen with her, though certainly Ellen had a better chance of making a career of art and writing in the East. Ellen began to search for pupils in music and painting. Emily, who had not seen her younger sister for so long, found her "a queer little body," affectionate and "impressible," with "taste and ideality and activity, and yet some very disorderly and unpoetic streaks—a good deal of spirit and self-esteem and yet of timidity and lack of confidence." She regretted Ellen's lack of adequate education, which might have limited her emotionalism. In later years Elizabeth always spoke of the family in youth as having divided into pairs: Anna and Marian, Sam and Henry, Emily and Ellen, Howard and George, which left Elizabeth alone and shut out. Yet there was never much closeness between Anna and Marian, or much understanding between Emily and Ellen.

Elizabeth had been urging Emily to come East, but not energetically enough to satisfy Emily's demands for love. Yet Emily needed to see Elizabeth again "to judge how far I can work with her and whether we can be really friends." Even Emily's search for God was a search for "belief in an ever present friend." "Why am I alone, perplexed in a labyrinth of impenetrable mysteries, fettered in restraints within and without, and not I only but every human soul that thinks and feels and aspires in vain for its life—its home. . . . God if thou art our father—Christ if thou art our brother, speak to me."

In spite of continued plaints about her lack of friendship, she seems to have had a continuing warm relation with her brothers. That spring of 1852 she went on long botanical rambles with George, on walks with Sam. Henry went with her to call on doctors in search of recommendations which would help her gain admission to the Cincinnati medical school, where she had reapplied.

By summer the frustration of her efforts reached the point where she decided to borrow money, go East and apply for admission to Dartmouth. Late in July, as she was leaving, word came that she had been accepted at "the little Cincinnati College"; but it seemed too late to change her plans, and she went East. She stopped in New York, where Elizabeth and Marian were living, though not together. It was Elizabeth whom Emily had come to see. For five days they talked almost constantly. Elizabeth told her sister "of her Parisian experiences, particularly with regard to M. Blot." If reassurance was possible to Emily, she should have felt reassured. Elizabeth found with joy that they shared "the same hopes, the same determination . . . she has a noble intellect, clear and strong . . . warm affections and lofty aspirations." [3] Emily, less secure and less generous, found Elizabeth "not nearly as particular and fidgety as I had the idea"; but was troubled about her in another way, for Elizabeth was learning that male physicians would not allow women in their hospitals or dispensaries, and that even women patients did not seek out women doctors. Marian was in difficulty too. She was trying to support herself by teaching, but that winter Sam had noted that she had only one pupil for two hours a day.

Emily went on to Dartmouth, where she was refused, and returned by way of Pittsfield with the same result. Even Elizabeth's alma mater at Geneva, which had been censured by the State Medical Association for granting her a degree, was afraid to accept another woman student. In fact, temporarily at least, Elizabeth's success had made it, if possible, more difficult for a woman to enter medical school. The unthinkable had happened, and the forces of conservatism were determined that no such unfortunate error should occur again.

When Emily returned, disheartened, to New York, Elizabeth took her to meet Horace Greeley, editor of the *Tribune* and staunch supporter of woman's rights. "He looked up with his blue eyes under their colourless lashes and brows," and promised to help her.

Elizabeth was finding life slightly less grim. In the spring of 1852 she had delivered a series of lectures, later published, on the physical education of girls. A small but intelligent group of women had attended, some of them Quakers, a sect always more liberal than others in its view of woman's role. Several of these women took Elizabeth as their family physician, and became her close friends as well. By late summer Emily could report that Elizabeth had had three patients in a week and earned twenty-five dollars.

At about the same time, Emily, though refused admission to Bellevue, was given permission, through Horace Greeley's intervention, to go on ward rounds with the doctors and to attend operations "like any other student." At first the young men stared, and once a picture labeled "strong-minded woman" appeared on a blackboard, but soon she was taken for granted. She worked at Bellevue for several months.

Still she was no nearer a medical degree, and decided to try her luck in Chicago. On the way she had to stop over in Detroit, "a country-looking place—streets and pavements of wood—houses mostly of white frame" with gardens around them. At Rush Medical College in Chicago, the faculty received her cordially, and on November 2, 1852, she was registered there as a medical student. A professor, introducing her to the class, said, "Americans have the reputation of being a very gallant nation. I need not tell you you will be expected by your conduct this winter to maintain the national character." The students applauded. Emily even started to work in the office of one of the doctors, but some of his patients objected and she had to leave.

She hoped to become a surgeon, the best in the United States. Yet her reflections on the practice of medicine led her to the conclusion that she desired not so much "to be a great physician . . . but to aid effectually in the development of a free and noble social era." She studied the possibility that "some means might be found placing conception under the control of the individual," and that the "process of gestation" might be made "much more endurable." Male physicians had over the centuries "felt no special interest in the matter." Medical training was a farce, even the best of the graduates being "imbued with the shallow false principles they have been taught."

She planned to return to New York in February 1853, at the end of the term. She was eager to help in the new clinic Elizabeth had opened, but was discouraged at the thought of the "weary three days imprisonment in the cars to get there," and upset to learn that though the trip to Chicago had cost seventeen dollars, the return fare would be two dollars and sixty cents more.[4] She did return, however, only to discover that she was now to be excluded from Bellevue.

That spring Ellen and Henry came East to attend antislavery conventions in New York and Boston. In Boston they visited such eminent people as Emerson, Garrison, Wendell Phillips, Horace Mann. Henry had been writing poetry, and hoped to interest a publisher. The rhythms were the conventional rhythms of his time, the emotions those familiar to idealism and reform:

> Oh! 'tis no easy matter to be free;
> Most men in bonds go limping to their graves,
> Groping, because they do not will to see,
> Victims of Impulse, voluntary Slaves! . . .
>
> Mankind in solid Phalanx shall unite
> In perfect Liberty and perfect Law! [5]

But, though his offerings appeared from time to time in newspapers and magazines, he did not find a publisher for a volume.

Their mother came East that summer too. Also in New York was the doctor whom Emily had assisted in Chicago, her chief sponsor there. Emily learned with dismay that he was not returning to Chicago in the fall, fearing that, without his support, she might be refused readmission. Nevertheless she worked on her thesis.

Her twenty-seventh birthday was in October. In November 1853, she returned to Chicago, where her fears proved real enough. She decided to try Cleveland, and there, with the help of a family friend, gained admission to Western Reserve Medical School. Sam had left his work to help her, first in Chicago, then in Cleveland.

In the middle of February 1854 Emily took her final examinations. She read her thesis, which was received with congratulations, and she was graduated with high honors. It was hard to believe that her "long course was over," and that at last she was a doctor. She had given up an idea she had long contemplated of going to Paris disguised as a man to finish her training. She had decided instead to go as a woman to England. She went first to Cincinnati to say good-bye, then to New York for a few weeks.

Elizabeth's New York Dispensary for Poor Women and Children had been incorporated, and several well-known citizens acted as trustees. Among them were Horace Greeley, Charles A. Dana and Dennis Harris, whom Elizabeth's father had befriended so many years ago. The one-room dispensary, starting as a triweekly clinic, opened in March in a slum area near Tompkins Square. At first even poor and desperate women were afraid to come, but necessity drove a few; they spread the word, and slowly the number of patients grew.

On March 29 Emily sailed from Boston. The transatlantic trip now took only eleven days. She stopped over in Birmingham to meet Anna and Howard, then went by way of London to Edinburgh, where she had had the good fortune to be accepted as assistant to the great surgeon James Simpson, Professor of Medicine at Edinburgh University, one of the first to use anesthesia in surgery. Here she "gained invaluable surgical experience . . . in his extensive practice in female diseases."[6] Any young man just graduated from medical school might well have envied her.

After a few months there, during which she made careful notes on maternity cases for Elizabeth, and even sent pessaries back to New York, she felt she should move on. But where? Elizabeth, in a letter, again went over the question of disguise in France. However, Emily wisely remained at Edinburgh for several months more, then, after a stay in England, where she worked at Children's Hospital and at St. Bartholomew's, finally did go to Paris. There, as a female, she studied with Dr. Pierre Huguier, and, against Elizabeth's advice, entered the cloistered confines of La Maternité to learn midwifery.[7] By the end of her European experience, she was one of the best-trained physicians of her time. In a testimonial letter given her when she left Edinburgh, Simpson had written, "I have rarely met with a young physician . . . better acquainted with the ancient and modern languages, or more learned in the literature, science, and practical details of his profession. . . . [I]n your relation to patients, and in your kindly care and treatment of them, I ever found you a 'most womanly woman.' "[8]

When her former teacher received a baronetcy in 1866 in honor of his contributions to surgery, Emily was probably very little impressed. She had recorded her feelings about such matters in the summer of 1854. "I was annoyed by Dr. S. introducing me to a Lady Agnes Duff—Cousin of the Queen—who asked to meet me and then, as I thought, was very rude—it is astonishing how rank imposes on these people. Dr. S. seemed to think her condescending to stare at me with impertinent curiosity quite an honour." [9]

Emily had still been in England in the fall of 1854, when the supposedly invincible British army was engaged in its disastrous venture in the Crimea. In Scutari the filthy and dilapidated base hospital was packed with men dying of wounds and cholera. By then Florence Nightingale, whose delicate, languid appearance concealed a will of iron, had successfully defied the conventions of her family and of the civilized world. For a year she had been the effective superintendent of an Institution for the Care of Sick Gentlewomen in Distressed Circumstances. In October 1854, by appointment of the government, she was setting out at the head of a group of nurses for the Crimea and fame.

Barbara Leigh Smith urged Emily to go with Miss Nightingale; but, though tempted by the opportunity for such wide experience, Emily decided against it. Elizabeth applauded her decision not to accept this "insane suggestion." For Florence Nightingale, Elizabeth said with surprising disdain, "the episode might be an instructive and every way useful one—she will probably thus sow her wild oats, in the shape of unsatisfied aspirations and activities and come back and marry suitably to the immense comfort of her relations." [10] For Emily, who expected to return to New York to work with her sister, experience or reputation gained in the Crimea would be of little use. Seemingly the Crimean War was a better preparation for matrimony than for medicine.

During Emily's two European years, Elizabeth reported her own doings regularly by letter. Besides the slow increase of her practice and the modest success of the dispensary, several important events had occurred. The family's friend Mr. Alofsen had lent her money to buy a house at 79 East Fifteenth Street, part of which, in the family tradition, she let to boarders, the earliest of whom were Mr. and Mrs. Vail, family friends and former housemates. The purchase had been necessary because the belief that a woman doctor must be indecent made it almost impossible to rent a respectable place where she could receive patients.

In the spring of 1854 she wrote to Emily that she had finally found a student in whom she was much interested. Her name was Marie Zakrzewska, a young woman who had appeared one day to offer help in the newly opened dispensary. In spite of her name, Marie was German. Her mother was a midwife in Berlin and, after assisting her for some time, Marie had been trained in midwifery at the medical college of the university there, and against powerful opposition had attained the status of teacher and chief of midwifery at the Royal Hospital, a position from which she was soon ousted by her enemies. She had been in America a year when she came to see Elizabeth. She was still only twenty-four. She spoke almost no English, and Elizabeth began to teach her. That summer Elizabeth was able to arrange for Marie's admission to Western Reserve Medical School, from which Emily had graduated. She even managed to get lecture fees on credit and board paid for the desperately poor girl. Marie left for Cleveland in October.

Most important for Elizabeth, in the fall of 1854, "the utter loneliness of life became unbearable," and she decided that, since it seemed unlikely now that she would marry, she ought to adopt a child. She went to the immigration center on Randalls Island to find an orphan girl, and there deliberately selected the most pathetic child she saw. "When I took her to live with me," Elizabeth wrote two years later, "she was about seven and a half years old. I desperately needed the change of thought she compelled me to give her. It was a dark time, and she did me good—her genial, loyal, Irish temperament suited me. Now I look forward with much hope to the coming events of this year." [11]

But at the time she took Kitty, her motives were either quite different or she was unwilling to reveal her loneliness to Emily, for she wrote this account of the acquisition of a child before the days of social agencies. "I must tell you of a little item that I've introduced into my own domestic economy in the shape of a small girl . . . whom I mean to train up into a valuable domestic, if she prove on sufficient trial to have the qualities I give her credit for. I chose her out of 400 children . . . no easy thing to do . . . no living soul claims her, her name even seems doubtful, but she is called Catharine Barry—she was a plain and they said stupid child though good, and they wondered at my choice—I thought otherwise, she wanted to come with me . . . I gave a receipt for her, and the poor little thing trotted after me like a dog. Instead of being stupid, I find now that she is withdrawn from blows and tyranny, that she is very bright, has able little fingers that are learning to dust, and wash up, and sew, and much perseverance and energy for so small a child—she is a sturdy little thing, affectionate and with a touch of obstinacy which will turn to good account later in life. Of course she is more trouble than use at present, and quite bewildered me at first, but still I like on the whole to have her, and it is quite pretty to hear her in the morning, sitting up in bed, waiting for permission to get up, and singing. . . . She is not pretty, but has an honest little face, something like Howard's when a young child—and it is growing brighter every day under happier influences than the poor child has ever yet known."[12]

Kitty's own account, when she was an old woman, seems even more to have suffered the blurring of time. Dr. Elizabeth came at the "sunset hour, and found me with my hands clasped behind me, gazing at the setting sun. She asked me, would I be her little girl? I squeezed her hand, but had to see the end of the fast-fading lights."[13] It is to be hoped that no abandoned orphan child ever turned her eyes away from her own future with such inhuman unconcern; and young Kitty was far from inhuman.

To Kitty, Elizabeth was always "Doctor." There is no better indication of the specialness of Kitty's life in those male-dominated days than her amazement at meeting a male physician. It seemed so strange to hear a *man* called doctor.

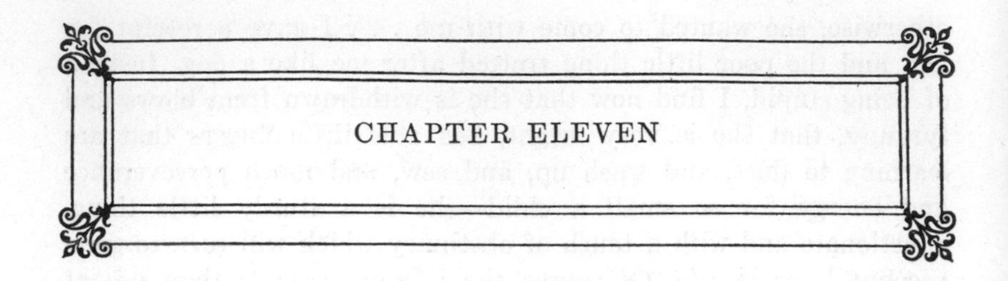

CHAPTER ELEVEN

When Henry met Lucy Stone in 1850 and found her attractive, he not unnaturally thought of her as a possible wife for his elder brother rather than for himself, though even Sam, a year and a half older than Henry, would still have been young for Lucy. She was thirty-two, Henry twenty-five. Years later he wrote unflatteringly enough of their first encounter that "a young middle-aged" woman had come into the store; but she was small, round-faced, clear-eyed, and he was charmed by "her sweet voice, bright smile, pleasant manner and simplicity of dress and character." [1]

That day in Cincinnati she was an anonymous individual. By the time he saw her again, she was very well known indeed. That same fall of 1850 Marian and Ellen had met her and heard her speak in Worcester at the First National Woman's Rights Convention. They had been greatly impressed; but Elizabeth, reading reports of the meeting, thought the women had shown "much right feeling, great energy, but not a great amount of strong clear thought." [2] A reader of the *Liberator,* Henry must often have had news of Lucy as an antislavery and woman's rights speaker, for she was becoming famous or infamous, according to the point of view, as the first woman to devote whole lectures to the cause of woman's rights. "I was a woman before I was an abolitionist," she had said. "I must speak for the women."

Henry did not see Lucy Stone again until the spring of 1853 when he and Ellen went East to attend antislavery meetings in New York and Boston. In New York he heard her make a speech in which she described a Negro mother fleeing with her baby, when a pursuer's bullet struck the baby's head and scattered its brains over the poor mother as she ran. She told the tale so movingly that the entire audience wept.[3] In Boston she must have heard him deliver a lecture on the Constitution as an antislavery document. Finally he met her again in the Anti-Slavery Society offices in Boston. She was wearing a bloomer costume.

For several years a small number of "strong-minded" women had been expressing rebellion by wearing a costume intended to give them ease of motion as well as spiritual freedom. What it had so far given them was ridicule in the press on both sides of the Atlantic, and mobs of rowdy boys who followed them, shouting insults, whenever they dared appear on the street. As to comfort, the long trailing dresses and tight corseting of the day must have been miserable garments to have made bloomers appealing. An uglier, more cumbersome costume would be hard to imagine. The revolution consisted of a waist not pinched in, and of a pair of shirred harem-type pantaloons which covered the ankles and were themselves partly covered by a skirt, shorter than the usual dust catcher with its layers of supporting petticoats, but hanging well below the knees. Above the waist a conventional high-necked, long-sleeved blouse covered by a jacket was customary. Yet this outfit made it possible for women to breathe without a sense of suffocation, to bend from the waist and to carry the baby upstairs without fear of tripping over a trailing skirt. Because of the disruption it caused in their lives, lady reformers soon abandoned the garment, but when Henry met Lucy again, she was still wearing bloomers.

Henry had recently begun to be much interested in a young widow, Nancy Clark; but now, in spite of the bloomer costume, the spirit of which he preferred to its appearance, Miss Stone's "superior moral character" won the day, and Henry, who had barely spoken to her, decided that she should be his wife. Characteristically he also decided not to waste Mrs. Clark, with the result that Ellen, writing to Sam about one of his current romances, advised him not to rush into matrimony. "Elizabeth and Harry are very anxious you should see Mrs. Clark before you decide, and I am sure you would be very much pleased with her."

Of Lucy in those days, Henry long afterward said, "There was such a life and spirit and individuality about her as I have never known in any other woman—before or since." And the direction of this spirit was calculated to appeal to him. He had long ago concluded that his "standard of female excellence [was] so high and definite that [he would] not easily get caught"; [4] and when he was caught, it was by one of the few women of his time who in ideals, determination and refusal to accept woman's traditional lot resembled his sisters.

If he was "caught" by Lucy, it was in an entirely emotional sense, for he pursued her with a vigor only exceeded in the early days of their acquaintance by her resolve never to marry. Lucy's background was very different from the Blackwell sisters', her struggle far grimmer. There was no liberal conviction, no intellectual family tradition to sustain her. She grew up on a Massachusetts farm, where her father, a harsh, inexpressive but not cruel man, was the master whose command his wife and children obeyed. Had he been a sadistic drunkard, his word would have been just as powerful. The law gave him the right to rule. His stern Congregationalist religion confirmed it. His Bible admonished women: "Thy desire shall be to thy husband and he shall rule over thee." The accidents of life fortified his authority.

The night before Lucy was born, her mother, left alone in the house because of a farm emergency, milked the Stones' eight cows. Time did not lighten her load. Mother Stone bore nine children, of whom seven lived to grow up. She did the cooking, scrubbing, clothes making, washing, for them and for the farm helpers. Lucy did not need to look far to see that a woman's lot was hard and a man-made society unfair to the fair sex. Why did she rebel? Her sisters did not. Her neighbors did not. But from her earliest days it seemed intolerable to Lucy to accept a man's domination. One way to evade it was not to be content with the reading, writing, sewing, manners, usually taught to girls, but to attain an education equal to a man's.

Her father was not uneducated. In his youth he had been a schoolteacher, and he helped his sons, one of whom was to be a minister, to achieve college educations. Yet when Lucy announced that she was going to college, he thought her literally insane. Not too surprisingly, for when she made her extraordinary claim, though there were several ladies' seminaries, there was not a single institution of college level in the United States which admitted women.

The first college to accept women on an equal basis with men was reformist Oberlin in Ohio, a college which in 1834, in its first circular, announced its intention of elevating the "female character, by bringing within the reach of the misguided and neglected sex, all the instructive privileges which hitherto have unreasonably distinguished the leading sex from theirs." It was not until 1843, when she was twenty-five, that Lucy, defying her father, alternately studying and teaching, learned enough and saved enough—all of seventy dollars—to get herself to Oberlin for at least a term. Once there she worked to exhaustion to be able to stay on. Lucy was rebellious even at rebel Oberlin, where abolitionism was of a brand less fiery than her own, where religion was more orthodox, and where equality for females extended to allowing them to enter a coeducational rhetoric class but did not permit them to take part in the weekly debate required of their male colleagues, nor permit lady authors of winning graduation essays to deliver them at commencement. Nevertheless Lucy was graduated in 1847, the first Massachusetts woman to attain a college degree, one of the first in the nineteenth-century world.

To her family's horror she now proposed to dedicate her life to public speaking. Eccentricity had already gone too far; this was disaster. Not that lecturing was a disreputable profession. Lectures were one of the only forms of education in largely uneducated communities, one of the only group entertainments in a society without motion pictures, radio or television, a society in which orthodox religion condemned theatre and dancing as immoral. But for a woman to appear on a public platform, and few had done so, was a badge of immorality. For her to lecture on two such unsavory topics as abolition and woman's rights was nearly suicidal. She would be—Lucy was—hosed with icy water, physically threatened, refused a place to speak or even to sleep. In Indiana after one of her early lectures, the local newspaper reported that Lucy, described by a more sympathetic listener as "a prototype of womanly grace . . . fresh and fair as the morning," had been found "in the back room smoking a cigar and swearing like a trooper." [5] Yet in spite of opposition from church, press and public, Lucy and a few others were determined to make women's traditionally soft voices heard.

So much courage in so small a person won Henry's heart. Having decided to marry her, he went to his father's friend William Lloyd Garrison, who knew Lucy well through her antislavery connections, to ask for an introduction. Garrison warned him that Lucy was determined never to marry. But Henry would not be diverted. He appeared a few days later at the door of Lucy's farm home to find her standing on a table whitewashing the kitchen ceiling. From then on he bombarded her opposition to matrimony with argument, conciliation, affection. He courted her largely by letter, since his home and business were in the Middle West, and since in those years Lucy was traveling about the nearly impassable country at a rate which led her undaunted suitor to comment that she seemed to have been "born locomotive." He went to meet her whenever he could: in Niagara, Cleveland, Pittsburgh, Louisville, Madison, Chicago.

He had more allies in his courtship than he realized. If Lucy's convictions were against matrimony, some at least of her impulses were not. She told a friend that her heart ached "to love somebody that shall be all its own." And "It is horrid to live without the intimate companionship, and gentle loving influences which are the constant attendant of a true love marriage. . . . but nothing is so bad as to be made a *thing*, as every married woman now is in the eye of the law." [6] He had an ally in Elizabeth too, for to rebellious women everywhere Dr. Elizabeth and her battle were guiding stars. In fact on Lucy's trip through Cincinnati in 1850, she had driven past the Blackwell home and had been elated at the thought that Dr. Elizabeth had once lived there. Now, when her travels took her near Cincinnati, she came to stay with Henry's family. They "quite adopted her." In "her quiet decision, steady purpose and lofty principle" she reminded Sam of Elizabeth; and Hannah Blackwell, whose daughters were scattering over the world, took this highly recognizable young woman to her heart. To culture-starved Lucy, the Blackwells, with their intellectual tradition, their celebrated friends, their independent women, represented a world of which she had only dreamed. She feared she could never live up to them.

Some of the absent Blackwells were less enthusiastic. Elizabeth, who had considered it unladylike to walk in her own graduation procession, though she admired Lucy's dedication to woman's freedom, found the public nature of her protest inacceptable. Lucy, she told Henry, had as yet only come before her "in the eccentricities and accidents of the American phase of this nineteenth century, in bloomerism, abolitionism, woman's rights-ism." [7] And from Europe Anna sent words of warning and a tirade against Yankee women. These letters Henry, with childlike naïveté, immediately passed on to Lucy.

On her side, Lucy was surprisingly scornful of Henry's concern with business, although he had explained that "in every human probability, in three years more" he would "realize" a position in which he could dedicate himself to bettering the world without jeopardizing "the relatives and friends" whose fortunes were linked to his. At the same time he expressed doubt as to how he should proceed in the reform movement, with what group he should cast his lot. "I find in every question . . . wheels within wheels, difficulty beneath difficulty! The more I consider it the more complex it becomes." [8] Lucy replied impatiently that she regarded "moral independence as far more needful than pecuniary independence," [9] and pointed out that one might delay decision from year to year until one died. She herself was not given to doubt, believing even that the Union should be dissolved rather than exist half slave and half free. She had little patience with doubters. She had broken her own ties with the past, and yet been able to earn enough to live simply and put aside a good deal for the future. In this happy outcome Henry had played a major role, for while traveling about the country on horseback, carrying on the business she so scorned, he was able to arrange lecture trips for her, trips on which whenever possible he met her, on which she sometimes came to stay with his family. So effective was Lucy's influence that a mere two months after expressing his uncertainties to her, Henry made a speech at the Fourth National Woman's Rights Convention. It was a continuation of his courtship.

By December 1853 Lucy was admitting that she loved Henry, but still insisted that marriage was impossible. Immediately he began persuading her that a marriage of *equals* was desirable. "Will you permit the injustice of the world to enforce upon you a life of celibacy? The true mode of protest is to assume the natural relation and to reject the unnatural dependence."[10] He had already explained that his concept of marriage involved "no sacrifice of individuality but its perfection."[11]

It was characteristic of Lucy that it was not protestations but action which crumbled her defenses. In the early fall of 1854, during an antislavery meeting in Salem, Ohio, where Henry was a speaker, news was brought that a little slave girl was being transported from Pennsylvania to Tennessee in a train that stopped at Salem. The Ohio Supreme Court had recently held that a slave brought into the state by his master was free if he declared his desire to be freed. Here was an opportunity to make use of the ruling. After the meeting adjourned, "1200 persons assembled at the depot." A committee of four, one of whom was Henry, one a "respectable colored man," boarded the train. There they found "the little girl, only eight years old," who was traveling with her master and mistress and their small baby. "The child was asked if she wished to be free, and replied 'Yes,' "[12] whereupon, after a struggle in which some of the passengers tried to snatch the girl back from her rescuers, she was taken safely from the train.

Cincinnati, only a river's width from slave-holding Kentucky, had many proslavery inhabitants, among them a number of the hardware store's customers. The local papers were abusive and, according to Henry, misrepresented the affair, claiming among other slanders that he had assaulted the lady and tumbled the baby onto the floor. "So you see, Lucy," he wrote, "that, with all my love of approbation, I am not, at present, on the road to popularity, apparently." He was so far from popularity that for some time thereafter Kentuckians would come into the store and stand staring at him, saying they wished to be sure to recognize him if he ever set foot in Kentucky, where a reward of ten thousand dollars had been offered for his capture. It was then less than seven years before the outbreak of the Civil War.

Lucy was won by Henry's militancy as she had not been by his love-making. "I felt nearer to you then, dear Harry, in all that constitutes nearness, than I ever did before." And "you will be richer with your self-respect, even though you may have less in dollars." But business had suffered, and his partners did not share Lucy's scorn of dollars or her dedication to Henry's soul. Much to her disgust, he promised them not to take an active part in the 1855 Anti-Slavery Convention, but assured Lucy that he was determined as soon as possible to dissolve a partnership which imposed such restraints. That spring, still a partner, he nevertheless took part in an attempt to test the legality of freeing slaves on a boat which had docked on the Ohio side of the river, and again the proslavery press urged that he be tarred and feathered.[13]

Even Henry's abolitionist family failed to share Lucy's enthusiasm for his new radicalism, which was disrupting his first successful business connection. Just after the Salem adventure, Elizabeth told Emily that Harry seemed "to be ruining himself through injurious influences acting on his morbid craving for distinction." [14] Two months later she defined the "injurious influences." Harry had written that the firm was to be broken up, and that he had "'*quite determined to live east!*' . . . This announcement . . . is totally at variance with all his preceding plans, so that of course it is Lucy's influence." Elizabeth had already protested to Henry that all his ambitions must be satisfied. "You have distinct and superior *business* talents which will need exercise in order to give you the greatest efficiency." [15]

Ellen wrote to Lucy about the Salem affair that, although she preferred Harry to make noble mistakes rather than to be cold and selfish, she did not think "the use of force justifiable, except in cases where the person concerned appeals for . . . help. Then even a mob is justifiable." Undoubtedly the problem had been discussed in family conference, for Sam had expressed himself in almost the same words to Harry some months earlier. Ellen, perhaps on newspaper evidence, stated that the slave girl had clung to her mistress and begged not to be taken, but had been "rescued" anyhow,[16] a statement completely at variance with Henry's account.

Early in his courtship Henry had told Lucy that, if ever she consented to marry him, he would wish to give up his legal superiority; and at the beginning of 1855, when she had consented, he began to draft protests "such as seemed . . . needed and proper as a declaration of principle and a model for imitation."

There was much indecision about their wedding plans. Largely because of Henry's aid, Lucy was now so busy a lecturer that she did not feel she could take time to be married until spring. She suggested coming to Cincinnati to be married, but Henry, for once conventional, worried that people would criticize her for coming to him.

They were married early in the morning of May 1, 1855, at Lucy's home, "a high little farm house, round which the misty sky shut down, revealing only rocks and barns and cattle."[17] The ceremony was performed by the feminist-abolitionist-associationist preacher Thomas Wentworth Higginson, Lucy's good friend, and linked to the Blackwells too by his marriage to William Ellery Channing's sister. The Higginsons had been in Brattleboro when Marian was taking the cure there.

The wedding party was small, those of Lucy's family who still lived on the farm: her mother and father, her elder brother and his young family. One of Lucy's brothers and two of her sisters had died. Her remaining sister was married and away from home, as was her eldest brother. The only outsiders were Mr. Higginson and his wife, a semi-invalid who had with difficulty come as a tribute to Lucy, and Charles Burleigh, an eccentric, long-haired abolitionist. None of the Blackwells came. Marian and Elizabeth, who were in the East, had promised to be there, but just before the wedding Elizabeth wrote that Marian would be unable to come—perhaps because of one of her frequent illnesses—and Elizabeth herself did not appear.

It was a conventional wedding even to orange blossoms and cloth of gold roses. Henry wore a "proper white waistcoat" and Lucy a beautiful silk dress of "ashes-of-roses color." What was not conventional was the marriage protest, which Henry, standing beside Lucy, read before the ceremony.

While we acknowledge our mutual affection by publicly assuming the relationship of husband and wife, yet in justice to ourselves and a great principle, we deem it a duty to declare that this act on our part implies no sanction of, nor promise of voluntary obedience to, such of the present laws of marriage as refuse to recognize the wife as an independent, rational being, while they confer upon the husband an injurious and unnatural superiority, investing him with legal powers which no honorable man would exercise, and which no man should possess.

We protest especially against the laws which give to the husband—

1. The custody of his wife's person;
2. The exclusive control and guardianship of her children;
3. The sole ownership of her personal and use of her real estate, unless previously settled upon her, or placed in the hands of trustees, as in the case of minors, lunatics, and idiots;
4. The absolute right to the product of her industry;
5. Also against laws which give to the widower so much larger and more permanent an interest in the property of his deceased wife than they give to the widow in that of her deceased husband;
6. Finally, against the whole system by which "the legal existence of the wife is suspended during marriage," so that in most States she neither has a legal part in the choice of her residence, nor can she make a will, nor sue or be sued in her own name, nor inherit property. . . .

Thus reverencing Law, we enter our earnest protest against rules and customs which are unworthy of the name, since they violate justice, the essence of all Law.

No statement could better have defined the situation, close to bondage, which was the lot of the nineteenth-century wife, should her husband care to enforce his rights.

Elizabeth could not have been pleased. "You haven't the vulgar vanity to wish to make a fuss about your marriage," she had written to Henry, again putting the blame where she obviously thought it belonged, "and do not take the human nature out of it, by crushing it with platforms and principles." It was in bad taste, she went on, to drag "one's private, personal affairs into public notice. . . . I think that Lucy, and you, too, have protested enough, in all conscience, both by public and private parlance, to define your position."[18] But for Henry, a stronger influence had at last superseded Elizabeth's.

Higginson, who thought Lucy "one of the noblest and gentlest persons" he had ever known, and who approved of every aspect of this union, sent a copy of the protest to the Worcester *Spy*, and the newspaper published it. It was widely reprinted and received much publicity. A dissident view was expressed by the Washington *Union:* "Mr. Blackwell, who last fall assaulted a Southern lady and stole her slave, has . . . married Lucy Stone. Justice, though sometimes tardy, never fails to overtake her victim."[19]

Higginson, appropriate as he was, had not been Henry and Lucy's first choice of a minister. Their first choice had been Antoinette Brown, Lucy's close friend at Oberlin. Like Lucy, Antoinette was a rebel, and her rebellion had led her to become the first ordained woman minister in the United States.

Antoinette, born in Henrietta, New York, grew up on a farm; but, though her background was much the same as Lucy's, her battle against tradition was less lonely and less arduous. Not that life was easy. She was the seventh of ten children, three boys and seven girls, four of whom had died before Antoinette was grown. Her father, not only a farmer but the village magistrate as well, was far more considerate of his womenfolk than was Father Stone, and more aware of his daughters and their needs. He permitted Antoinette to attend the academy in Henrietta where boys were prepared for Dartmouth, and she studied everything they did except Greek. Just before her sixteenth birthday she began to teach.

Luckier than Lucy, she went to Oberlin with her father's consent and with some financial aid from him. She was twenty when she entered Oberlin in 1845, and so far advanced in her studies that she was placed in the third-year class of which Lucy, almost seven years her senior, was a member. True, the requirements for her entry were less stringent than Lucy's, because Antoinette had enrolled in the Young Ladies' Course, and was a candidate only for a special diploma, not for the Bachelor of Arts degree to which Lucy aspired. Life for Antoinette at Oberlin was easier in another way too, for whereas Lucy worked to exhaustion throughout the college term and between terms, Antoinette had chiefly to teach between terms.

The two girls were instantly drawn to each other by their convictions, determination, limited funds, and by a less tangible rapport. Her first night at Oberlin Antoinette found Lucy, for whom she had eagerly been looking because she had been warned by a family friend to avoid that dangerous radical. She saw "a small round-faced girl" who "appeared to be about sixteen." Lucy must have seen in Antoinette a girl more self-assured and determined in manner than herself, more vivacious, with clear blue eyes and wavy brown hair. Antoinette was more frivolous and feminine too, and once exasperated Lucy to tears by insisting on wearing a gay, flowered hat. This frivolity was the more amazing since Antoinette was highly religious, far more so than Lucy, with whom one of her chief disagreements was that Lucy adhered to a group of abolitionists who believed in leaving a church which did not stand firmly against slavery.

Antoinette had been six years old when her parents were converted to militant Christianity by the famous revivalist Charles Grandison Finney, who later became one of Oberlin's leading spirits. Finney's convincing arguments for the religious life were, according to Antoinette's elder brother, not sensational, but "logic on fire." [20] At the age of nine Antoinette herself had joined the church on a profession of faith, and been much petted by a congregation which she led in hymns and to which, in her child's voice, she even preached. They agreed that dear little Antoinette would grow up to be a minister's wife. They did not guess that she was determined to defy St. Paul's verdict that women must keep silent in churches. To be not a minister's wife, but a minister, was her ambition.

Even Lucy was startled when her friend Nettie confided her secret hopes. A woman might conceivably aspire to be a speaker, but a minister! It was impossible. And if Lucy was amazed, the consternation of radical Oberlin and of Antoinette's conservative family, when they learned her plans, can be imagined. The authorities of Oberlin refused to enter Antoinette and another brave young woman as members of the Theological Department, though they could not refuse to let them take the course, since Oberlin's charter forbade them to refuse education to women. Nettie's family, even her minister brother William, himself a graduate of Oberlin's Theological Department, withheld support, hoping to force her home. Oberlin's Ladies' Board, stern watchdog of female morality, refused to let her earn money by teaching in the preparatory department. "I was reasoned with, pleaded with, and besought even with tears . . . not to combat a beneficent order tending to promote harmony . . . in the family and in the commonwealth. Established, ordained masculine headship everywhere was held to be indispensable to morality, and grounded in the inmost fitness of things." [21]

A man in whose school she had taught, the one person who had promised to help her, died suddenly. Still she did not give up. Finally a sympathetic woman, assistant principal in the Ladies' Department, learning that Antoinette had considerable artistic skill, arranged for her to teach a private drawing class. She was saved. By teaching the forty pupils who enrolled she could earn fifty cents an hour.

At the end, even Lucy decried Nettie's return to Oberlin as a "resident graduate, pursuing the Theological Course," a compromise which uncompromising Lucy considered "dishonorable." Not so Antoinette. "I came back here just on no terms at all. . . . I came back to study Theology and get knowledge. I do get it . . . I am not responsible for their conduct or decisions."

Without their authority she preached in nearby churches. She wrote an exegesis to prove that, in the original of "Let your women keep silence in the churches, for it is not permitted unto them to speak," the Greek word translated as *speak* meant literally *"chatter, to make the sound of monkeys.* Is it not then that St. Paul is merely cautioning women to speak wisely, and not to babble?" [22] Triumphantly she learned that her paper was to be published in the *Oberlin Quarterly*. She had breached the wall at last. Nevertheless, when she left Oberlin in 1850, after completing the theological course, she left without a degree, without ordination, and without the young man whom she loved. He was going to Africa as a missionary, but she had refused to go with him. She was dedicated to her mission closer to home. She was determined to be a minister, and nothing, not even love, was going to stop her.

Shortly after her return East, at the Worcester woman's rights convention which Marian and Ellen Blackwell attended, Antoinette joined Lucy as a speaker; but she "felt that all the ladies had their elbows out a little bit,"[23] and decided it would be better to be a lone lecturer than to appear at meetings. She began to lecture around New England, which seemed to her "more ready for such things." She was invited to preach at Thomas Wentworth Higginson's church in Worcester, at George Channing's church in Brooklyn, best of all, at her brother William's church in Andover. She continued, like Lucy, to travel about the country lecturing: on antislavery, woman's rights, temperance. Unlike Lucy she never wore bloomers, believing them a diversion from the main fight for woman's rights. She came to know young Henry Ward Beecher, William Henry Channing, Charles Burleigh, Gerrit Smith. In 1853 Horace Greeley and Charles Dana offered her one thousand dollars a year and board to stay in New York and preach, but she felt herself too young and inexperienced for such large responsibility. Instead she accepted a pulpit she was offered that year in a small Congregational church "without steeple or bell," in South Butler, New York. The New York *Independent,* a religious newspaper with a general circulation, announced that any woman who would be ordained was an infidel and any church which would ordain her an infidel church. It neglected to print Antoinette's reply, only commenting that Miss Brown disclaimed being an infidel.

That fall, Antoinette went as an accredited delegate from the South Butler Temperance Society to a World's Temperance Convention in New York. It was a "World" which refused to admit a Negro delegate or to let a woman speak. When Antoinette tried, "There was a great furor, and I stood on the platform for three hours except when someone brought me a chair, and I did not have a chance to open my mouth. So much stamping and pounding with canes that [the] air was full of dust. . . . Regular hubbub."[24] And her revolutionary intention had been only to thank them for admitting her, a woman.

She returned for two more days with much the same results.

Greeley's New York *Tribune* reported the noisy and vituperative meetings in four short sentences which became famous in the annals of reform:

First Day—Crowding a woman off the platform.
Second Day—Gagging her.
Third Day—Voting that she shall stay gagged. Having thus disposed of the main question, we assume the incidentals will be finished this morning.

From New York Antoinette went to South Butler, where on September 15 she was "ordained to the work of the Gospel Ministry." [25] The preacher chose as his text "There is neither male nor female; for ye are all one in Jesus Christ." Two months after her ordination, Antoinette wrote in her diary, "This is a very poor and small church and my salary is three hundred dollars a year, ample . . . in this small community. . . . To get humanity condensed into so small a compass that I can study each individual opens a new chapter of experience." [26]

Yet her tenure at South Butler lasted less than a year. On July 20, 1854, she was "at her own request dismissed from her connection." Her faith was not shattered, but it was no longer the faith of the congregation or the church in which she was ordained. She could not preach eternal damnation. She had refused to condemn and ostracize an unmarried girl whose baby had died, or to preach a sermon on infant damnation on that occasion. She had refused to force a dying boy into conversion, as his parents had demanded, by terrifying him with threats of hell-fire. How bitter to have struggled so long only to find in victory another defeat! How strange to have battled against such odds to be a minister, without perceiving that success involved preaching every tenet of her sect!

It was at South Butler that Antoinette learned that the young man she had loved at Oberlin had died in far-off Liberia. It was there too that she first met Samuel Blackwell. He was on a trip to Boston, and on Harry's advice—had not Harry for years been looking for a wife for Sam almost as eagerly as for himself?—he stopped to visit Lucy's friend. It was a cold, rainy day in early November. "She received me very pleasantly," wrote Sam in his diary, "took me to her room and I forgot my drenched boots and the rain and wind without while busily talking with her for 3 hours. . . . She is a lady of pleasant, intelligent appearance, about 30. Strong and robust in form. . . . We had a confab beginning with 'Woman's Rights' and ending with metaphysics and theology. She seems to me to be a lady of judgment, very kind disposition and with the best principles and high aims. She has . . . that breadth of sympathy and hearty toleration which are so clear an evidence of a magnanimous and cultivated mind. I enjoyed the visit exceedingly."[27] A more judicious if less passionate appraisal than in some of his earlier attachments.

They had much in common besides the fact that his brother was in love with her closest friend. They were believers in woman's rights, abolition, temperance, but most important they were highly religious and, at the time they met, both losing their orthodoxy.[28] They began to correspond, and their correspondence continued after Nettie left her pulpit and went home to Henrietta to rest. Afterward Nettie returned to lecturing, and now, like Lucy, stayed with the Blackwells when she was near Cincinnati. Like Lucy she won their hearts.

In 1855, at Greeley's suggestion, Antoinette dedicated herself to unpaid social work in New York's filthy slums and miserable prisons, earning her simple livelihood by occasional speeches and sermons. At an antislavery convention that year she expressed her philosophy: "I pity the man or woman who does not choose to be identified with the cause of the oppressed."[29] She was making verbal her own social protest in Mr. Greeley's daily *Tribune,* in articles telling of the pitiful creatures she encountered in her work. The series was called "Shadows of Our Social System," and the first article explained the title: "Polished, enlightened, civilized, Christianized society has yet the black shadow . . . on its vine-trellised cottage . . . and its halls of learning . . . on the cheek of the little maiden, and on the brow of the grave judge."

In August Sam came East, met her in Springfield, and spent three glowing days with her there before they returned together to New York by boat. Sam asked her to marry him, but Nettie, without Lucy's convictions against matrimony, nevertheless continued to believe herself dedicated to causes too important to sacrifice to marriage. In early December Sam visited her again in Henrietta.

"The love of her whom I love best on earth," he wrote in his diary, "is now wholly mine." She had said she would marry him. Yet only two weeks later she had to urge him not to send her love letters on to his sisters. "They are for you Sam dear, and full of haste, bad spelling and confidences." And added, logically enough for anyone not a Blackwell, "Elizabeth can easily get acquainted for herself." [30]

Of this outcome Ellen, who knew Elizabeth better, was less sure. Nettie and Elizabeth ought to be friends, she told Nettie, but "I'm afraid you will not just at first because you are both rather reserved." And added significantly, "You will not find her cold or critical when you get a little farther in. You are striving both in your own way towards the same end." [31] Except that one of Nettie's purposes was to marry Sam.

Sam and Nettie were married on January 24, 1856, in the snow-covered farmhouse in Henrietta. The town magistrate, who happened also to be the bride's father, performed the ceremony. Like Henry and Lucy nine months before, they made a marriage contract, but a simple one, dealing only with financial arrangements. They declared themselves "joint owners of all properties, real estate and moneys." Nettie was to leave her property to Sam, Sam half of his to his wife, half to his "widowed mother and unmarried sisters for their support." Then Sam, handsome in Henry's wedding waistcoat, brother William's gloves and his own black trousers, was married to the Reverend Antoinette Brown. He might, as Lucy put it, "rejoice in the fact that he alone of all men in the world has a Divine wife." [32]

CHAPTER TWELVE

Henry and Lucy's marriage, in true farm fashion, took place at an hour which permitted the wedding party to leave at 7:45 A.M. to catch the morning train. On their way to Cincinnati, Henry and his bride spent their first night together at Elizabeth's house, having bought tickets by way of New York at "no additional expense." Elizabeth had arranged a wedding soirée, but Lucy took to bed with a sick headache. For years she had been subject to migraine, and one of her debates with Oberlin's Ladies' Board had been whether she might take her bonnet off in chapel if her head hurt. In the period after her surrender to Henry's love the attacks had grown unusually, and perhaps significantly, severe.

A century later self-consciousness might have limited Henry's and Lucy's jests about their marriage, but in 1855 Lucy had been able to write to Nettie that she wanted her help in "putting Lucy Stone to death," and on his wedding day Henry described to a friend how he, the "Unenviable," had entangled himself beyond the possibility of release, and ended: "Ora pro nobis." A few weeks later he wrote in more serious vein: "Well, Lucy and I are *married.* A very respectable, sober, affectionate couple, neither of us *very* young, nor very sanguine, but both of us desirous to aid each other in living out what remains to us of life to the very best advantage." Henry was all of thirty.

Yet they had not "had the shadow of a shade of a quarrel," and for Henry who called himself "one of the most captious, snappish and hasty tempered of mortals this is saying wonders."[1] He was no more astonished than the Blackwells' friend and neighbor Harriet Beecher Stowe, whose "capital little story" had now shaken the nation and drawn more tightly the strengthening lines of pro- and antislavery. Mrs. Stowe, who had known Henry from boyhood as the gayest and most worldly of the serious Blackwells, expressed amazement because "that wild boy" had married Lucy Stone. But so in love was Lucy that, though she found the West "antipathetic," she had consented to move into the Blackwell home, making this concession to Henry's business obligations, for the hardware store was still unsold.

Lucy's sense that Lucy Stone was dead rested partly on the loss of a woman's name and identity in her husband's. She had made her name known. Must she now submerge it in Lucy Blackwell? Their wedding card had read Henry B. and Lucy Stone Blackwell, but a year later she was asking the Woman's Rights Convention to omit the Blackwell altogether. She was to be Mrs. Lucy Stone.

Her decision was acclaimed by her feminist associates, even by Elizabeth Cady Stanton, who was so firmly Mrs. Stanton. Susan B. Anthony, who had been converted to feminism by Lucy's speech at the Worcester convention of 1850, had become a close friend of Lucy and Antoinette. A confirmed spinster, she had looked on the marriages of her two friends as defections from the cause of woman's rights, and perhaps from herself. Now she found some small comfort in Lucy's intransigence. Henry too applauded Lucy's decision, though it was awkward when they traveled together, and gave currency to reports that they were not legally married. Later, for a professional woman to keep her own name became common enough, but in Lucy's day it was a courageous protest against woman's social and legal loss of identity in marriage. Into the nineteen-twenties and thirties married women who used their maiden names were widely known as Lucy Stoners, so that, ironically, Lucy was better remembered for this small dramatic gesture than for her years of tedious commitment to women's freedom.

She had no sooner settled into the Walnut Hills house than she was away again lecturing and attending conventions. That summer she went as far as Saratoga Springs, New York. Henry meanwhile continued his business travels, so that their relationship was almost as often carried on by correspondence as by personal contact.

The tightening bonds of sectional differences—economic, social, emotional—were moving the country step by rapid step toward disunion and war. That year Henry and Sam took part in the founding of the radical, antislavery Republican Party.[2] The antislavery forces in Ohio were divided into two groups, the Liberal Party and the American Party. The American or Know-Nothing Party had a single principle: Protestant Americanism unpolluted by Catholics or foreigners. It had a chameleonlike coloration, and in Ohio in 1855 this adaptation dictated a free-soil line. At a mass convention to nominate delegates to the Republican State Convention, the two factions threw the meeting into such turmoil that the convention was nearly broken up. The head of the Liberal Party asked Henry to try to save the organization. Henry protested, but was finally induced to rise and speak. At the sight of him, the Know-Nothings increased their clamor. "Englishman!" "Throw him out of the window." Finally his supporters lifted him onto a chair and "pale with excitement, [he] began in a trembling voice" which grew firmer as he went on, begging the factions to join forces in order to win. After the battle was over they could go their separate ways.

His triumph was complete. Englishman though he was, he converted the Know-Nothings. A delegation was elected, which at the state convention tipped the balance to nominate Salmon P. Chase, who became governor.[3] When the chairman of the Cincinnati meeting was chided for letting an "unknown young man" carry off his meeting, he replied, "I have just heard the most eloquent speech that ever fell from human lips. Unknown young man!" [4]

So, following their separate paths, the newlyweds were busy. In the fall, largely because the National Woman's Rights Convention took place in Cincinnati that year, Lucy was at home; but between November and March she was scarcely there.[5] They were both away most of January and February of 1856, and when Nettie and Sam, after their marriage, also came to live in the

Walnut Hills house, they saw Henry very little and Lucy not at all in their first months there.

Even though they had been so much less spectacular in their marriage than Henry and Lucy, Sam and Nettie were welcomed by the Cincinnati press in doubtful terms, one paper going so far as to suggest that their marriage by a mere justice of the peace was most irregular and that perhaps the "famous lady preacher" was not really a legal wife. [6]

Efforts to sell the hardware store continued. By now Sam had begun to feel that he too would move East, where those members of the family still in the United States were congregating. Emily was returning from England, persuaded perhaps by Elizabeth's conviction that the brilliance of English society was not the best setting for the slow, laborious task they had chosen and that, "bad as America is, it has thrown off so many shackles for men, that there seems an almost providential necessity of woman's work first being planted here."

The Blackwell brothers were again caught in one of those widespread financial crises which followed each other with such disheartening rapidity in a laissez-faire economy. It was hard to collect outstanding bills. It was nearly impossible to dispose of a business for its full worth. But by spring they had managed to sell their interest, and Henry was traveling with one of the new owners, teaching him the business. Years later Henry described their financial situation: they sold the business "on credit, taking in exchange a farm near Chicago, and owing a cousin in England for it. What Lucy had earned by her lectures, some $5000, she had placed in the hands of my brother and myself, and held our note secured by western land certificates. What little property I had was also invested in western lands which paid no income, but on the contrary were a heavy load to carry." [7]

Two years before, Henry had told Lucy that he had speculated in ten thousand acres of land in Bad Axe County, "a new county northwest of Wisconsin river," and that he was going to see them. He and Sam had bought land, largely on government credit. Now, before moving East, Henry decided to go again to their Western lands, which had to be surveyed and "certified" before he could sell them and make the fortune that was to release him from the bonds of commerce. He begged Lucy to join him. "Let us not be separate any more, but live and act together." [8] She said she would go.

It was their first truly married life, and a strange one. They met in Chicago on the last day of May 1856, and in their "own carriage" drove across wild country to Viroqua, Wisconsin, a distance of two hundred and fifty miles over direct roads; but roads were sometimes nonexistent, rarely direct, often mountain paths, forest clearings, bogs "frightfully deep." For nightly shelter there were farmhouses, where sheets might be dirty and accommodations far from private. On one occasion, Henry told Sam, "We got with some difficulty into bed (while our six roommates stepped out to give us the opportunity)." Their clothes were torn, were lost. They reached Viroqua expecting so little that they were delighted to find "at least thirty shanties visible to the naked eye." Yet it was a happy, an intimate time, to Henry in later years "like a lovely dream."

From Viroqua they went on to La Crosse. Lucy described arriving at the junction of two rivers which "rushed past wild and high. . . . A young man came and told us to cross the Otter by a log; but alas! the log was swept away. So he went far up the Kickapoo and swam down, whirled like a straw by the current, our men pulling him out." Next day Henry went on foot to see some of their land. Lucy, in spite of her scorn for finance, was delighted that property bought last spring for eight hundred dollars would within a year bring three thousand. "And if Harry had not come home with the skin all off his ankles, so that he could not get his boots on, we should have been satisfied." [9]

The Blackwell brothers did not concern themselves only with each other's love lives. Their financial ventures were as usual intertwined. George and Sam traveled together to Bad Axe that July, and Sam spent early August with Henry and Lucy, inspecting his land. He decided to put up a thousand acres for sale, holding only five hundred for investment.[10] By then the hardware business was out of their hands, and Sam planned to move East rather than "look for a situation" in Cincinnati. He had been hanging on at the hardware concern until the Walnut Hills house should be sold, but on July 7 he had written to Henry that he could not cover expenses going on as he was, working half-time for half-pay.[11] Antoinette and Mother Blackwell went straight East, and stayed for a while with Nettie's family in Henrietta. On August 22, Sam came from the West to call for his pregnant wife and take her to New York and the care of his doctor sister.

So when Henry and Lucy returned from their Wisconsin adventure, the Walnut Hills house had been abandoned, and they followed the family East. By late fall Mother, Marian, Sam and Nettie, Lucy and Henry had moved into Elizabeth's house at 79 East Fifteenth Street. Kitty was already there. Dr. Emily came home from Europe, and Dr. Marie Zakrzewska from Cleveland. Kitty later remembered that the Walnut Hills furniture arrived in fifteen carts which lined up in front of the house. Elizabeth had eagerly anticipated this mass invasion. "I have been more than eight years without a family circle," she had written to Emily. "I can now appreciate one, and bear and forbear as I never did before." [12] Certainly she could no longer complain of being lonely. And in November, just before Lucy and Henry arrived, Nettie gave birth to a daughter, who was named Florence and called Floy.

Marian had dutifully settled back into the role of housekeeper. In recent years she had made various attempts to remove herself from her family bonds. For a time she had lived in the East with the Alofsens, whose daughter Frances was one of several people later said to be Dr. Elizabeth's "first baby in private life." [13] But in November 1854 Elizabeth had told Emily that Marian and the Alofsens were getting on each other's nerves and that Marian was planning to return to Cincinnati. She had been asked by Miss Peabody that summer to come as school mother in a new experiment in communal living, but had refused, fearing that the position would be a mere extension of the dull, familiar domestic duties.

In the spring of 1856 Marian accepted an offer to teach in Orange, New Jersey. Orange, today a busy suburb, was then wooded, hilly country. She was happy there. Whenever she did anything on her own, it turned out well, she now told Henry, forgetting her wanderings about New England six years before. She asked him to lend her money to buy a house, so she could live in Orange and cultivate a garden. She was pleading for "a hand out of the mire both temporal and spiritual in which [she had] been well nigh smothered the last 10 or 15 years."[14] Marian's dyspeptic attacks had become so frequent that in November Elizabeth described her as having a "health spell"[15] and working hard.

Ellen, in spite of her mother, had escaped the family ties which held Marian. All the Blackwells had artistic abilities; they could write and sing and play musical instruments, and most of the girls could draw skillfully. Only Ellen, though, had developed her artistic talents. For several years she had been determined to go to Europe to study. In 1854 Düsseldorf was her aim, "but," Elizabeth told Emily, "I imagine like so many of her plans, it will serve the purpose of interesting her at present, and then be dropped as it is not wise in itself—Ellen is not suited to professional life of any kind, and just at her age it would be a pity to see her withdrawing from society. I believe we are all anxious that Ellen should marry."[16]

Ellen was the sister they had decided must marry, their one tribute to convention, perhaps because she was the baby who needed to be cared for. But Ellen was more like her sisters than they had realized. She had not married. She had not gone to Düsseldorf either. Instead, in 1855, taking Anna as her example, she had arranged to support herself in Europe by sending weekly newsletters to two Philadelphia papers, no routine matter for a woman in those days. She went first to join Anna in Paris, where for a short time she studied at a school of design for girls. Then she settled in London, which she described as the smokiest place under heaven. She was now studying drawing under no less an authority than John Ruskin, who must have appealed to her as much by his reformist impulses as by his extraordinary critical faculties. At thirty-six he had already produced the first volumes of *Modern Painters,* as well as *The Seven Lamps of Architecture* and *The Stones of Venice.* Only son of a rich father, Ruskin's concern with teaching was selfish—to train engravers to the precision he required in illustrations of his works. He himself was a skillful draftsman, transcribing precise details of architecture and of nature; but he was not a creative artist, nor did he ever attempt to paint. Ellen wrote to Lucy that she had permission to paint in the National

Gallery and was going to copy "a lovely little picture of Claude Lorrain's. . . . I think I shall like Mr. Ruskin on the whole, but shall not limit myself to his plans for drawing." [17]

Howard, in England too, had been having financial problems. The formerly prosperous English cousins had had such reverses that, although Cousin Sam was holding onto the family business and fighting what Howard considered a useless battle, Kenyon had taken a job. In 1856 Howard had what seemed like his first stroke of luck. He was chosen out of a great number of candidates to go to Bombay as representative of the East India Company to examine Indian mines and report on the practicality of making iron there on a large scale. The salary was one thousand pounds a year and travel expenses, and "for a poor devil of a bankrupt iron master . . . quite a Godsend." [18] He might also have said that for a young man not yet twenty-five it was a considerable undertaking. Apparently Howard had always suffered from an appearance of responsibility which placed him in positions of too great responsibility; he had been just nineteen when he went off to Wales to be in charge of five blast furnaces.[19]

At closer range the Blackwells had revised their views of the English cousins whom they had so fully loved and trusted. Howard now called them "such crooked sticks that as relations they are of little use." Emily, when Henry briefly considered going to England, warned him that Cousin Sam was a man of high ideals but no caution, "always in hot water" and the most annoying man in the world to deal with.[20]

Anna, now living chiefly in Paris, was supporting herself by corresponding regularly with papers in the United States and in English colonies. A column signed "Fidelitas" consisted of lively news items combining politics with a rather gossipy account of life in Paris. She was a successful poet too. As long ago as 1846 in Charleston, before Elizabeth herself was famous, she had learned to her surprise that she had a famous sister, when a gentleman asked her whether the Anna Blackwell who had written *The Song of the Stars* was related to her. "He said it was highly spoken of in the reviews, and he had read extracts which he admired greatly . . . I could not lend it to him, for I had not seen it." [21] In 1853 a collection of Anna's poems had been published in England, a solid volume of two hundred and forty-eight pages. There were a few light and charming verses, a few poems of love lost, but the tone in general was of faith in a brighter future.

> And we shall scale, through that sublime conspiring,
> The widening gyres of Being's glorious scope;
> And life o'er top our loftiest aspiring
> With fulness ever nobler than our hope. . . .
> Then shall we know that every seeming Ending
> Is but a new and happier phase Begun;
> Extremes of orbèd movement ever blending
> In golden cycles round th' Eternal Sun.

But whatever the public expression of her private thoughts, in relation to her family Anna had not changed. "Anna is what she always was," Emily told Henry after meeting her sister again after so many years, "impulsive and unreliable in judgment, but very good, generous and affectionate, having got over her first horror at yr marrying a 'Yankee' she now begins to feel extremely kindly." [22] To Anna, feeling kindly meant interfering now on Lucy's behalf. Having learned that Lucy had given up bloomers, she put her own construction on the matter and wrote to Henry that he was limiting Lucy's freedom and that she ought not to give up the "short dress" for his sake. And so powerful still were the dictates of his elder sisters when they did not conflict with Lucy's, that Henry promptly wrote to his wife about the costume he disliked, "I shall have to go on my knees to you to induce you to resume the short dress . . . I want you to feel that I aid you, not retard you." [23]

CHAPTER THIRTEEN

"I had a vision of a family Phalanstry when I came east," Hannah Blackwell wrote, "but it has faded as earthly visions do."[1] Yet her children had not dispersed to any great distance. In October 1856 shortly before Florence was born, Sam obtained a position at twelve hundred dollars a year as bookkeeper for an old, established firm, and with an assured income, Sam and Nettie ventured to take a house of their own. New Jersey, where they had lived as children, continued to lure the Blackwells. Marian had spent the summer in Orange, and longed to settle there. And even before he came East, Elizabeth had told Henry, "we all want to see you with a mountain home in Orange,"[2] and suggested that if he would buy a house there, she would try to, too. In April 1857 Sam and Nettie moved to their country home at the end of what is now the teeming thoroughfare of Market Street in Newark. It was an odd little house, tall, thin, perched on a rise, and Henry promptly christened it The Pepperbox.

At about the same time, Henry and Lucy moved to Orange. Henry, after prolonged difficulty because his economic and personal connections were centered in the West, had acquired a new business interest. It was an agricultural-book publishing house, and Henry's function was to travel through the Midwest setting up farmers' libraries based on the firm's publications. Again his life with Lucy had to wait on better days. A week after they moved, she was left alone to cope with "carpenters, masons, housecleaners and gardener etc." But at least they had a home, though neither spent much time there at first, for Lucy continued to travel and lecture. After a few months she gave up her public life and stayed at home. With Henry away it was consoling to know that Sam and Nettie were only a few miles distant.

Her loneliness must have been magnified by feminist Susan B. Anthony's protests at her unexplained desertion of the movement. At last in July, though modesty decreed that even modern women must not lightly reveal such matters even to their closest friends, Lucy confided to Susan that she was shortly to have a baby. She could not, in this crisis, have been much sustained by Henry, who, from far away, poured out his fears with the same lack of restraint which had permitted him to reveal to her his sisters' objections to their marriage. Lucy was thirty-nine, and the danger of death from childbirth was real enough in those days. "Lucy dear," wrote her devoted husband, "*however* this great crisis may eventuate, whether it result, as I hope and believe, in *our* assumption of new duties and cares, or whether in leaving me *alone* in this strange, uncongenial world—I will try to *meet* my responsibilities *worthily* and *well*." And in a sort of premature farewell, "Dearest! You have made me *very happy* in spite of surface cares and excitements." [3]

In spite of forebodings, on September 14, Lucy successfully gave birth to a daughter. Henry was at home, and Dr. Emily was there as obstetrician. Elizabeth described the baby as "so like Harry 'tis quite funny," [4] and months later said her looks were an improvement on his, her eyes "large, darker grey with black lashes, and very bright." [5]

One of the first problems was a name. Daughter of Lucy Stone and Henry Blackwell, what should she be called? They decided she should have both names: —— Stone Blackwell. The blank remained for almost a year, while her parents debated a first name. For a time they settled on Sarah, much to Ellen Blackwell's disgust; her given name had been Sarah Ellen, and she wrote that she had always been grateful for a second name to fall back on.

Whether for this reason or not, at long last the baby was named Alice, and so she remained.

Fortunately, shortly after the birth of Lucy's daughter, Sam moved his little family—Nettie was pregnant again—to a house nearer his brother's. Henry and Lucy, barely settled, had also moved that summer. The Blackwell brothers continued to trade properties, both eastern and western, and to move whenever a good trade made moving desirable. Any surplus earnings of their sisters they also invested in land. In the Fifteenth Street house Marian had replaced her two brothers and their wives by boarders, who were soon joined by young George, come to New York to study law by apprenticeship in a legal firm.

The doctor sisters and their colleague, Dr. Zakrzewska, were busy indeed. As long ago as 1855, excluded from practice in established male institutions, Elizabeth had begun to plan for a large hospital where poor women and children could be cared for by women doctors. In England, Emily had begun collecting money from friends and sympathizers. In New York, Elizabeth's Quaker circle had organized sewing groups which at weekly fair meetings made small objects and sold them; but they collected pennies, and dollars were needed. Dr. Marie became impatient. More practical than Elizabeth, she decided the plans were too grandiose, the efforts too small. They ought to settle on a smaller hospital to be opened in a year, and collect money and articles for a large fair. She had already visited Boston, wealthy center of liberalism. She went there again, and found a group eager to help and astonished by Marie's report that few of the rich women in New York "dared to connect themselves with such radical reformers as we appear to be."[6] Marie collected a hundred dollars and the promise of a large table of fancy goods for a fair.

A sympathizer described the enterprise in the *Liberator* as "a Christian charity for the sick poor." Yet even for so respectable a purpose, no one seemed willing to give the lady doctors a room in which to hold their bazaar, until, after long searching, they were offered a loft at Stuyvesant Institute, which they eagerly put in condition to be used. Greeley's *Tribune* carried a notice on December 5, 1856; and ten days later reported that, at the fair, held on December 11, the ladies had realized "over $1,100 from sales and money donations, besides leaving quite a large number of articles . . . which will form a basis for a similar effort at a future time, as it is designed to raise $5,000, the sum required to rent and furnish a suitable house for the accommodation and support of forty patients, with a dispensary for outside patients attached." A second trip to Boston netted Marie an additional six hundred and fifty dollars, and a promise of the same amount for each of the next two years.

With enough money to make a start, they rented an old Dutch house at 64 Bleecker Street. It belonged to a New York family named Roosevelt. Mr. James Roosevelt had died ten years before, and the house was leased from his widow. No prescience declared that their grandson James, then nearly thirty, would in his middle years have a son named Franklin Delano.

May 12, 1857 was Florence Nightingale's thirty-seventh birthday, and, as a tribute to her now famous friend, Elizabeth decided to open the New York Infirmary for Indigent Women and Children on that day. It was a day which fell during Anniversary Week, the week when religious and radical organizations held their yearly meetings. The Anti-Slavery Society, the Home Missionary Society and the Temperance Union were among the national societies meeting in New York, insuring the doctors a wider range of sympathizers than usual. The *Times,* describing the opening ceremonies, said that "the parlors were well filled with friends of the institution." It was a day of achievement and sentiment. Henry Ward Beecher, son of the Blackwells' friend and neighbor in Walnut Hills, came from his church in Brooklyn to speak at the ceremonies. Dr. Elder, Elizabeth's landlord, friend and supporter in her early days in Philadelphia, was also among the speakers. Elizabeth herself, in her white doctoral sack, made her report.

The four floors of the house were on display, from the dispensary downstairs, through the small wards, through the maternity floor, to the attic where servants and four medical students were to live, one of the purposes of the Infirmary being to give practical training to graduates of the two "Female" medical schools, who, inadequately taught, could in no way receive supervised clinical experience. Since so much had been donated, the furnishings were a "mixture of elegant old furniture and cheap stands and chairs." Before a month passed, the beds were filled and the dispensary was caring for more than thirty patients a day. Elizabeth was director; Marie moved from Fifteenth Street to become resident physician, housekeeper and manager; Emily was the surgeon. Five distinguished male physicians acted as consultants and teachers. Patients who could afford to pay were charged four dollars a week; the rest were treated free. The entire budget for expenses—food, wages, heat, lighting—was twenty-two dollars a week.

But their battle for acceptance as physicians had barely begun. A patient died of childbed fever, common enough in those days, yet it was taken by the neighborhood as a sign that the lady doctors were killing their patients. Dr. Marie remembered that "an immense crowd collected, filling the block . . . howling and yelling and trying to push in the doors . . . so that we were beleaguered in such a way that no communication with the outside was possible." At length, after moments of terror, two policemen came running and dispersed the crowd. Again a mob armed with stones attacked the hospital after a patient died of a ruptured appendix. The little hospital survived this attack too.

That summer and fall, Elizabeth had an English visitor. Barbara Leigh Smith had recently married Dr. Eugène Bodichon, a well-to-do Frenchman sixteen years older than herself, who, like her, devoted his life to philanthropy and reform. Algiers was his adopted home, and throughout the years of their happy marriage, she divided her time between Algiers and England, sometimes staying in England for months without him. He was an eccentric who even in England and the United States wore a burnooselike over-garment. Their wedding trip was slightly eccentric too, for they visited the United States, spending some months in the South to observe the workings of slavery, and some in the North enjoying a view of democracy and reform. Elizabeth went with them on a trip to Niagara Falls.

Because England was even more backward than the United States in accepting women in professional roles, Elizabeth's English friends constantly urged her to return there to help the cause of medical education for women. Elizabeth was eager to go. She had become a naturalized citizen of the United States in 1849; but, for her, England continued to be the homeland. And by the summer of 1858 the Infirmary was running so smoothly that she felt able to leave it for a year in the competent hands of her two associates.

A further inducement was that so many of the family were now on the European side of the Atlantic. In June Ellen had written to Lucy from the Isle of Wight, where she was vacationing with "Aunt Eliza, my uncle's widow." Aunt Eliza was the Blackwell children's nurse of long ago, who had come from England with them and bigamously married their Uncle Charles. Ellen, "after roving so much about alone," was happy to be with this small, gentle woman. Anna, she said, had recently returned to France after having nursed Uncle Charles in his last illness. She had seemed in better health and spirits than usual in spite of this strain, and had welcomed Ellen "with much greater cordiality than ever before." The "same funny Anna as ever," she had dressed soberly and with dignity for her trip to France, then at the last moment put on a nightcap under her bonnet. The frill stuck out oddly all around, but Anna "stood there arranging it as if it were the most ordinary costume in the world," and Ellen could not persuade her to take it off. Yet odd as she looked, odd as she must have been to look as she did, she as usual made "acquaintances all along the road . . . and had a pleasant journey."[7]

Anna had lent Ellen money, and since, in the Blackwell tradition, Ellen had invested her small earnings in land, she asked George to transfer some property to Anna in payment. Ellen reported that two of her pictures were in an exhibit of lady artists in London, and one had received special comment in the press.

On August 18, 1858, Elizabeth and little Kitty embarked for England on the Cunarder *Persia,* the combination sail and steam vessel on which Emily had returned the year before. Years later Kitty still remembered the watch pacing in the night from prow to stern, calling "All's well ahead!" Elizabeth and Kitty were both very seasick.

Howard met them when they landed. He had just returned from India, driven away by the Indian mutiny, which had finally and belatedly removed the ruthless East India Company (his employers) from all governmental authority. Howard was a small man—all the Blackwell brothers were short—and Kitty thought him "just the counterpart" of George.

When they reached London, eleven-year-old Kitty was sent to Surrey to a coeducational boarding school of which reformist Madame Bodichon was a patron, and Elizabeth went to Paris to visit Anna, who had a flat near the Champ de Mars. There Elizabeth retired to write three lectures, their subject the medical achievements of women in America, and the value to women of physiological and medical knowledge. With the help of Lady Byron, she also established relations with the Countess de Noailles, a rich and enlightened French lady who was interested in endowing a woman's hospital in which to demonstrate the life-saving value of sanitary reforms. Elizabeth seriously considered remaining in England to head such a hospital, if Emily could come as her associate. "I will accept nothing that is not offered to us both . . . we cannot separate in practice."[8]

In England, Kitty was unhappy at school, but the authorities of this modern institution would not permit her to tell Elizabeth. Ingeniously she acquired a stamp, wrote a letter, and carried it in her pocket until, on the pupils' daily walk, they passed a post office where she slipped it into the mailbox. On receiving the letter Elizabeth did not hesitate a moment. Kitty was instantly rescued and sent to London, where Ellen was sharing a flat with Howard. It was Kitty's first sight of Ellen.

A little later the eleven-year-old girl traveled alone to Paris. At Dieppe she was put onto the Paris train by a friend of Anna's, but in Paris she missed Elizabeth at the station. Terrified, she nevertheless, as became the brave foster daughter of a brave family, found a carriage and set out for Anna's address. On the way she met Elizabeth, who had been directed to the wrong station.

Kitty stayed on in Paris and went to a boarding school for Americans. In later years she recalled that in London Ellen, asking no one's permission, had bought clothes for her. She remembered a "brick-dust red dress with pin-point black spots" and a "green bonnet." Anna disapproved and, asking no one's permission, burned the clothes without giving Elizabeth opportunity or money to replace them.

Kitty's foster mother was busy. She went to the Riviera to confer with Madame de Noailles, then, in January 1859, returned with Kitty to England. In London Elizabeth stayed mostly with

Cousin Kenyon and his French wife. Cousin Kenyon was now Chief Inspector of Mines for Great Britain, very successful and very rich. Part of the time Elizabeth traveled, lecturing not only in London, but in other English cities, and returning once to the Riviera for conferences with Madame de Noailles.

Meanwhile Kitty went to day school, and lived with Ellen and Howard. Howard, determined not to return to India, but to stay in England and have Anna come there to keep house for him, "hunted Britain over" for an interest in a mine, but found nothing. He read *A Tale of Two Cities* aloud to Kitty, as it appeared serially.[9] Kitty loved books, and, at this unsupervised period, reading late into the night by the light of a single candle, she injured her eyes so that they were always afterward weak.

That Easter Elizabeth, Ellen and Kitty went to join Anna, who was vacationing on the Isle of Wight; and Anna helped Elizabeth prepare an English edition of her book *Laws of Life*. Elizabeth was trying to decide whether or not to stay in England. Her emotions fluctuated. She wrote to Emily that she saw the charms of working and living in England as clearly as she had on going there;[10] but a little later, and in a different mood, confessed that she felt "no personal . . . enthusiasm" for Britain.

In certain terms her year in England had been a great success. Her lectures had been enthusiastically received and had had practical results. Young Elizabeth Garrett heard one, decided to study medicine, and became the pioneer of the English movement for acceptance of women as physicians. A committee had been formed to collect money for a hospital for women's diseases to be staffed by women physicians. Elizabeth's own name had been enrolled in the newly established Medical Register of the United Kingdom, as a doctor of foreign qualification practicing in England —the first woman to be so honored. No woman trained in Great Britain was included for another eight years.[11]

But she was having problems with her supporters. She began to find Madame de Noailles oversensitive and changeable, and was afraid to depend on her promises. Florence Nightingale was so dedicated to nursing that she had no interest in any other aspect of medicine, and tried to persuade Elizabeth to devote herself to establishing a school for nurses. Only Lady Byron continued to live up to expectations. To her Elizabeth confided in June that, though she had made headway in educating the English public, it was "uphill work, not remunerative (my tour was an expense to me); a repetition, to a great extent, of our last seven years' work. . . . I shall therefore endeavour to prepare others for English work by receiving and educating students in America. In America, as here, it is a life work."[12] She had decided to return to New York and the Infirmary.

Ellen too had had enough of England. She complained of constant sore throats and colds in the raw English climate, though her doctor sister believed her to be suffering as much from "hysterical symptoms, and general debility."[13]

Elizabeth, Ellen and Kitty sailed in late July. Elizabeth took with her an eight-hundred-pound contribution from Madame de Noailles to be used for establishing a country sanitarium, because the countess believed that "in seven cases out of ten" women's complaints could be cured by fresh air alone. Elizabeth hoped that a tract of land might be found for the sanitarium where all the Blackwells could have homes and help with the work.

In the United States both before and after Elizabeth's departure, her family had been involved in difficulties. In the spring of 1858 Henry had still not managed to find employment that would keep him in the East with his wife and daughter. For a short time he had had a bookkeeping job but had soon reaffiliated himself with an agricultural-book publisher and was off to the West once more. Again he was full of enthusiasm, delighted at performing a social function by providing libraries where, by paying one dollar, a farmer's family could have the use of books worth sixty dollars or more. And the project was very successful.

Yet his enthusiasm was in battle with his more intimate emotions. Lucy had two attacks of pleurisy that spring. She also had boils, so prevalent in the days before modern sanitation that they were widely believed to be a healthy, if inconvenient, outlet for bodily poisons. Every common laborer, Henry wrote, could afford to live with his wife and children. Why must he be for months away from home?

In Springfield Henry and an associate had occasion to consult an Illinois lawyer, who was also a leader of the young Republican

Party. They found Mr. Lincoln "as he was coming out of the Court House with his law books under his arm—a tall, middle-aged man with kind eyes and a frank, quiet manner who impressed one with sincerity, sense, and benevolence. He had then attained only local celebrity."[14] But that year Abraham Lincoln achieved national fame. It was the year he made his "house divided" speech, the year too of the Lincoln-Douglas debates.

In the East that spring, Lucy, lonely and deprived of the work she loved, finally succumbed to Susan Anthony's pleas and consented to lecture in New York, leaving the baby with a neighbor; but the baby "took a dreadful cold," and Lucy decided not to leave her again.

In April Marian, still keeping house in Fifteenth Street, told Lucy that she could no longer bear the responsibility of caring for her mother—and perhaps for Elizabeth, Emily and George as well. She must do something for herself, as her sisters had. She asked whether she and her mother could move into Lucy's house, living separately from Lucy. Then if Marian found work, her mother would not be alone. Lucy consented, and they came.

That April too Nettie gave birth to a second daughter, and received a congratulatory rebuke from Susan Anthony. Mrs. Stanton had "devoted 18 YEARS out of the *very heart of existence*" to having children, Susan said, "but *I say* STOP NOW, once and for all, your life work will be arduous enough with *two*."[15] Whether or not to prove her wrong, Nettie agreed to speak in May at the Woman's Rights Convention in New York; and she and Sam went to Boston to attend antislavery meetings there. After that Sam persuaded her to stay home with him and the children. It was fortunate that he did, for at the end of July the baby suddenly developed a high fever. Elizabeth, soon to leave for Europe, came out to care for her, but it was no use. A few days later the baby died. Nettie was desolate.

By November Henry was so distressed at his continued absence from home that Lucy, who in any case was not working, consented to bring year-old Alice and join him in Chicago. They lived in Evanston, "a very pleasant village with a beautiful grove and public park extending to the Lake shore" where they had a bathhouse.

From the East Sam reported that Emily and George had spent Christmas with the rest of the family in New Jersey. George and Emily "jog on together quietly and to their mutual satisfaction." George had taken to the law with characteristic "settled, interested indifference." [16]

In the spring of 1859, while Elizabeth was in England, Emily's second associate left her. Dr. Marie's visits to Boston had had a result beyond the collection of funds for the New York Infirmary. She was invited to manage a hospital in connection with the recently opened New England Female Medical College, and to teach obstetrics. Having completed the two years she had promised to give the Infirmary, she left in June with Emily's reluctant consent.

From Evanston that summer came news that Lucy had lost a premature baby boy. In her grief, the religion she sometimes scorned stood her in good stead. "He is garnered from all harm," she wrote. And "The circle widens on the other side, that will welcome us when we go." By the end of the summer Henry's work was completed. He had taken orders for fifteen hundred libraries. They returned to New Jersey.

Lucy's reaction to the loss of her baby was to direct her attention even more toward Alice and away from the lecturing and propaganda which would keep her so much from home. Nettie's response to the death of her child was quite different. To free herself of grief, she returned vigorously to preaching and speaking. Indeed early in July of 1859 she left little Floy with her family at the farm in Henrietta, and went for several months on a lecture trip with Susan Anthony, speaking in Lake George, Niagara Falls and other parts of New York State. At last, homesick and guilty at having left her husband and child so long, she suddenly gave up the trip and returned home. With Elizabeth and Ellen back from England, and Lucy and Henry back from the West, the family phalanx was regrouping in and around New York.

Of the Blackwell women, only Elizabeth, who had undertaken medicine with such reluctance, seemed never to question the basic direction of her life. Marian, Ellen, Lucy, Antoinette were suffering doubts and confusion about their chosen roles. Emily was not immune. Like Antoinette, who, having attained the ministry, had quickly lost her faith and relinquished her gains, so now Emily, who had with such heroic effort achieved the impossible and earned a medical degree, was uncertain of her aims. In the summer of 1858, just before Elizabeth left for England, Emily confided to her diary, "An agony of doubt has burnt in my heart for months. Oh my GOD, is the end of all my aspirations . . . to be that this long earnest struggle has been a mistake—that this life of a physician is so utterly not my life? . . . I could bear anything but the feeling of failure: Show me the way! be with me!" It was no passing doubt. More than two years later, when their success was assured, Elizabeth told Barbara Bodichon that Emily had "taken an extreme dislike" to medicine, and when—if ever—she had "collected a small competency," intended to travel and devote herself to art.[17] Perhaps it was the battle more than the career that drew these courageous rebels to fight the customs and conventions of their time.

CHAPTER FOURTEEN

Now the trend of the restless Blackwells was away from Europe. In the fall of 1860 Howard gave up the fight to make his fortune in Britain, and briefly cast homesick eyes on the United States. "What a life mine is. I have been so long without any fixed home, I've been so knocked about and so completely without a circle of relations or even friends that I can hardly realize the fact that I have brothers and sisters if I could only get hold of them. Life is really worth very little under such circumstances and although I don't know that I ought on the whole to regret having left America and separated from you all I certainly should hesitate if it were to be done over again." Yet in the end he decided it would be folly to give up "such an opening as I have in India."[1]

There were compensations. In spite of the vicissitudes of his career, at twenty-nine he had done well enough so that he found it necessary to indicate that he was not as rich as his American relatives imagined. He valued his capital at about two thousand pounds, though in actual present shares he was worth only about one thousand. This explanation was presumably occasioned by a suggestion that he contribute to his mother's support, and he now offered twenty pounds a year to the joint enterprise.

Mother and Marian were in financial straits. Marian had bought the longed-for home in Roseville, New Jersey, and she and her mother were living there, with a maid who would give Marian the freedom she so longed for. Marian was working, but even so, there was not enough money. Fortunately Ellen had decided not to join them, but had opened a small studio in New York where she was happily teaching drawing to young ladies.

In October 1860, Marian told Henry that Elizabeth and Emily had offered to pay for the maid Marian had realized she must give up. She went on, like a bookkeeper totaling an account, "You will remember that for a year and one month from Sept 1st 1857 to Oct 1st 1858 you felt unable to contribute anything to Mother's support; while Sam and George have paid regularly month by month." Since then, besides his monthly contribution, Henry had sent Mother one present of thirty-five dollars and advanced Marian seventy-five, so, to be even with Sam and George, he still owed fifty-two dollars and fifty cents. Marian pointed out rather sharply that she had never asked for extra money. "I mention this because you have sometimes spoken as tho' my unlucky purchase of the house was involving you all in money difficulties." [2]

Perhaps it was the two marriages rather than the accustomed precariousness of their economic situation that injected an unaccustomed note of irritability into the interlocking finances of the family. In April 1858 Lucy had with "gladness" allowed Henry and Sam to use some bank stock as security for a land purchase. Yet only six months later, when Sam suggested a division of their obligations, Sam repaying Mr. Harris two thousand dollars and Henry taking over the debt to Lucy of twenty-one hundred dollars minus fifty, Henry replied with such indignation that Sam felt obliged to explain that he was merely trying to simplify the transaction, not to reduce Lucy's security. He told Henry that his employers had promised him a retroactive raise to fifteen hundred dollars a year. It was much needed. In the past year he and Nettie had used up their entire savings.

Although Emily had been left alone with the vast task of managing the Infirmary, it had prospered in her competent hands; but the expense and inconvenience of separate living quarters troubled her, and when Elizabeth returned, Emily persuaded her to sell the Fifteenth Street house and to move the Infirmary to a larger building where they could work and live. They found a suitable place for sale, "a large, handsome house" at 126 Second Avenue on the corner of Eighth Street, and moved there in April 1860.

At Fifteenth Street, with the house full of boarders, Emily had "slept in the garret and dined in the cellar, when [she] dined at all." Sometimes she had eaten in a cheap restaurant, more often nibbled oranges, dates and bread, or cooked a little piece of meat over an alcohol lamp.[3] Patients never invited her to dine with them, and even the most ardent Infirmary supporters would send up a tray if she happened to pay a house call at mealtime, for it would never do to ask a guest to share a table with so odd a creature as a lady doctor. Now on Second Avenue, though the Infirmary instead of boarders occupied the center of the building, Emily and Elizabeth again slept in the garret and ate in the cellar. Nevertheless their lives and finances were much simplified by the move.

Emily, in spite of her doubts about her profession, continued to take chief responsibility for the Infirmary, while the more verbal Elizabeth carried on outside practice and lectured extensively. Yet it was Emily who, with one of the women trustees, went to Albany to ask for the thousand dollars a year which the legislature granted to all New York dispensaries. The subsidy was not only a great financial gain, but gave them the acknowledged status for which as women they had had to struggle so fiercely.

Elizabeth, writing to Barbara Bodichon, told her that she and Emily had decided they must stay in the United States for a few years. She reported Anna as being angry at the decision and feeling particularly abandoned in Europe now that her beloved Howard had been forced to return to India. Elizabeth herself had been disappointed at first, but she was now reconciled. Her desire to go back to England seems astonishing when she discusses the gossip and malice which surrounded her English visit. Hardly less strange is her reason for feeling content to remain in the United States where she has "no wish to enter society, and [does] not care for the people sufficiently to mind ill-nature." [4]

The year 1860 was of course a momentous one in her reluctantly adopted country. In that year the Democratic Party split on the issue of slavery in new territories, with the result that in November

1860 Abraham Lincoln, candidate of the young, vigorous, united Republican Party was, to the delight of the Republican Blackwells, elected President. This growing power of the North, even should slavery be permitted to flourish, was intolerable to the South. South Carolina seceded, and was followed by ten other states; and on April 12, 1861, the guns of the Confederacy were turned on Fort Sumter in Charleston Harbor.

When, six weeks later, Emily wrote to Barbara Bodichon, change was already everywhere. "The whole look of [New York] is coloured by the war—all the parks are filled with rows of wooden barracks, and the streets are always resounding with military music as the regiments move in and out." In these early days of the war, optimism was the mood of the North. Yet then, as now, European views of America were dim. Emily explained that to Europeans "this crash of war indicates an utter break up of the union, and a total failure of republican institutions. Here the feeling is universal that the North will come out on a higher ground than it has previously occupied." There would inevitably be complete derangement of business and great suffering among the poor. Yet "the people are cheerful and hopeful. . . . How far it will destroy slavery speedily can not be told, the half loyal Border States tie the hands of the gov't in the matter at present, and the popular sentiment is not yet clear on the point. It is curious to see how the lines are dividing the country more and more clearly on this point . . . more because it is a Southern Institution and they are growing bitter against the South than from any other feeling. . . . It will be a great good bought at a terrible price, but progress must always pay a tax to the Devil."

"We are very busy," Emily continued, "as we have taken part in the work of selecting and registering women to be trained as nurses for the Army. We have given a great deal of time and labor to the work. . . . The Gov't has appointed Miss Dix 'Matron General' and given her full authority to superintend the nurses of the army—and has directed that a part of the nurses shall be women." This was stipulated against the wishes of the War Department, and only because of public pressure. "Miss Dix, though in many respects an estimable and sensible woman, is deficient in the power of organisation, and has no idea of the details of Hospital management. . . . I think there cannot fail to be much confusion."[5] Dorothea Dix was then fifty-nine years old, a Boston schoolteacher who had dedicated herself to correcting the barbarous conditions in so-called lunatic asylums, where the mentally ill were treated like wild animals and often turned into animals by their treatment. At the outbreak of war the courageous Miss Dix joined the Massachusetts troops traveling to Washington, and there, in the general confusion, was assigned to create a new army branch—nursing. Elizabeth described her as acting "without system but with intense benevolence."[6]

As soon as the war began the Blackwell sisters had called a meeting of the lady managers of the Infirmary to discuss the training of nurses, for there were no adequately trained women to care for the wounded. Somehow an announcement got into the New York *Times,* and at the hour of the meeting the parlors of the Infirmary were suddenly and astonishingly crowded with ladies eager to help. There was "a perfect mania among the women," Elizabeth said, "to 'act Florence Nightingale'!"

A further meeting was scheduled at Cooper Institute, and there a Woman's Central Association of Relief was set up. The movement spread throughout the North, and dedicated women collected funds and necessities to alleviate the hard lot of the soldiers. From these small beginnings at the Infirmary grew the famous United States Sanitary Aid Commission, appointed that June by President Lincoln. It was an official organization, though without official status or funds. Its funds were provided by the unremitting efforts of thousands of women throughout the country, who made bandages, collected supplies, organized fairs. The Sanitary, as it came to be known by the grateful soldiers, was the U.S.O., the Red Cross, the hospital unit of the Civil War. It saved men, and often made life bearable in the essentially intolerable situation, in the first years of the war, of a volunteer army enlisted by the states, unequipped, untrained, and enrolled not for the duration, not for a year, but for periods of three months.

In June 1861 Emily described the budding organization, which was almost solely responsible for attempting to improve the well-being of the army, as "an influential organisation here which we aided in forming and with which we are connected." But already there was such fear among their associates that the presence of lady doctors would make the work unpopular that the Blackwells had "to a great degree withdrawn as the affair went on." Before that, Dr. Elizabeth had been appointed by the Central Relief Association to interview the hordes of would-be Florence Nightingales and to select those moral, intelligent and disinterested enough to be trained at the Infirmary, Bellevue or New York Hospital for army service. Because of the pressing need, this training period was one month. Elizabeth herself gave the trainees a series of lectures ranging from sanitary rules, through care of patients, to moral and religious precepts; and Emily wrote a monograph on *The Selection and Training of Nurses* which became the authority for thousands of Sanitary Commission auxiliaries.[7]

On Lucy and Nettie the war had a very different effect, for in the early war years both the woman's rights and antislavery movements were swept away in the whirlwind of the conflict. In the days before Lincoln's election, radical abolitionists like Garrison, Higginson and Lucy had advocated the secession of the North from a compact with slaveholders, and Lucy believed that the slaves should be encouraged to rise and overthrow their masters. In October 1859, when John Brown and his handful of followers were captured, after their tragic, Quixotic tilting at the government arsenal at Harpers Ferry, the man who had performed Lucy and Henry's wedding ceremony took part in two wild and hopeless plots to rescue them from the gallows.

The abolitionists expected Lincoln to free the slaves, and were disaffected when he did not. In the days after Lincoln's election, however, fear of the dissolution of the Union and of civil war had created in the North a mood almost as strongly opposed to any suggestion of emancipation as in the South. Rioters broke up antislavery meetings and attacked the speakers. When the war started, the abolitionists decided to call off their scheduled meetings and support the government, slow though it might be to fulfill their hopes. The woman's rights movement, which had had unprecedented success in the months just before the war, also stopped its meetings and propaganda.

Lucy's earlier retirement from public life had ostensibly been to care for her home and child. Yet there had been more to it than that. With her acknowledgment of love there had come the sickening migraine headaches which immobilized her; and in her further retreat from activity there was an element of uncertainty as to her abilities, a fear of speaking before audiences which had never troubled her in the days of her loneliness and self-sufficiency. It was only a few months before the war that she began to appear on the platform again and to "find again the old inspiration." The war drove her back to her home, and in its first years her contribution consisted, like that of any New Jersey housewife, in scraping lint for bandages.

Henry and Lucy had by now moved to a remodeled farmhouse with woods and an orchard on a hillside in West Bloomfield, today part of busy Montclair. Elizabeth had a country house there too. West Bloomfield was the place she had chosen for Madame de Noaille's sanitarium, and after her return from England had built a cottage where she now spent Sundays and sometimes weekends. The house looked over "charming undulating country to New York Bay in the distance; and with my telescope, I can see the white sand of Coney Island and the ships sailing on the Atlantic beyond."[8] She had tried in the first year of her return to open a sanitarium, but there had not been enough funds to carry out the plan.

In the second year of the war, Henry and Lucy rented their house in West Bloomfield and boarded in New York. Henry was working in the city, and the trip from West Bloomfield took one and a half hours each way. From the time he returned East, Henry had occupied himself entirely in real estate, buying, exchanging, selling his own land, selling and renting on commission. He had offices in Orange and New York, and while he tended the New York office, Lucy, taking little Alice with her, presided over the New Jersey office.

With the outbreak of war real estate became a prosperous enterprise. Property owners, frightened about the outcome of the conflict, were eager to sell at any price. Yet it was at this very moment that Henry found "the load of interest and taxes" too heavy to bear, and transferred his business to George. George took over and prospered to the extent that he eventually became a multimillionaire, proving that the expediency he had advocated to

Emily in their philosophic walks in Cincinnati had the practical results for which it was intended. The idealistic members of the family prospered in reform, but were never entirely free of economic pressures. After he left the real-estate business, Henry held several positions as salesman, and in the third year of the war became for a while salesman-bookkeeper at the excellent salary of three thousand dollars for Dennis Harris in the sugar business.

It seems hardly credible that a war on their very doorsteps should have had as little effect on the lives of the Blackwells as it did. True, it turned Elizabeth's and Emily's attention to the medical and hygienic needs of the army. It temporarily retired Lucy and Antoinette from active participation in the battle for woman's rights. But in general they led their lives undeviatingly. Ellen in her New York studio was teaching drawing to her young ladies. The three brothers were going about their jobs.

None of the brothers, even the two committed to creating a union free of slavery, fought in the war—a war in which, despite a belated national draft instituted in March 1863, it was possible and customary for a man who had the money to do so to pay someone less fortunate to take his place. Henry, at least, was drafted and, like most men who could afford to, paid three hundred dollars for a substitute, a low enough price for avoiding—or undertaking—the dangers of disease and battle in 1863. Thousands of men found substitutes or paid the official three hundred dollars to have their names withdrawn.

In the summer of 1862 Lincoln wrote to Greeley, "My paramount object . . . is to save the Union, and is not either to save or to destroy slavery. . . . What I do about slavery . . . I do because I believe it helps to save the Union." In September he issued the Emancipation Proclamation which, from January 1, 1863, freed the slaves in rebel areas, leaving untouched the institution of slavery in the loyal border states. This did not satisfy the abolitionists. In 1862 Henry wrote an article appealing to Lincoln to enroll a Negro battalion from the seceding states. In 1863 he wrote a plea for emancipation in the border states.

But if emancipation was not enough for the reformers, it was too much for the common man. In industrial centers throughout the North discontent grew. The draft sent working men to fight, while it kept rich men safe. Almost worse, the white worker going to war believed that, while he was gone, his job would be usurped by a freed Negro. In various industrial centers riots broke out. The most violent were in New York, where, for three fatal days in July 1863, rioters took possession of the city. Armed with rifles captured in an armory raid, they looted and burned buildings, including a Negro orphanage, and murdered hundreds of Negroes, until they were finally subdued by Federal troops.

The Infirmary was, by design, in a poor part of the city. To make matters worse, at the time of the riots it housed some pregnant Negro women fleeing from the South, who were waiting to give birth to their babies. White patients demanded that these Negroes be turned out. Elizabeth and Emily refused. The second night of the rioting, when the glow from burning buildings was already clearly visible from Infirmary windows, the rioters set fire to a group of houses only a block away. The doctors covered their patients' eyes to shut out the awful glare, then waited in terror for the next, seemingly inevitable event. It did not come. The Infirmary was not attacked, and the flames did not spread.

In 1863, after Lincoln had freed the slaves in rebel territory, women reformers found a cause of national significance in which, even in wartime, they thought it proper to make their voices heard. A call to the loyal women of the nation, signed by Elizabeth Cady Stanton and Susan B. Anthony, announced a convention to be held in New York on May 14. At the first meeting Lucy presided. Nettie made a spirited speech pointing out the impossibility of combining two such inimical forces as democracy and slavery.

These leaders had been waiting impatiently for the moment when they might end their truce. In one of those ironic advances often made in the regressive years of war, American women had attained a new freedom of motion and action, speech and thought. Their country had recognized a need for their services as never before. Yet in another way, they had lost. In New York, for instance, where shortly before the war their demands had forced the beginnings of a married woman's property law, most of the advances were repealed two years later by a legislature unharassed by protesting women.

But many of the women who came from far and wide to the

convention did not conceive of loyalty as involving rights for either women or Negroes. When Susan Anthony offered resolutions including, "There never can be a true peace in this Republic until the civil and political rights of all citizens of African descent and all women are practically established," an indignant debate broke out; but in the end the resolutions were carried by a large majority. The Women's National Loyal League was formed, its chief function to set up affiliates throughout the country to spread the creed of total emancipation and to collect signatures appealing for a constitutional amendment outlawing slavery everywhere and forever. By the next year over three hundred and fifty thousand signatures had been collected and presented to Congress. The work stopped only when the Thirteenth Amendment, abolishing slavery, was passed in 1865.

By the fourth year of the war, women in medicine were sufficiently accepted so that Elizabeth was invited to Washington by the Sanitary Commission. She wrote home to "Kittychen" describing her experiences, her pleasure in traveling through Maryland, which had just freed its slaves, of seeing colored workmen on the roads, "no longer slaves." Washington itself was grimmer and more stirring. The "wounded have been arriving here since Monday." From her window, Elizabeth saw the sad procession move by, watched the efforts to steady the swaying carriages so that the jolting would not further agonize the wounded men. She visited Miss Dix, "making acquaintance with the lady, and watching her style of working." Best of all, escorted by her old Philadelphia friend Dr. Elder, she was received by the President.

"A tall ungainly loose jointed man was standing in the middle of the room; he came forward with a pleasant smile and shook hands with us. I should not at all have recognized him from the photographs—he is much uglier than any I have seen, except a little one which was given me yesterday in the treasury, and which I supposed then to be a libel. I never should have given him credit from a passing view of the ability to regulate affairs and to write excellent documents which he certainly possesses—his brain must be much better in quality than in quantity for his head is small for the great lank body, and the forehead very retreating."

Dr. Elder mentioned to the President that Elizabeth was the

second woman ever to become a United States citizen. "I added that I believed Queen Victoria reserved the privilege of shooting me. 'Why yes,' said he, 'that was the chief cause I believe of our war of 1812'—and then he plumped his long body down on a corner of the large table that stood in the middle of the room, caught up one knee, looking for all the world like a Kentucky loafer on some old tavern steps, and began to discuss some point about the war." [9]

Within a year slavery was officially ended, the Civil War, in its fighting aspects, was over, and a few days later the great man who had received Elizabeth with such friendly informality was dead. He had achieved his ends, though he was killed too soon to see the final results, too soon to institute the moderate peace he had designed. But the Union had been saved.

CHAPTER FIFTEEN

In human experience the plans, dreams, projects never fulfilled are often as illuminating as those brought to fruition. In spite of her supposed talents, Marian alone of the Blackwells, perhaps because of the ailments, real or imaginary, which weighed her down, achieved no worldly success. Among the others, the most dramatic of those unattained hopes was Elizabeth's longing for love, for marriage, for a family. In 1860 she wrote to Barbara Bodichon, herself a wife, a mother and a painter, "How good work is—work that has a soul in it! I cannot conceive that anything can supply its want to a woman. In all human relations the woman has to yield, to modify her individuality—the strong personality of even the best husband and children compels some daily sacrifice of self . . . but true work is perfect freedom, and full satisfaction." [1] And four years later she pondered how strange it was that there should seem "almost an antagonism between love and work—in other words that the man who stood nearest should have the least sympathy with the woman in the expression of . . . the very part of her nature which really colours her love and makes it so noble and precious to him. . . . This anomaly, which is not selfishness, was a stumbling block in my life for many years; and although I have quite outlived the pain, and gained strength by the necessity of self centered life, it is still a fact which I am analysing with intense interest." [2]

When it seemed clear even to her that she would not marry, she for many years planned to adopt two or three more small girls and boys of "good English" stock. This she did not do; and it is perhaps significant that the one child she did take she did not make entirely hers. She never legally adopted Kitty, never gave her the Blackwell name. It was only after Dr. Elizabeth died and Kitty herself was an aging woman that she called herself Blackwell.

Henry struggled throughout his life to make a fortune quickly so that he could dedicate himself to reform, or if this proved impossible, to make his living in some enterprise which would improve the human lot. In the spring and summer of 1861, his mother, who with Marian lived not far from him in New Jersey, was unusually concerned about his worldly plans, and as always about his lack of plans for the world hereafter. About his life on earth, she wrote imploring him to move from remote Bloomfield, not to New York but to his own house in Orange, and not to give up the real-estate business which he had developed. "You are too disposed to change and . . . there is great virtue in *perseverance*." [3] She did not say, as she might have, that she had learned this bitterly from his father's career, and that Henry was reproducing his father's pattern.

"Do try to give yourself and Lucy present enjoyment, and this is to be found in your present competence, not in future fortune." [4] She gave more specific and more revealing advice too. "Do attend to your outer man, if you go shabbily dressed, with head down and hands in pocket, it will affect your reputation, for it is wonderful how far appearances go in this world. And do be considerate of the feelings of nervous, fidgety persons,—men or women, and don't get out of patience with them." [5] But she did not abandon his soul. The true motivation of these letters was that her granddaughter Alice, now three and a half years old, was receiving no religious training, and this to Hannah Blackwell was mortal sin. Eternal salvation depends on prayer, she wrote to Lucy when her appeals to Henry failed, and "I cannot endure the thought of separation hereafter." [6]

She did not, in her terms, save Henry's soul, nor did she convert him to perseverance. A year later he moved to New York, then from job to job. It might have been supposed that a well-paid position with Dennis Harris, whom he had known since boyhood and by whom he had been employed before, would have solved Henry's problems; but he had worked for him little more than a year when he became uneasy about Mr. Harris's way of doing business. At this point Henry was again seduced by his dream of dedication and, being "out of debt and with several thousands in his pocket," in the fall of 1864 he decided not to work, but to campaign for Mr. Lincoln's re-election.

Lucy and Henry were apart again. Lucy and Alice spent that summer and autumn with Lucy's ailing father at Lucy's childhood home. The mother Lucy had so loved had died four years before, and at the end of September her father died too. Yet even his death did not send her back to Henry. She was determined to live in the country for a period, not to be shut up in a city boarding house with a small and active daughter. "I want you all the time," she wrote, "for speech, and for silence, for rest, and sympathy, and all good things, Harry dear." [7] Yet she decided, for her state of mind and for their finances too, to remain for a time at her sister's home in Gardner, Massachusetts.

Lucy was forty-six, and the menopause was having a profound effect on her; but at the farm she had suffered less of the "mental confusion" that had "so tormented" her, and had begun to believe that after "the inevitable change" was over, she would again go out "into the world with words that *must* be spoken." [8] Meanwhile she was far removed from either of the conflicting roles she had assumed. She was neither wife nor rebel.

Nettie had continued to have babies. By 1869 there were five. As though feminism were expressing itself even in reproduction, they were all daughters, a single boy having died shortly after birth. Yet Nettie, partly by inclination, partly by financial necessity, found energy to go from time to time on lecture and preaching trips. From Toronto on one such trip she wrote to Sam, "There is only one luxury that I long for and that is yourself. . . . Even the babies are not wanted here. The truth is it is an immense relief to be quite away from them. . . . I should be as fidgety as

Mrs. Greeley is, or any other nervous lady, if I were tied to my children as they are to theirs." [9] And again, "I fall in love with you anew every time we separate. . . . I suppose lover's quarrels have something of that character; but as we never quarrel, taking a trip somewhere for a few days answers the purpose very well." [10]

After the birth of one of the babies, Elizabeth agreed to rent her New Jersey house to Sam and Nettie, and set the price at ten dollars a month. Her letter to Sam contained an amusing note. "I have only one fear, which I will tell you frankly—I should be horribly vexed if you brought bugs into the house. Servants are such pigs. . . . I have not got one bug in the house yet . . . and it would wring my heart to have it come in!" Otherwise she claimed not to be "fidgety" about her property as Marian and Lucy were.

From Anna in Europe came news of a very different sort. Before she returned from England in 1859 and before Howard went back to India, Elizabeth had written, "I am really sorry for Anna—compelled as she is to live in France, and disliking it so much—she has very strong affection too for her family, which if she knew them all, would be a great resource in her life. It really will be a source of great regret to leave her and Howard . . . a very fine fellow and depending much on his family for society—How shall it be reconciled—it seems wrong to give up either half the family!"

But Anna was making a living in France as a newspaper correspondent, and seemed to dislike France, if anything, less than other places. To live with Howard would have been her choice if this had been practicable, but Howard never settled anywhere long. In 1866 he was back in England. The rigors of Indian life had been too much for his health.

Now from Europe came the saddest of news. Emily wrote in her diary, "Received the news of dear Howard's death. The circle is broken—oh dear Howard! Poor Anna!" [11] Poor Anna indeed. "My darling Howy," she wrote, "my idol, for whom I wd have joyfully given my very life." If only she had left her work and gone to join him in England when he came back from India! But she had been in Paris, not even knowing he was ill; he had not let anyone notify her "because of the fearful tempest that raged, all that week, in the Channel." Then "on the Sunday afternoon just before the last relapse came on," he had dictated a letter, saying he was not getting proper care and asking her to come and nurse him. When she received it, he was dead.

None of his physicians—he seems to have been at a water-cure sanitarium—had any idea "what caused the terrific infection." But Anna's homeopathic doctor told her of "cases in which the liver, in India or Africa . . . formed minute attachments to the ribs. . . . He says he has had several such cases, and has cured them all in a few hours with arnica." According to Anna's advisor, Howard's case was neglected, and he ruptured the attachment "in that violent kick in bed." The ruptured spot bled and gangrene set in. Anna believed he might have been saved, that she might have saved him. This "gives to my hopeless sorrow an additional agony that drives me nearly mad. . . . Whether I shall really be able to outlive this loss I have no idea—I have been at Death's door . . . I should be glad to follow my deepest affection into the other life." She was unable to work, and a friend wrote her columns for her.

For consolation, she had one of her mother's stern religious reminders, and answered it. "I do earnestly hope that my letter, tho' of course it will not shake her faith in her horrible creed, will at least convince her that I have a religion of my own, and help her to take a view of my darling Howard's state and prospects less outrageous to him, to Heaven, and to common sense." [12] Did she in those days hear again her mother's words that morning so long ago when the other Howard had died: "It has pleased God to take our little Howard in the night"?

Cousin Kenyon and his wife, Maria, came to be with Anna, so lonely and far from home. This was a tribute to the deep family feeling of the Blackwells, and to the fact that among them the tensions which grew so easily seemed to dissolve, leaving at least no visible scar, for, toward the end of the Civil War, Cousin Kenyon had been caught up in the bickering which now from time to time shadowed the formerly relaxed and cordial financial dealings among the Blackwells. Kenyon's short period of affluence was past, and he wrote asking for the money he had lent Sam and Henry to go into the hardware business fifteen years before. He believed them to be using surplus funds to speculate in real estate instead of paying their debts. Henry hastened to reply that the land they had acquired had been in exchange for Western holdings, not for cash. They intended to pay their debt, but since United States currency was much depleted, to pay in European funds would involve great loss to them. Would he accept United States bonds or money?[13] Kenyon promptly and not unreasonably replied that this would involve great loss to him.[14]

Yet two years later Kenyon and his wife came to help Anna, who was so grief-stricken that Elizabeth and George decided to make the long trip to France to be with her. They stayed for several months. In October Elizabeth wrote to Marian that she was studying music seriously, her eyesight being too bad for much reading. One of the pleasures of the trip was a renewal of her friendship with Monsieur Blot. He had a wife and two charming children whom Elizabeth liked very much.[15]

In January 1867, when she was back in the United States, Elizabeth wrote to Barbara Bodichon that Lucy and Henry's nine-year-old daughter, Alice, was living with her and Emily. Many years later Alice remembered that during that winter's stay she had "trembled with awe before that very kind and harmless lady" her aunt Elizabeth, but had been less afraid of Emily, who gave her chocolate drops. She also remembered that when someone expressed surprise that Elizabeth was so short, Kitty had remarked that there were occasions when she could look "at least six feet high."[16] Little Alice, according to Elizabeth, had been committed to them for guidance and restoration, " 'tis funny how our household becomes a gentle reformatory for little unmanageable nieces! We never punish, but we live them into right ways."[17]

This view of Alice's presence at the Infirmary may be accurate enough; but there was perhaps a simpler explanation. For more than a year at the end of the war, Henry, Lucy and Alice had lived together in New Jersey, first in a rented house in Roseville, then in a house Henry bought near Sam and Nettie's, near also to the house which Marian, Mother Blackwell and George now shared. But when the woman's rights movement was reorganized after the war as the American Equal Rights Association, linking the demands for woman and Negro suffrage, Alice's mother gradually returned to full activity. Her father too, free for a time of business commitments, was traveling about the country with his wife, helping her rebuild her still wavering confidence in her abilities.

That spring Alice was still with the doctors. Henry and Lucy were in Kansas, stumping the state for equal suffrage. The battle for freedom had been bloodily fought in Kansas from its earliest days as a territory, for it had been largely settled by men determined to keep slavery out. "Only three years ago," Henry wrote to Alice from Lawrence, "this town was attacked by wicked slaveholders and burnt down. . . . But now the houses have been built anew and all the people who were not killed have come back." [18] Kansas had now been a state for six years, and its legislature had decided to put before the voters in the fall elections the questions of whether women and Negroes should be given the right to vote. The woman's rights movement had made huge strides in the twenty years since its beginnings, when its few adherents had been afraid to mention suffrage. Women had made great gains in courage, some improvement in status and in property laws. Now suffrage was the rallying point, not only woman suffrage but Negro suffrage as well.

Lucy and Henry covered the state, moving over the bumpy roads at the rate of twenty-five to forty miles a day in a carriage or "an open wagon with or without springs." They held meetings; they handed out tracts. Lucy spoke again with the old vigor and self-assurance. And they were confident of victory. In the fall Susan Anthony and Elizabeth Cady Stanton took up the banner; but in September, when Henry went back to Kansas, he felt that the battle had been lost. The Republican Party, while officially for equal suffrage, was split by factionalism, and in November, in spite of so much valiant effort, the free state of Kansas rejected Negro equality by a vote of 19,421 to 10,483, and the equality of women by 19,857 to 9,070.

When Lucy and Henry returned East that summer, they spent some time on Martha's Vineyard, the beautiful island off the Massachusetts coast. Henry, Lucy and Alice had gone there first toward the end of the war with the Blackwell brothers' friend and Walnut Hills neighbor Ainsworth Spofford, whose father was now Congregationalist minister in the island town of Chilmark. Ainsworth Spofford and his wife came from Washington to join them. In 1864, Spofford had been made Chief Librarian of the Library of Congress, a position which he held for many years. The party went to the island by sailboat, and boarded, romantically enough, at the

Gay Head lighthouse. They fell in love with the rolling countryside, the precipitous dunes, the blue bay and the bluer sea.

What one Blackwell liked, whether it was a woman, an investment or a place to live, he instantly recommended to the others. The second summer Henry and Lucy rented a furnished house on the island. When Hannah Blackwell became seriously ill with a carbuncle, she came, with Marian as nurse, to recuperate there; and others of the family came and went. By 1868 it was their established summering place. They liked its primitive quality in spite of "serious privations" and real "difficulty in obtaining supplies." Later the family bought a tract of land sloping from high dunes above the sea on one side to gentle Nashaquitsa Pond on the other. Their houses are still standing, and some of the Blackwell descendants have homes on the island.

Marian had almost reached the end of her nursing days. In the fall of 1867, Mr. Alofsen, with whose family she had lived for a while in the East, asked her to go to Europe for an indefinite stay with him and his daughter Frances. Elizabeth was pleased, because Marian had been "rapidly falling back into the old dyspeptic misery." [19]

Henry was still considering the possibility of returning to business. In the summer of 1868, in spite of his earlier discontent with Dennis Harris's business methods, he suggested that he and Sam go into the sugar business with his former employer. Sam, who had recovered from his earlier financial slump, was skeptical, and outlined a series of conditions before he would either enter the business or lend Henry money to do so. He refused to involve himself while Henry was "undertaking any other [presumably reformist] enterprise simultaneously"; Mr. Harris must have paid off all his debts; the business must be a joint partnership with twelve thousand five hundred dollars invested by each partner, and a stipulated amount drawn by each monthly.

When the scheme fell through, Sam expressed relief. He had almost decided to lend Henry part of the money if he "really wished to go into it alone." As for him, he preferred to give his "present mode of life at least a longer trial." [20] In this he was unlike much of the rest of his family, for whom sudden shifts and changes were in the making.

CHAPTER SIXTEEN

Emily, in spite of doubts, was more firmly entrenched in medicine than ever. From its earliest days one of the projects of the Infirmary had been the eventual founding of a medical college for women. In December 1863 at an Infirmary meeting, Elizabeth, in an address composed by both sisters, was able to state that "the practice of medicine by women is no longer a doubtful, but a settled thing." Several hundred women doctors had been graduated in the past ten years, and many were practicing successfully. The problem lay in the kind of medical education they were receiving.

It was in general inferior even to the education of male physicians, which was sketchy enough, and the reputation of women as doctors suffered because women doctors were in fact inadequate. Their premedical education, as well as their medical training, was often insufficient. There were no endowments to help them or even libraries where they could work, no professional societies or companionship to encourage them, no professorships or hospital posts to look forward to. Like many men students, they received no clinical training, but this was because no hospital would take them in. In Europe, four years of medical training were required, during which at least ten months a year must be spent in instruction, including lectures, laboratory work and hospital training. In the United

States there was no such legal necessity, though the best medical schools were now trying to expand their requirements.

It was hoped that the projected college would overcome these sad defects. Students were to be "called upon to communicate as well as to receive knowledge." They were to be taught to practice medicine, not just memorize words out of textbooks. Examinations for graduation were to be in all branches of medicine, and were to include demonstrations by students of bedside care.

When the college finally opened in November 1868, Elizabeth spoke eloquently of their long dream of such a moment. "We have been facing . . . two perpendicular cliffs—money and skill—for fifteen years." Three years of study were required by law for physicians, she said, but only two sessions of five months each need be at a college. The other twenty-six months could be spent reading, and were often wasted. The Infirmary hoped to require at least eighteen months of training at its Women's Medical College.

The great Dr. Willard Parker, one of the nation's foremost physicians, spoke too, and he appeared in the prospectus as Examiner in Surgery. Most of the eight professors were men. Elizabeth was Professor of Hygiene, Emily, of Obstetrics and Diseases of Women. The new college offered a combination of theoretical and practical courses unusual at the time; and in the years ahead, it increased the period of study to three and then to four years. It was one of the first medical schools in the United States to require a four-year program.

Great emphasis was placed on the study and practice of hygiene and nutrition, subjects not then ordinarily included in medical studies. Elizabeth had told Madame Bodichon that she had searched for some time for a "proper subject of enthusiasm" and thought she had found it in hygiene. She claimed her coprofessors did not share her enthusiasm, but perhaps this exempted Emily, who, a year before the college opened, said, "I think hygiene bears the same relation to domestic and social life, that mechanics does to building or engineering."[1] These were advanced views. Even in educated and well-to-do groups, there was little realization of the importance of good diet, rest and the sensible use of water inside or outside for the sick. Among the poor there was no awareness of such matters. But from its beginning the Infirmary had spread the surprising doctrine that sick people must be kept clean and given fresh air.

As early as 1866 the Infirmary had assigned a sanitary and nursing visitor to go into the homes of patients who obtained "medical prescriptions from the Dispensary." This checking on treatment made it possible for the visitor or, as she would now be called, social worker to go into a home "without seeming to intrude." She took with her a bag of soap, disinfectants, clean linens, pamphlets translated into various languages or read aloud to the illiterate, and her own good sense. In 1872 Dr. Rebecca Cole, a graduate of the Infirmary college and the first Negro woman to become a physician, was the Infirmary's chief sanitary visitor. Conditions in crowded tenements and sweatshops without sanitary requirements or facilities defied reform, but knowledge was a beginning.

In June 1869, at the end of the first school year, Emily told Barbara Bodichon that the college had achieved a greater success than she had anticipated. Though it was not the ideal they had dreamed of for so long, it was much respected, "better than anything we have had yet, and . . . a step forward."[2] In the same letter she said that Elizabeth was sailing for England in July.

Elizabeth was going to live for an extended period in England. At the very moment of its success she was leaving the Infirmary and College toward which she had for so many years directed her hopes and energies. Emily, who had such doubts about being a doctor, was to carry the major burden alone.

Elizabeth recorded in her autobiography that by 1869 "the early pioneer work in America was ended," the "free and equal entrance of women into the profession of medicine was secured," and she was going to England to assist English women to attain equal freedom there. But when Kitty Barry was an old woman, she remembered that Elizabeth and Emily had had serious disagreements, which must have begun before Marian went to Europe late in 1867, for "Aunt Marian told Dr. Elizabeth that she had alienated and was alienating Aunt Emily. My doctor wrote to Madame Bodichon about it and Madame Bodichon urged her to come to England and settle there." And indeed in 1867 Elizabeth had written to her friend that she would prefer to live in England,

and hoped within two years to have a sufficient income—about one thousand dollars a year—to afford to do so. Either she had forgotten her earlier doubts about English life or her dissatisfaction with the United States had increased. Emily, she said, was willing to have her go but would not join her; and Elizabeth obviously no longer felt that they *must* practice together.

In May 1869 Cousin Kenyon died suddenly in England. Elizabeth, leaving Kitty temporarily behind, sailed from New York in July. She went almost at once to see Marian, and presumably Anna too, in Paris, then returned to London, where she stayed for a time at the Leigh Smiths' family home in Blandford Square. Later Marian came to England to visit Elizabeth, who had never changed her view of Marian as her closest and most admired sister. Elizabeth told Madame Bodichon that she would find Marian, "in spite of her indigestion," an excellent "intellectual companion."

A few months later Marian returned to the United States, where her mother was growing frailer. In 1870 Marian, Ellen and their mother were living in a house in Lawrence, in the Rockaway section of Long Island. Kitty was with them. In January Elizabeth had written that, since Kitty was obviously better off in the country and Elizabeth could not "practice amongst cows and sheep," they must seriously consider the problem of where to live. Meanwhile Kitty ought to remain for a time with ailing Mrs. Blackwell and under "Miss Marian's admirable tutelage and care." [3]

A few weeks later she told Kitty that, sooner than return to her old life, she would live in an attic in England, where she had friends and consideration she could never achieve in the United States. She felt that Kitty ought to come "unless Mrs. Blackwell needs you," [4] but warned that, before deciding, the young girl must realize that Elizabeth was poor and it would be a long time before she could go back to America to visit. Elizabeth addressed her adopted daughter affectionately as "Dear Kittykin" and signed herself "Your own doctor" or "Your affectionate doctor," but she always referred to her family as Miss Ellen, Miss Marian, Mrs. Blackwell; and Emily, writing with easy intimacy to Kitty, signed herself not "Your aunt," but "Your friend."

In May Elizabeth asked Kitty to come as quickly as possible. Significantly this letter was written soon after Elizabeth had stopped living with Barbara Bodichon, with whom she had spent the winter, and whose busy life and entree into the literary and artistic life of London she had shared. It was a glamorous world, including the Rossettis, Charles Kingsley, the Carlyles, Herbert Spencer, George Eliot, Ruskin, the entire spectrum of England's great men and women. Elizabeth's admired Lady Byron had died in 1860. Now Barbara had left, presumably to return to Algiers, and Elizabeth had moved into her own, more lonely, quarters.

The letter contained another small indication of financial conflict within the family. "Miss Ellen writes me, that Mrs. Blackwell does not want the best china to leave the country, in her lifetime—if that really be so, of course I have not a word to say, because I would not, I need hardly say, cause Mrs. Blackwell even a shadow of annoyance; but I cannot help thinking it is Miss Ellen's idea rather than Mrs. Blackwell's." Elizabeth had written to Miss Marian, and Kitty was to do whatever Marian advised.[5] Whatever Marian then decided, Hannah's wedding china at some time followed Elizabeth to England.

Ellen's situation had grown increasingly domestic and difficult. In the spring of 1869, while Elizabeth was still in New York, an indignant letter from Ellen to Henry revealed a host of grievances. Ellen explained that she had received messages from her mother saying she was ill and alone; Henry and Lucy, with whom she had been living since Marian went to Europe, were both away, and she begged Ellen to come. Ellen went. As a result she not only received a letter from Henry reproaching her for staying uninvited at his house, but a rebuke from Emily for having left Second Avenue, where during Marian's absence she had fallen into the role of housekeeper. Ellen wrote that she need never enter Henry's house again unless their mother required it, but if she had to go there, he ought not to make her "position unendurable by such remarks" as had been repeated to her "on all sides." Ellen pointed out that it had been her custom to spend Tuesdays at Henry's house, visiting her mother and giving Alice lessons. She could stop this. She appended an itemized bill for fifty-five dollars for two years' tuition.[6] Yet this difficulty too blew over, and later letters were in the old, affectionate vein.

A quite different element in Ellen's life was suggested by a letter to Barbara from Elizabeth shortly after her arrival in England, inquiring about H.B., an Englishman who had visited America and who "has a fancy for my youngest sister, which I did not encourage . . . he seemed so very odd—I see it still lingers—it is very important for me to know him intimately—I should like him much, as a brother,—and think how valuable to me to have one of my own family settled here! But your word 'tyrannical' frightens me, and I *must* know him better, before I would raise a finger to help." [7]

In Elizabeth's autobiography she refers to "Mr. Herman Bicknell, F.R.C.S. . . . a fellow student of the St. Bartholomew's days," who, after the death of his wife, was traveling in America, no longer practicing medicine, but devoting himself to reform and to translating Persian poetry. Elizabeth called him "a man of great though eccentric talent." It is to be wondered whether this distinguished man was forty-one-year-old Ellen's incipient and unencouraged suitor. If so, he ended up unmarried to Ellen, but Elizabeth's close friend for the rest of his life.

The Blackwell family, except for Sam and Nettie, were leaving their homes in and around Roseville, which had been as near to their mother's dream of a family phalanstry as they ever came. At the end of 1869 Henry and Lucy moved permanently to Boston. This change in their lives was the result of forces far larger than themselves. The woman suffrage movement had arrived at that point in its growth to which every reform movement seems to come. Reformers are single-minded people; the approaches to any reform, and in some measure the ends to be achieved, are many. Sooner or later in their efforts to reach a better world reformers come to a crossroads and choose different paths to their destination.

Perhaps the split in the suffrage ranks had begun as long ago as the developing temperaments of its leaders. It first expressed itself ideologically at the end of the Civil War, when many of the old-line abolitionists, formerly supporters of woman's rights, declared that women should withdraw their claims until the Negroes had gained their rights. "This is the Negro's hour!" was their cry. Susan Anthony and Elizabeth Stanton moved toward the other pole. Let the Negroes wage their own war; women must fight only for themselves. In the embattled area between stood Henry and Lucy. "We are lost if we turn from the middle principle and argue for one class," Lucy said.

The argument was complicated by Susan and Mrs. Stanton's alliance in Kansas with George Francis Train, a sort of burlesque crusader for any cause which momentarily caught his volatile fancy. He had made a fortune in speculative finance. He was a Fenian, a woman's righter, a violent anti-Negro. He was tall, handsome and, even when traveling through pioneer Kansas, wore black pants, a tight blue coat with brass buttons, patent-leather boots and lavender-colored gloves. His speeches for women's rights were more harangues than arguments. But Susan and her cohorts were inclined to be forgiving when Train supplied her with money to start a woman's rights paper. The *Revolution* began publication in January 1868.

At the end of 1868 Lucy and Henry went to Massachusetts to help launch the New England Woman Suffrage Association. It was attacked by the *Revolution* for being too "conservative." By 1869 the feud had split the Equal Rights Association wide open. Out of the ruins Susan and Mrs. Stanton secretly developed the National Woman Suffrage Association, leaving Lucy and Henry out. By fall Lucy, Henry and their sympathizers were able to call a national convention which met in Cleveland to form the American Woman Suffrage Association.[8] It was a necessary move if they were to continue to function in a movement to which they had given most of their lives; but it was misunderstood by many supporters of woman suffrage. One national organization already represented the small movement. Why must there be another? The *Revolution* enthusiastically encouraged this misunderstanding.

Yet there were basic differences between the methods of the two societies. The National believed that suffrage must be won by Constitutional amendment. The American worked to attain small gains on local and state levels, convinced that when women voted in enough states, national suffrage would follow. At the American convention were Nettie, Garrison, Higginson, Julia Ward Howe. Lucy was to have her own paper, the *Woman's Journal.* It began publication in January 1870, just a year after the *Revolution,* and endured until 1917, when victory was nearly won. Susan had to give up the *Revolution,* abandoned by Train and overwhelmed by debt, only a few months after the *Woman's Journal* appeared.

Hannah Blackwell's family had never been more scattered than in the summer of 1870, but on August 21, all those who could be assembled were at the Long Island house. On that day Mother Blackwell died. "She died," Henry wrote to Lucy less than an hour later, "with her head in George's hands—He has stood by her day and night almost without cessation and is fairly overwhelmed with grief at her loss. All the children were around her but Sam, to whom I telegraphed . . . but who could not come out in time." She was seventy-seven.

A touching memorial was published in the *Woman's Journal.* "Mrs. Blackwell's life fulfilled the most conservative conception of the sphere of woman. . . . As wife and widow, she was the presiding genius of a beautiful home. . . . She was a consistent and active member of the Presbyterian church . . . and never wavered in her adherence to the literal verities of the Calvinistic faith. Yet with conservative opinions and ardent religious feelings, she united genial sympathies and freedom of thought on moral and political questions. In the best sense of the word she was a constructive radical." There followed an account of her abolitionist activities.

The obituary ended with the heartening story of a woman's faith and determination. In 1868 it had been decided among suffragists that they would test woman's right to equal citizenship by attempting to vote in the presidential election. On election day in various parts of the country a few courageous women, willing to endure ridicule and certain defeat in order to publicize their cause, went to their local voting places.

"In company with her daughter-in-law, Lucy Stone, and leaning upon the arm of her son, the venerable lady . . . walked quietly to the place of voting in Roseville, and offered a straight Republican ticket. The Inspectors of Election received it respectfully, but declined to let it be deposited in the box. When a majority of the wives and mothers of America who cherish the same conservative religious opinions, and exhibit the same domestic fidelity as Mrs. Blackwell, awaken to a similar sense of political and social responsibility, the Woman Suffrage movement will be an accomplished fact."

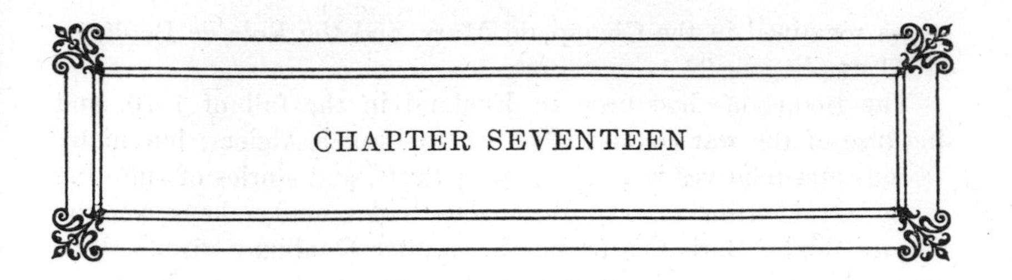

CHAPTER SEVENTEEN

In September 1870, after the French armies had been ignominiously routed by the Prussians, Paris was besieged. "You know, I suppose," Kitty wrote to Alice in late November, "that the poor people of Paris have no way of communicating with the outside world but by balloon and carrier pigeons. . . . Paris is said to have bread enough to last two months." In fact the city held out until the end of January, when starvation and cold had long passed the point of endurance.

Two months later the workers of Paris seized the municipal government and held it against the rest of France in a bloody civil war that lasted from April 1 to May 28. Revenge thereafter was fierce and frightful. Buildings were fired by Frenchmen to prevent their being taken by the French; and in the last week of May an estimated fifteen to thirty thousand Parisians were slaughtered by French soldiers. Order was restored and a republic established. Kitty, visiting Paris six months later, described it as less devastated than she had supposed, yet surely damaged enough, "the fronts of the houses everywhere peppered with rifle balls from street fighting . . . few houses destroyed, but most of the grand public buildings are burned, and the ruins stand everywhere derisively marked 'Liberté, Egalité, Fraternité.' " No tree or blade of grass remained in the Champ de Mars, and the Bois de Boulogne was "simply gone." [1]

The Bodichons had been in England in the fall of 1870, and because of the war could not return to French Algiers; but many friends and relatives were trapped in Paris, and stories of suffering there were harrowing. The Bodichons had rented a house on the Isle of Wight. Barbara's friend the painter Daubigny visited them there; his entire family were cut off in the battle zone. Kitty reported that the doctor seemed the same odd fellow as always, "walking about in his extraordinary flannel garment, never appearing at any meal except dinner. At dinner Dr. B. has three dogs seated by him and feeds them on crackers and cheese, and as the dogs *always* quarrel, it is very unpleasant." [2]

By now Barbara Bodichon had to her credit the first woman's college connected with Cambridge. She and her friend Emily Davies had organized it the year before. It was in Hitchin, some miles from the university town, but the students were taught by Cambridge lecturers and required to pass Cambridge examinations. There were five students the first year. Two years later, with twelve students, the little college moved to Girton, just outside Cambridge; but it was not until 1947 that the university gave the ladies equal status with men.

Anna, who had escaped from France and found refuge with Elizabeth and Kitty in England, was, at fifty-four, odder than before, though still "certainly very handsome." Age, as it often does, had solidified her eccentricities, and Howard's death had further magnified them. Elizabeth found her a difficult companion. She "catches up every word and intonation of voice, till sometimes I almost tumble down with weariness." [3] She was also having "mysterious communications" from the spirit world; and Elizabeth, who hoped to win Anna back "in great measure to ordinary earthy life," had tried to please her sister by sitting for two hours with her hands on a round table, though she herself did not share the current passion for spiritualism, and had warned Kitty not to have anything to do with planchettes.

Elizabeth had a full household. That spring, when Kitty was still in the United States, and reluctant to leave her only homeland, and the Blackwells, her only family, even to be with her beloved doctor, Elizabeth had written, as an inducement to her "young housekeeper" to come to England, that she had taken a "little baby patient, whose parents are to be away . . . a charming little fellow of eight months old, who will be under my care, probably for some years." [4]

There is a certain mystery about the baby's background, his connection with Dr. Elizabeth, and his sudden appearance in her home. He came of a wealthy family, and seems to have been related to Kenyon's young French wife, Marie, who was suspected by the Blackwells of having an affair with a Mr. Drousart during Kenyon's lifetime, and who certainly married him shortly after Kenyon died. One of the reasons Dr. Elizabeth had consented to take the boy was that she knew it would delight Kitty, who had a passion for babies and dogs; and it did. "Our small baby, Paul Harvey," Kitty reported, "is a charming little fellow." Yet she was somewhat disappointed, for "a baby who has two nurses, and the devoted attention of Miss Durant," his French foster mother, hardly needed the attention she had hoped to give him "when Dr. undertook the care of him." [5]

To Alice she wrote in the fall of 1871 that Paul chattered French baby-talk enchantingly. George Blackwell, who was spending a gay social winter in London and had rooms nearby, found Paul a rather sour-looking child; but Kitty suspected Uncle George of not liking children. A year later, little Paul was learning English rapidly. Miss Durant still insisted on his having two nurses besides herself, Dr. Elizabeth and the devoted Kitty. "Is it not absurd?" Kitty asked. But by sometime in 1873 they had lost Paul, who had been with them for nearly three years, and he in melodramatic fashion had lost not only them but the rest of his past as well. His parents had died. The adoring Miss Durant, who had "adopted him," had taken him on a trip to France, and there she too had died. Now he was being kept in France by "M. and Mme. Drousart (Cousin Marie that was)," and brought up in a fashion of which Kitty and Elizabeth disapproved. The Drousarts, who were paid a handsome sum for his maintenance, refused to let Elizabeth and Kitty see him. On their only visit, Paul had begged to go home with them, and was "almost broken hearted" when he could not. Elizabeth hoped, with the aid of some of the trustees of the estate, to get him back.[6] Kitty was desolate at his loss. She had taken him utterly to her heart and made him hers.

A few years before, Elizabeth had promised her adopted daughter that when they had enough money Kitty might adopt "first one and then another tiny urchin, so that you shall have a little family always with you." [7] At no time does it seem to have occurred to anyone that Kitty, who was twenty-three the September she joined Dr. Elizabeth in England, might be expected to marry and produce inalienable children of her own. In spite of a shyness magnified by physical defects—she had weak eyes and was slightly hard of hearing—she was an attractive, gay, energetic girl, a good pianist, an excellent cook, competent in French and Italian, an omnivorous reader and "a perfect encyclopedia on a wide variety of subjects." Why should she not have married? After Kitty's death, Alice remembered her having had an unrequited passion for George Blackwell. If so, it was secret indeed. She was Dr. Elizabeth's young housekeeper, who fitted herself "into all Elizabeth's angles like an eiderdown quilt," and though the family loved her and made her almost one of themselves, this career, in a family in which none of the women married, was accepted as an ultimate and presumably satisfactory role.

Between Alice and Kitty there was throughout their lives the warmest of attachments. When Alice was four and Kitty thirteen, they had become "engaged," and the letters they wrote regularly over the years often began "Dear Betrothed." Kitty's were sometimes signed Captain Kidd or Robert Kidd. The rest of the family seems to have accepted and even entered into this game. At least, Marian, departing for Europe in the spring of 1872, told Henry she would see them before she left, and "carry to Captn Kidd the last views of his dear betrothed."

Alice had many changes to report to Kitty. In the early months of 1870, after her family's move to Boston, she had been sent away to school. Her mother declared herself desolate at the separation, but she was also too busy moving, forming a suffrage association and publishing a magazine, to undertake the simultaneous care of a young and demanding daughter. Alice, following her mother's pattern, was beginning to suffer from severe headaches. After one bout, she had stopped taking lessons, and reported that, as soon

Hannah Lane Blackwell, mother of the family

Eliza Lane,
first governess,
then aunt

Anna

Marian

Emily

Elizabeth
*(sketch made in 1859
by Countess Clarice de Charnace)*

Samuel and his wife, Antoinette Brown

Lucy Stone and her husband, Henry

Alice

Kitty Barry with an honored friend

Agnes, Grace, Edith, Florence, Ethel, daughters of
Samuel and Antoinette

Emily (seated), Emma, George, Alice, Henry

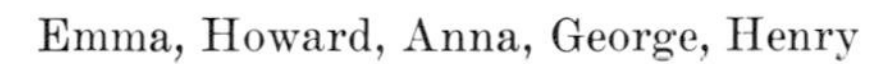

Emma, Howard, Anna, George, Henry

Samuel

Antoinette

Lucy Stone

Emily

Elizabeth

Alice and Antoinette riding in state in a suffrage parade

as the lessons were resumed, the headaches returned; but "when Mama had driven them away with magnetism they did not come back."

In a letter ending, "Tomorrow I shall be 45 years old. —I look and feel 60," Henry told Elizabeth Alice was doing so well at school in Newburyport that they would keep her there as long as they could; but money was short. Even so, he might never go back into business, for "Lucy's occupation is so absorbing to her that . . . the practical effect of doing so would be to separate us almost entirely or else to involve her withdrawing from active work . . . for which she has a genius." [8]

When Alice returned from boarding school a few months later, the family still had no home, but lived in a tiny makeshift apartment over the offices of the *Woman's Journal* until December 1870, when they bought a great white house in Dorchester, a town recently annexed to Boston, but still open country. It had a large garden and an orchard and from the upper stories a clear view of the city on one side and, on the other, boats on the blue sea. Alice loved the sound of the wind roaring about it.

Less than a year later, while Henry and Lucy were away at a series of conventions and Alice was at home with the servants, a fire broke out which destroyed most of the house. Much was lost, Henry told Elizabeth, by the imbecility of the servants and the inability of Alice, who threw silverware and valuables out of the window and in the confusion forgot to gather them up, but who "worked like a (child) hero," and rescued much of the furniture. Their loss was more than three thousand dollars above the insurance. "We are increasingly impecunious and will have to curtail." [9] Irretrievable at any price were the lost letters and papers, public and private, of thirty years.

Family letters sent to and fro across the Atlantic were, unless specifically marked private, dispatched from one family group to another until everyone had read them. News from the United States to Europe indicated that it was not only Elizabeth who had suddenly acquired a child. In the letter in which Henry wrote that Alice was still away at school, he said also that their little orphan girl, Annie, had died. They had hoped for an "eventual affinity between her and Alice." Annie had in fact died two months before, and

Henry had written then to tell Alice about it. "Annie loved you and loved us all. . . . If she had lived, you would have learned to love her dearly as you grew older, because you would have found out her good qualities." Apparently Alice's feeling for Annie had not begun to approach that "eventual affinity," a fact scarcely to be wondered at, particularly as it must have seemed to Alice at school that Annie had supplanted her at home. True, Annie may have been installed partly to help Lucy, as happened later with another orphan girl, but Lucy and Henry obviously looked on her as a second daughter, for in reporting her death to Elizabeth, Henry went so far as to say, "so now we have only Alice."

In February 1871 Alice told Kitty that both Emily and Ellen had adopted baby girls. They had delayed long before undertaking the lifetime responsibility of raising families. Emily was forty-four that year and Ellen forty-two; but Emily had had no leisure, nor had they had the financial security to undertake such obligations. Not only was the hospital now in a sounder position, but the real-estate exchanges their brothers had made for themselves and their sisters over the years now gave them at least some small economic stability.

"Miss Ellen" told Kitty that her child, a "poor tiny little dark baby . . . only weighed 5¼ lbs, but is a child of educated parents." The baby was about to be sent to a foundling asylum when Ellen decided to rescue it. If it turned out to be a nice child—how would she discover this and when?—she planned to give it her mother's name, Hannah Lane.

In the end though, it was Emily who preempted the name Hannah for her fair-haired, blue-eyed baby; and the child having been named Hannah, though she was called Nannie, the family began to find that she looked like, and even was like, their mother. This went so far that sometime later Alice told Kitty that "Aunt Marian suspects that Grandma's spirit has transmigrated into it. Did you ever hear of such an absurd idea?" [10]

Ellen's baby had become Cornelia Howard and was called Neenie. When Lucy went to see the new babies and Ellen asked her if she didn't think Neenie pretty, forthright Lucy found it necessary to say no. In fact she thought the little girl very dark and ugly.

Ellen had bought a house in Lawrence "on extraordinary terms," and instantly tried to rent it in order to meet even those terms. When she failed to do so, Emily paid her a hundred and fifty dollars to use it for the summer, and they turned it into a nursery with Ellen in charge, and servants and a wet nurse in attendance. Nettie, Sam, Henry came by turns to spend a few days. Marian had a house nearby, but spent most of her time with Frances Alofsen and her father, who were about to return to Europe. To George, already in Europe, and therefore probably to the other European members of the family as well, Ellen wrote that Marian, at fifty-three, was "decidedly older and feebler"; she had sold her Roseville house at a good profit and talked of going to Europe to live, but she ought not to do this unless Elizabeth could offer her a home. She ought not to live alone wherever she was.[11]

In December 1871 Emily wrote to Lucy, "You will be glad to know that I shall probably take Ellen's little Cornelia on trial and if she and Nanny get on well, take her off Ellen's hands. Ellen begins to feel the burden more than she can carry, and to feel that if it wd work it wd be the best arrangement."[12] Yet only six months later Ellen had taken another baby girl, "and meant to make the Rockaway place a great baby house."[13] Emily thought a third child one too many, as well she might when she had already had to take the second off Ellen's hands. At Christmas 1872 Ellen had cheap tintype pictures of the children made to send to the family in Europe. She told them she hoped to bring all the children to Europe to be educated.

Alice who had "rather sympathize[d] with Cornelia, because everyone but Aunt Ellen seems to like the other best," finally saw her late in 1872, when the entire American family except Henry and Lucy spent Christmas with the Samuel Blackwells in Somerville, New Jersey. Uncle George had told her in somewhat grim jest that little Cornelia "formed the connecting link between man and monkey, all of which I believed; and was prepared for something monstrous. Therefore I was agreeably surprised to see a merry-looking little brown baby, with very fine black eyes, and all the forehead she needed. . . . I think she is prettier than Nannie."[14]

Alice was ready enough to sympathize with the dark, unpopular, little girl. She had told Kitty six months before about her own "dismal frame of mind produced partly by having made no friends among the girls at school, who flirt like sixty, nearly all of them, and are not my sort at all; wherefore I am lonesome, and solace my mind with nervousness,"[15] and with strange forebodings of mysterious diseases.

Marian had left for Europe, after attempting to settle near Sam and Nettie in New Jersey, and finding them too absorbed in their own lives, and Somerville too far from New York and too lonely. From France in the summer of 1872, she sent Alice news of her "Captn Kidd," who was visiting Marian and Anna. Kitty seemed unchanged, though the top of her head which had begun to grey before she left them was a little greyer. "She is the same warmhearted old Kitty as ever." There followed a description of Kitty, and in a sense of Alice, which explains much about these young women, who now formed an intermediate generation between their aunts and uncles and the newly acquired babies. "She dresses neatly in a grey alpaca suit, and a grey hat trimmed with a tuft of black ribbon and a black veil—which is quite becoming. She wears her dress *rather* short as she cannot see very well to keep it out of the mud." Otherwise she follows the fashion and "wears a double skirt looped up like other people and crinoline enough not to look 'slinky.'" Marian found this wise, since in New York, when Kitty did not trouble to look like other people, she was stared at, "and the boys would sometimes hoot after her." Then a revealing admonition: "'Go thou, and do likewise.'"[16]

Marian's young friend Frances Alofsen, now almost like an adopted daughter, for her own mother had died, had returned to Europe with her father in August 1871, and in November, undeterred by the example of her adopted family, had been married. Kitty went to Paris to attend the wedding and a dinner at "Vefours" for thirty-five people. The next October Frances gave birth to a small boy with a long string of given names and Gerken as a surname. The baby, called Leon, was sickly, and Frances's life was not easy. From the time they married, Mr. Gerken did not work, but presumably lived as best he might on his wife's money. Frances's father died five years after her marriage, and Frances, still in her early twenties, turned to the Blackwells, and especially to Marian, as her only family.

CHAPTER EIGHTEEN

When Elizabeth returned to England in 1869, she was not sure that the move was permanent, but her life there and the group she quickly entered drew her from the start. She had been desperately seasick on the voyage over, and still felt so ill when she landed that her friends urged her to go to the Lake Country, where, like any lover of English poetry, she wandered in the shadow of Wordsworth, Southey, Coleridge. After that, with Herman Bicknell, she attended the Congress of the National Association for the Promotion of Social Science. It happened that the meetings of this radical organization, which represented the English humanist movement, were held that year in Bristol.

In Bristol, Elizabeth pulled together the strands that led back into her past and forward to the future. She visited Corn Street, where Uncle Browne's goldsmith shop had been. Across from it, in front of the Merchant's Exchange, she saw again that row of flat-topped bronze trading-posts, known as Nails, from which, according to Bristol tradition, came the expression "cash on the nail." More intimately, she returned to the house on Nelson Street where she had lived as a girl, opposite it the familiar medieval arch over Broad Street, and the ancient wall in which an oriel window was set above a beautiful lion's head basin. The basin had been repaired since her childhood, and bore, as it still does, an inscription stating that the conduit granted to the Vestry of St. John in the fourteenth century was redone in 1866. The streets, the houses were filled with memories of her beloved father and of her lost girlhood.

She paid a visit to her father's two remaining sisters, Ann and Lucy. Ann, grown very old, tiny and wrinkled, still wore a foot-and-a-half-high cap. Lucy, the only sister who had married, proudly produced her husband, a disagreeable old man whom Elizabeth never learned to like.

So much for the past. At the congress two important influences for the future entered her life. She was introduced to an exceedingly tall, thin, swarthy-skinned gentleman, who fixed her with his bright gaze and said with the excited tenseness she later learned was characteristic, "You are one of my heroes." He was Charles Kingsley; and Elizabeth was filled with astonishment that this famous clergyman-novelist had known of her existence. She grew to be a close friend of Kingsley and his wife in the five years until he died, and visited them at Eversley Parsonage, and later at the Deanery in Chester. Kingsley, the Christian Socialist, became her mentor and turned her attention to social problems she had never seriously considered.

Her interest in association was reawakened too by the hope that Kingsley and religious reformers like him could introduce into the new Utopia a "religious element" which the old had certainly lacked, and offer a promise "which no attempts based on a limited view of material well-being [could] afford." In the summer of 1872 her renewed interest led her to make a strenuous trip by diligence across France to the Familistère at Guise on the Belgian border. This amazing community had been designed and built by a philanthropic manufacturer for his workers and their families. Monsieur Godin, himself formerly a workman, had created a model factory and self-sufficient cooperative town where his employees lived in a fashion far beyond their individual earning capacities. But as so often with Elizabeth, her dream dwindled in the face of reality, and after several days in the energetic and prosperous community, she found life there too intense and overpowering, and left, never to return.

The second revelation of the Congress came when she was asked to attend a meeting on what was politely called "social" disease. Women, although freely admitted to membership in the association, were excluded from this session, to which as a doctor Elizabeth could be admitted. The meeting had to do with an effort to force the repeal of the Contagious Diseases Act, an act which, in an attempt to control the spread of venereal disease, required prostitutes to be licensed and to submit to periodic physical examinations. The laws of England placed criminal responsibility on the offending woman, while exonerating her male customer. Elizabeth, whose education had been radical but restricted, was horrified to learn of the legalized degradation of women and the double standard of morality. She felt that legislation for vice, which did not tend to repress it, was immoral and served only to educate the community in evil.[1] In her enthusiasm she even argued that the extent and danger of venereal disease were much exaggerated by proponents of the law. The new knowledge, she said, "moulded the whole of my future life. . . . My eyes were now suddenly opened, never to be closed again, to that direful purchase of women which is really the greatest obstacle to the progress of the race." [2] An extreme statement, but one that embodied her belief.

In view of this dedication, it was an unkind accident that, when she opened her first medical office in London, she found that her respectable sign was being used to cover the less respectable activities of the rest of the household. She broke her lease and moved her office to 6 Burwood Place, where she lived and worked after Barbara Bodichon went back to Algiers.

Early in 1870, she delivered an address on "How to Keep a Household in Health," and included in this subject, as she had since the days of her first little dispensary in New York, advice on teaching sexual principles to the young of both sexes. A letter containing an inaccurate and unfortunate account of her speech appeared in the *Pall Mall Gazette* on March 21. Its author, who signed herself "A Brooding Hen," apologized for being impelled by "maternal anxiety" to defy modesty and discuss so delicate a subject. Yet someone must reply to "The Shrieking Sisterhood" who shamelessly made such matters public. She singled out Dr. Blackwell, who had recommended that the child-bearing woman limit her family to the number which could safely be cared for in her household, advice which encouraged infanticide or its equivalent. As a result of this unsavory publicity, Elizabeth began to receive "anonymous letters, and letters from persons in all classes of society, requesting medical advice on the most important and delicate subjects—subjects . . . only suitable for the confidential counsel of the physician's consulting-room." These she sensibly refused to answer.

Elizabeth's prescription for moral hygiene, enlightened though it was for a time when the subject was prudishly avoided, was primitive enough. Children must be taught self-restraint. "Self-abuse" was evil, demoralizing, enervating; indulgence in sexual relations without love corrupting. Boys should be encouraged to marry young—twenty-five was her optimum age—and should be as pure until then as the girls they married. She spoke of herself as a "Christian physiologist," and of this betterment of the race through morality as the Christian ideal.

In the United States Elizabeth had dedicated herself and the Infirmary to a battle for hygiene and prevention of disease. Now in England she continued her fight. A meeting in her drawing room at Burwood Place was the beginning of the National Health Society, with its motto, "Prevention Is Better than Cure," and its policy of spreading knowledge of the little-known rules of sanitation as a means of preserving health.

Elizabeth's two chief protégées in England were Sophia Jex-Blake and Elizabeth Garrett. Sophia, an English girl who from early childhood had "undutifully" rebelled against her proper Victorian family, had in a final flare-up of revolt gone to America to seek a career. In Boston she met Marie Zakrzewska and worked for a while as secretary at the New England Hospital for Women. This turned her passionate energies toward medicine. She went to New York and enrolled as a student in the first class of the new medical college of the Infirmary, but after only a short period of study was called back to England by her father's fatal illness. Now this hot-headed girl with a group of other ambitious women was fighting tradition, and more specifically the powers of Edinburgh University, in an effort to enter the medical school. The campaign, begun in 1869, continued for years, and included in its bizarre history a libel suit and an act of Parliament, as well as a riot in which male students flung insults and mud at the female aspirants, presumably in revenge for their having achieved the highest academic grades. Finally, in 1877, Sophia received a medical degree, not at Edinburgh but at Bern; and after passing the examinations of Dublin's Kings and Queens College of Physicians, the first British medical school to admit women to practice, was at last enrolled in the British Register, the fifth woman to attain this distinction.

Meanwhile Elizabeth Garrett, Dr. Elizabeth's disciple, had more quietly gone about obtaining a medical degree. By nature gentler and more dignified than Sophia, she was happier too in having her father's support from the first, as well as experience in Barbara Leigh Smith's group of woman's rights fighters to teach her how best to proceed. Finding it impossible to enter a British medical school, Miss Garrett had managed to take sufficient courses at various colleges and hospitals to make her eligible for the medical license given by Apothecaries Hall, which, try though it did, could not escape, because its charter required it to license anyone fulfilling its requirements and able to pass its examinations. The license in turn permitted her enrollment in 1866 in the medical register, the first woman since Elizabeth Blackwell to be entered there. But it was not until 1870 that she acquired a full medical degree at L'École de Médecine in Paris. A few months later she also acquired an attractive and sympathetic husband in James Skelton Anderson, a wealthy shipowner, and in the course of time and marriage became the mother of three children. Elizabeth Garrett, more of a scientist and less a Christian moralist than Elizabeth Blackwell, disagreed with her about the Contagious Diseases Acts. Like the British Medical Association, she believed compulsory examination and hospital care of prostitutes might stem the spread of venereal disease.

To Lucy Stone in Boston, one bit of news about her sister-in-law Elizabeth, in November 1870, must have seemed a pleasant irony. Elizabeth, the private rebel, always somewhat scornful of the noisy struggle for woman suffrage, had become the first woman of the family to vote. For in England in 1869, municipal franchise was granted to taxpaying women, that is, to unmarried women of a certain economic class. The next year school boards were instituted, and Dr. Elizabeth Garrett was asked by the Working Men's Association to be a candidate for the London School Board. Elizabeth Blackwell as a ratepayer was entitled to vote for her, and did; and Dr. Garrett was elected by four times the vote of the next highest candidate. Six months later the *Woman's Journal* was wondering whether, as a married woman, Dr. Garrett Anderson, as she was now called, would be required to relinquish her seat.[3]

Henry, an advocate of freedom on every level, was in those years greatly concerned with the fate of Santo Domingo, which in order to avoid being swallowed up by its neighbor Haiti had asked to be annexed by the United States. Henry went to the island in 1871 as correspondent for *Hearth and Home,* attached to a presidential committee investigating conditions in Santo Domingo. Henry was passionately in favor of annexation, and tried to influence his friend Charles Sumner to support it, but Sumner did not agree. The fight for annexation failed; but the following spring Henry returned to the island with Julia Ward Howe and her husband, who had been a member of the president's commission. Mrs. Howe described the trip in a series of articles in the *Woman's Journal.* Henry and Dr. Howe were involved in a project to colonize the island with settlers from New England, their aim being to correct the Dominicans' "present immorality" by providing a healthy, and apparently irresistible, example of home life in the United States.

Not that Henry was entirely satisfied with life in the United States. In 1871, largely because of his perseverance, the Massachusetts Republican Convention made a bow to the ladies by endorsing woman suffrage in principle. In 1872, Henry attended the national convention in an effort to have the principle established there too, but the convention went no further than to express mindfulness of "its obligations to the loyal women of America," and belief that "the honest demands of any class of citizens for additional rights should be treated with respectful consideration." Even this almost imperceptible nod was greeted with acclaim by the woman's rights leaders, accustomed as they were to boos and laughter; and when the Democratic Party refused them even such formal recognition, they put their small strength solidly behind President Grant for a second term.

From a radical viewpoint the election of 1872 was an anomaly.

The reformer Horace Greeley had been nominated by a liberal Republican group that split from the party when the majority backed the incompetent Grant and his corrupt administration. The conservative and traditionally proslavery Democratic Party, in a realistic effort to defeat Grant, had joined with these dissidents to make Greeley its candidate. But Greeley, formerly a strong advocate of woman's rights, was now, for reasons probably stemming from his years of marital difficulties with his prosuffrage wife, almost hysterically opposed; so the suffrage forces fought bitterly against him. The Blackwells were united in their support of Grant. Only Sam and Antoinette, Greeley's old friend, were not carried into the opposition which defeated Greeley and broke his heart and health, so that he died less than a month after the election. Alice wrote to Kitty that she had been horrified to learn that Uncle Sam had voted for the renegade Greeley, and concluded that Aunt Nettie had talked him into it.

Aunt Nettie had been busy. Having produced a large number of children, she was now bringing them up in a fashion which appalled the other Blackwells. Young Alice, who may be assumed to reflect the adult view, found them insufferable nuisances, because they had learned they could get things by howling.[4] But Nettie, in spite of howling children, found time to write long volumes of Christian philosophy. In 1871 she published a book of quite another kind, a novel called *The Island Neighbors*. The setting was the Blackwells' beloved summer home, Martha's Vineyard. "The action of this book," states the preface, "drowsy with the languor of summer, quickened a little now and then by the sea-breezes, moves on with the easy footsteps of unhurried rural life; and there is no more thought of a moral in it than there is in the plays of children."

Despite this disclaimer, virtue and love triumph; but this was the literary style of the period, as were the book's hair-breadth escapes and heroic rescues. The tone is not moralistic. It is indeed so simple, charming and honest in its perception of human foibles and its description of island life that Antoinette is revealed as a woman of greater warmth and humanity than is common among rebels, even though the betterment of humanity is presumably their main concern. The heroine herself is unusual enough in a romantic tale, for though she is a pretty, gay, energetic Irish girl, she has a pockmarked face. Is it possible that Nettie was taking pretty, gay, Irish Kitty as her model, with her bad eyes and defective ears?

The reason for the permissiveness Nettie displayed toward her children, to the distress of the more rigid Blackwells, is suggested in a comment in the novel about elders interfering in the love affairs of the young, "till our badgered young folks, like fishes gasping out of water . . . jump from the frying pan into the fire below, while we fold our hands with the mocking consolation that we have done all we could to prevent it. The egotism of experience is very often intolerable."

The concerns of the Blackwells are reflected in the author's description of the island's Indian colony, in the sympathy she expressed for Cuba, then attempting to free itself from Spanish domination, in the decision of the heroine to give up her job as a servant, take the money she has saved and enter an independent profession. She has chosen typesetting. "Respectable American women were beginning to learn type-setting, and she knew herself to be the equal of these." It was a small bow to feminism in a book otherwise far from feminist.

The love of the Blackwells for their new island home finds expression too. "Even in the broad glare of sunshine the sky outline of those treeless, brownish-green hills was always beautiful; while . . . between the most distant, you almost always caught the gleaming of blue water—in one direction generally studded thickly with sails; and in others, quiet bays or inland ponds sleeping peacefully."

In far-off France, Marian was managing in 1872 to re-create Martha's Vineyard for herself. She and Anna were living at Wimereux in the Pas de Calais, where "down below the sand bank on which the house stands, is a little river running to the sea," like the stream, she remembers, where Alice and Floy spent so many happy hours when they were all at the Vineyard together.

CHAPTER NINETEEN

Though it was Elizabeth their father had nicknamed Little Shy, Emily was at least as retiring and self-conscious. Yet, because she was not small and blonde, she never received the sympathy so freely bestowed on her sister. Emily's stature belied her inner uncertainty, and as time went by, she grew ever more commanding in appearance and decisive in manner. To a student who knew her in her later years, Dr. Emily seemed to belong "to the tradition of the great pioneers. She inspired us all with the vital feeling that we were still on trial and that, for women who meant to be physicians, no educational standards could be too high." Not only her convictions were inspiring. She was "tall, broad-shouldered and commanding in appearance but . . . it was her face and her head that arrested your attention. I dislike to use the word 'noble' in a physical description but it is the only adequate way to portray her face. . . . When she entered a room full of students, there suddenly seemed to be only one person in that room and that person was Dr. Blackwell. . . . Her voice was low and calm and of an uncanny quality." [1]

Yet beneath these outward manifestations, there incongruously lingered the girl who had confided to her diary her "terrible self-doubt," her failures, the lack of understanding even in her own family. Unlike Elizabeth, she preferred not to appear before audiences or enter into literary controversy. When there were attempts in the United States to pass legislation on the European model for restricting prostitution, she had to be persistently urged by Elizabeth before she undertook the battle her sister had waged for years in England. Yet when she could be induced to speak or write, she did so with vigor, clarity and style.

Perhaps it was because she was doomed to be ever one step behind Elizabeth that she failed to capture either her family's imagination or the world's as her elder sister did. True, Elizabeth was the pioneer, but Emily's struggle to become a doctor was nearly as great, her accomplishment in sustaining and enlarging the Infirmary and in building the medical college as solid as anything Elizabeth accomplished. Yet it was Elizabeth, the activist, the speaker and writer for causes, to whom both contemporaries and posterity handed the laurels. Emily, her name linked with her sister's, was always a secondary figure. She might have fared better if she had had some other name than Blackwell, already preempted in medical history. As a result, like everyone who feels underestimated or misjudged, Emily became prickly.

In 1866 when, after Howard's death, Elizabeth had gone to Paris to be with Anna, she had met there again a young woman she had known and liked in the States. The girl was Dr. Mary Putnam of the publishing family, herself a competent writer. Little Mary, whose five-foot stature held more energy than is usually contained in far larger frames, had taken a degree in pharmacy, a degree in medicine at the Female Medical College in Philadelphia, had interned in Boston under Marie Zakrzewska (now regularly and more pronounceably known as Dr. Zak), and then, aware of the deficiencies of this education, had gone to Paris determined to continue her training. It was not until 1868 that Mary attained her ambition, and became the first woman to enter the École de Médecine as a fully accredited student. She had in the interim supported herself by writing articles for American magazines about life in Paris. She continued to do so, even remaining there through the siege of 1870, when most of those able to leave had fled. In 1871 she returned to New York to practice medicine and to fulfill a promise made to Elizabeth in Paris five years before to teach at the New York Infirmary's Medical College.

Like most promises, this was easier to make than to carry out. Within a week after she had begun to lecture on materia medica and therapeutics, her students had rebelled because her teaching made demands beyond their capacities. She in turn had rushed to Emily not merely to complain, but to recommend the total reorganization of the school's curriculum. Her plans were logical and progressive. She wished to abandon the custom prevalent in American medical schools of requiring a two-year course, and then repeating in the second year the same courses the students had taken in the first. Dr. Putnam asked permission to teach materia medica the first year and therapeutics the second.

Emily, who was accustomed to expressing her opinions freely, and whose letters to her family overflowed with unsolicited advice, like so many people who liberally offer suggestions, did not suffer criticism gladly. The Infirmary college had higher standards than almost any medical school in the United States. To have a teacher of a week's standing reorganize the curriculum was more than Emily could bear.

In the ensuing battle Mary Putnam wrote to Elizabeth that she must be released from her promise. She could not teach under such circumstances. In due time, Elizabeth's answer came back across the Atlantic. Elizabeth begged her not to leave, but "to live down this trouble and 'malignant criticism.' I shall care comparatively little for your temporary trials, and the anxiety it gives Dr. Emily can be borne," said Elizabeth generously from three thousand miles away, "if only you will be true to yourself and ultimately succeed; but to do this you must be infinitely patient. . . . Do, my dear Mary, be very prudent and patient! You are young enough to wait for brilliant success, *but you must not fail now!*"

With Elizabeth's distant help, Mary and Emily composed their differences so successfully that at graduation exercises in 1872 Mary gave an address on the imperfections of the present system of medical education. She continued to teach after her marriage a year later to Dr. Abraham Jacobi, himself a distinguished rebel, the first physician in the United States to consider children's diseases as a separate field of medicine. She went on teaching at the Infirmary for nearly twenty years, while the improvements she had sought became part of its educational pattern.

The differences between Emily and her younger sister were deeper and more difficult of resolution. Ellen's gifts, both artistic and literary, failed to support her and the children she felt so avid a necessity to take and care for, so it was perhaps natural that, when Marian had escaped to Europe, Ellen should fall into Marian's domestic role. Ellen did, it is true, teach painting when she was in New York, but she also lived with Emily, kept house for her, and took almost total charge of Nannie and Neenie and of the little blonde baby, Susie, whom she had taken after Emily had had to assume Neenie's support. Whatever the financial arrangements, Neenie continued to be far more Ellen's child than Emily's.

The job of housekeeping was no simple one, involving, as it did, buying the supplies and managing the housekeeping of both Infirmary and College. By January 1873, just before her forty-fifth birthday, Ellen was writing to Kitty that in the spring she must "struggle into something else; with a feeling that I must do it or die." For five of the best years of my life, she continued, "I have had my board and in all $400 which I have spent on getting the babies nursed."[2] But when Emily moved that year into a house she had bought on Twentieth Street, Ellen and the children moved with her, and Ellen continued housekeeping.

A year later Kitty, on a visit to the United States, reported that little Susie was not welcome in the house. Not even Ellen really wanted her, and Emily and George, who was living there to help Emily financially, considered her such an intruder that the child was kept mostly in the kitchen. Even so small a girl, Kitty felt, must sense that she was not wanted.[3] From Europe Elizabeth deplored the fact that Emily did not have "finer childish natures to educate," though what she could know of the delicacy of childish natures three thousand miles away it is hard to imagine.

Whatever difficulties existed within the family, their pull toward each other was always strong. Elizabeth said that when George spent some months in Europe in 1872 he was lonesome for his American brothers and sisters. And in spite of a clear knowledge of the difficulties among them, difficulties from which she herself had fled, Elizabeth told Henry that she hoped "something or other" might draw them nearer together, "for brothers and sisters who have grown up as we have grown up, must, to the end of life continue that feeling of kinship and comradeship which seems naturally to need near neighborhood."[4] She even toyed with an idea suggested by Lucy and Henry of building her a house near theirs in Dorchester, but fearful of her tendency to desperate seasickness, she did not in fact even cross the ocean for a visit.

She had been ill enough without that. Late in 1872 she had been so sick with "biliary colic" that, when she was able to return to work, she had to cut down her practice. The following year she gave up her quarters at Burwood Place and, in order to avoid the dank English winter, went with Barbara Bodichon, Kitty and Marian to the continent. Unable to work at her profession, she turned in these travels to an avocation of her youth, and then and later sketched the scenes of her extensive European trips. Her pen and pencil drawings have an accomplished and delicate charm, and supply a far more vivid account of her journeyings than the rather prosaic and jotty notebooks she also kept.

That winter of 1873–1874, Elizabeth, Kitty and Marian lived in Rome on the Via Quattro Fontane opposite the Barberini Palace. This location added considerable zest to their stay. The princess had rented some of the lesser rooms in the palace; and the Blackwell party were fascinated, as well they might have been, by the goings on across the way, where two diverse dramas were being enacted. The prince was sheltering priests and friars escaping persecution at the hands of the new Italian state whose unification they had for many years assisted the Pope in fighting. Rome had in fact been annexed to the liberal Italian monarchy only two and a half years before, and only after the Pope's protector, Napoleon III, had had to withdraw his troops for use in the Franco-Prussian War.

Equally interesting was the presence in the palace of Mr. and Mrs. Theodore Tilton, fleeing from the effects of her much publicized, much denied affair with Henry Ward Beecher, son of the Blackwells' old neighbor and friend Lyman Beecher, and now himself minister of a Brooklyn church. The Tiltons' conjugal trip took place in a lull in the Tilton-Beecher feud, which had begun in 1870 with Elizabeth Tilton's confession to her husband of an affair with their minister and friend, and had continued through Beecher's public denial and the subsequent lurid publicity. Unfortunately this publicity directly involved the suffrage movement, since it was the result of the naïve confidences of Mrs. Tilton's confidante, Elizabeth Cady Stanton, to an unsavory and unscrupulous newspaperwoman.

The lull at the Barberini Palace was followed a year later by a sensational trial in which Tilton sued Beecher for alienation of affection, a trial which, resulting in a hung jury, ruined Tilton and his wife without vindicating Beecher. It did, however, make the minister one of the most spectacular characters in the United States, and one of the country's most sought-after and successful lecturers. Lucy and Henry's wing of the suffrage movement, with no more apparent basis than that women were always more sinned against than sinning, stood solidly upon the assumption that Tilton was a scoundrel and his wife an innocent victim. In the *Woman's Journal* both Julia Ward Howe and Lucy came to Elizabeth Tilton's defense.

An amusing social note entered the letter in which Elizabeth described their neighbors. She intended to go to a fair that night, and if neither Kitty nor Marian could go, "I must hire my escort, a very respectable man, who escorts ladies during the season for a franc an evening!" [5]

In April Elizabeth returned to England to resume her practice. She needed the money, particularly because she had promised to let Kitty leave that spring for a six months' visit to the United States. Kitty, far more than Elizabeth, missed the country she always considered her own and the family who were perhaps dearer to her than if they had been hers. She had never reconciled herself to her separation from the American cousins,[6] and in spite of her reluctance to part with her doctor, had decided to make the trip. Elizabeth, left in England, was so lonely that she expressed herself far more warmly than was her custom. She kept thinking, she told Kitty, of her "little voyager," of "the poor little tearful face I was obliged to leave amongst strangers—a leave taking which gave me a sharp pang, and brought up my own tears." [7]

Elizabeth moved into lodgings in Dorset Square, and attempted to reestablish her practice, but frequent returns of her illness over the next years made this increasingly difficult. She did, however, undertake to become Professor of Gynaecology at the new London School of Medicine for Women which her friend Sophia Jex-Blake with the reluctant help of Elizabeth Garrett Anderson had just organized. Years later she publicly said of the beginning of the medical school that it was her "privilege and pleasure in some small degree to encourage these brave workers in their pioneer enterprise in England,"[8] but before time had smoothed away the rough edges of experience, she expressed less pleasure. In September 1874 she wrote to Sam that the movement to open a medical school was begun "rather prematurely by Miss Jex Blake . . . a dangerous woman from her power and her want of tact . . . and I now seem compelled to step in and try how far my experience and judgement can supply the control."[9]

To Barbara Bodichon she confided that she was trying to reorganize the school plans to safeguard against the "headlong energies of its most active member." She was full of doubts about Miss Jex-Blake, who wanted to live at the college and handle its funds. Her doubts were shared by the trustees. In 1877 while Sophia was in Dublin being permitted at last to take her qualifying examinations as a fully accredited physician, an honorary secretary for the college was to be appointed. Sophia was undeniably entitled to the position, but while she was gone, the board appointed Elizabeth Garrett Anderson. The new appointee, though she shared the board's fears about Sophia's unrestrained and belligerent nature, was horrified at so displacing her, and suggested a compromise candidate, who was accepted; but the damage had been done. Sophia decided to leave London and practice in Edinburgh, where her long battle to enter the profession had been staged. She remained a trustee of the London School until 1883, when Dr. Garrett Anderson was made dean, ending Sophia's hopes for that office. Then she resigned as trustee and established a woman's medical school in Edinburgh.

In 1875 Sam and Nettie decided, in spite of limited finances, to send their eldest daughter, Florence, to spend a year in Europe with her aunt Elizabeth. They had hoped that George would help pay for the trip, but there seemed no sign of his doing so. Whether

her parents were motivated by more than a desire to give their girl the benefits of a European trip is not clear; but of the opinion of the rest of the family there is abundant evidence. Florence was not robust. Elizabeth would doctor her. Florence was listless and undirected; she seemed chiefly interested in getting married—she was, after all, eighteen—and had several times come close to choosing young men the family thought unworthy. Elizabeth might encourage her to more lofty endeavors.

Elizabeth was not sanguine, though she found Floy docile and capable of being "both reasonable and affectionate as soon as her soul begins to awake from the lethargy of physical debility." [10] After two months on the Isle of Wight with Elizabeth and Kitty, Floy was more robust, plumper, and taking exercise "voluntarily." Elizabeth told Emily that if she could keep Floy with her for five years instead of one, the girl might benefit mentally as well as physically. She admitted that it was hard on Florence to take her suddenly from her companions and their "cabals about sweethearts . . . and force her into a better social influence." If any of Sam's children, she wrote, "could come over to me before the instinct of sex has got an upper hand in them—I could do very much more in the way of radical benefit." [11]

A few months later, though Elizabeth still complained that Floy's only interest was in meeting young men, she told Floy's father that the girl was physically stronger and "beginning to be a little ashamed of her indolence, and other mischievous habits into which she has dropped." [12] Yet she was afraid that the year's visit would not make enough change to warrant Sam and Nettie's great financial sacrifice. And Kitty commented to Alice that she hated Floy's returning to her parents. "How I hate the mischief Somerville has done and is doing our children." [13] Yet, aside from Florence's physical state, the only aberration attributed to her was her total interest in young men, a preoccupation which might have seemed less odd in a more marrying family.

That year there were other visitors from the United States. Just before his forty-third birthday George Blackwell had followed the pattern of his brothers and taken a wife. He had indeed followed it so closely that he had chosen his sister-in-law Lucy's niece, daughter of her sister Sarah. Pretty Emma Lawrence was twenty-four.

She must have made a strange wife for the middle-aged bachelor whose niece, Alice, in the privacy of letters to Kitty described as having a sarcastic, sneering manner. And "if a man will turn the disagreeable side of his character outward . . . and poke it at you on all occasions, you can't help getting rather to dislike him," then added naïvely, "so far as is compatible with relationship." [14]

Most of the American members of the clan attended the wedding; and there were the usual discussions about what to wear which such an occasion seems to engender among rebels as well as more conventional ladies. But Nettie wrote to Lucy that she had neither the time nor, more importantly, the money to go to the wedding. Things were not going well with them, and they had dug deep in their pockets to give Floy the opportunity of a year in Europe. Nettie would, however, go to speak at the annual convention of the American Woman Suffrage Association in nearby New York.

She seems to have taken along her third daughter, Grace, because Grace included in her letters to Kitty, which abounded in enthusiasm for wasps' nests and birds and gardening, a less impassioned appraisal of suffrage meetings. "I went to all the womans suffrage convention meetings. There were four and I liked to go pretty well." [15]

For their wedding trip George and Emma paid an extended visit to the European members of the family. They visited Elizabeth, who with Kitty and Florence was living in a rented house in Hastings on the Channel. Early in 1876 Elizabeth took Florence to Paris. George and Emma had gone there to spend two weeks with Anna, who had left her house on the French coast to winter in Paris. The two weeks stretched out. Anna, who liked Emma, had decided to convert her into a cultivated continental, and had arranged for her to study French and music. But, according to Elizabeth, she "carried the imperious regulating spirit too far, and G. has sometimes had to interfere, which is fatal." [16]

All the family tactlessness was not centered in Anna. From America, Lucy, whom Emma much admired, and who now as aunt and sister-in-law considered herself to have a double authority, wrote to the bride to stop the lessons at once and take a trip to Italy and Switzerland. Whether she was to consult her husband before doing so was not clear. Poor Emma. The fact was that, like Florence, she was young and frivolous, and that, like Florence, she had been brought up in a family always short of funds. Now she and her new niece became close friends and, to the disgust of Emma's intellectual sisters-in-law, spent hours talking about clothes.

The newlyweds stayed in Europe until summer; then George returned to the United States with his wife, who was far advanced in pregnancy, and his young niece. He must have looked more like a father with two daughters. His hair had greyed prematurely; and the year before, Elizabeth in Europe and Emily in America had been startled after not seeing him for a time to find his hair gone suddenly white, only to learn that for some time he had been dyeing it.

It was six months after the voyagers' return that Henry, who was not quite fifty-two, on a trip to Washington to visit his friend Ainsworth Spofford, wrote to Lucy of "a singular experience" he had had in the dressing room of the sleeping car. "I was shaving in front of a mirror . . . when to my surprize I saw in the glass close behind me an old gentleman with profuse bushy grey hair. 'What old fellow is that standing with his back to me so close behind me?' I asked myself and turned round when lo! he had disappeared. Nobody was there, but there was a long mirror. . . . I had seen for the first time in my life the back of my own head and figure. It was a very queer sensation." [17] The Blackwells were growing old.

CHAPTER TWENTY

The young and undeveloped country to which the Blackwells had traveled nearly forty-five years before had grown older and broader too. In 1876 the one hundredth birthday of the Republic was celebrated by an exposition in Philadelphia. There had already been five world's fairs, but this was the first to take placc in the United States. There were great advances to celebrate. Seven years before, a railroad had been completed joining the Atlantic to the Pacific shore. No more must one travel, as the Blackwells had, by boat and barge and train and coach to reach the Middle West. No longer need one voyage two months or even two weeks to reach the United States from Europe.

Since the Civil War the transition from a predominantly agricultural to a predominantly mechanical culture had been achieved, and the era of big business and great tycoons was under way. Carnegie, Rockefeller, Vanderbilt, Gould, Fiske and the others created their empires unimpeded by restrictions either moral or governmental. The great wave of new enterprises following the war drew thousands into manufacturing ventures. Machinery was king. Ahead were endless vistas of new enterprises and new markets. Industries burgeoned. It was a development too rapidly attained. The market was not large enough to absorb such production.

The turn began in 1871. In September 1873 several large and seemingly stable firms collapsed; and when Jay Cooke and Company, the country's most famous banking house, went bankrupt, financial panic followed. Two days later the Stock Exchange was closed for ten days. This did not avert disaster. The depression which these events signalized lasted five years. Mills closed; railroads defaulted on bonds. Unemployment reached its highest point in the country's history. It was the familiar pattern of business crises undeterred. No method of controlling these cycles had been discovered, and if one had been known, the laissez-faire philosophy which still gripped the country's economists would probably have prevented them from acting. The scandals which followed close upon Grant's reelection, when, with the support of woman suffrage advocates, he had overcome the liberal Greeley, did not help the situation or bolster the people's faith in their government.

In spite of the depression, it was decided to hold the Centennial Exposition planned before the crash, and in spite of the depression, there were enormous numbers of visitors. Among them were George and Emma, newly returned from Europe. They must have been particularly interested in the Woman's Pavilion; their sister-in-law and aunt, Lucy Stone, had already been involved in battle with its directors. It had been Lucy's suggestion that instead of celebrating a democracy in which they were governed without their consent and taxed without representation, women should appear on the streets of Philadelphia in deepest mourning. Lucy and other feminist leaders had for years protested paying taxes, and in the early days of her marriage Lucy had allowed her household goods to be sold at auction rather than permit herself to be taxed unless she could vote. She had finally made a restless peace with the managers of the Exposition when they consented to hang a small frame containing exhibits of tax protests in the Woman's Pavilion; but when the fair opened, the exhibit had been placed so high on the wall that it could not be read without the aid of a stepladder.

Yet women had much to celebrate, and the leaders of the woman's rights movement much to be proud of. Higher education was open to women, both in many existing colleges which had by now admitted them, and in the new little colleges, like Smith and Wellesley and Vassar, exclusively for women. The right of women to practice medicine and law had been established, though opportunities were painfully limited and the way to a career almost impossibly difficult. Women's clubs, where women could meet to listen to lectures and to discuss the problems of the day, flourished throughout the country. In some states married women's property laws, though still far from equitable, had been liberalized, and a married woman was no longer a legal pauper and her husband's chattel. In the Territory of Wyoming women voted and sat on juries, as they also did in Utah, though later in Utah they were disenfranchised by Congress, acting against the Mormons. In a few states they were permitted to sit on the school boards which considered the education of their children.

The Woman's Pavilion paid little tribute to these achievements. It did show inventions patented by women, and art and textiles produced by them. It told of their entrance into the medical profession. Julia Ward Howe found even these acknowledgments "encouraging." She must have found far more encouraging the bold act of Susan Anthony and Mrs. Joslyn Gage in slipping onto the platform at the great Fourth of July ceremony, the culmination of the Exposition, and forcing on the unwilling officials of the liberty celebration a declaration of woman's rights, passed by the National Woman Suffrage Association, which had cleverly arranged to hold meetings in Philadelphia at that time.

In spite of the fair's success and the false attitude of hope this engendered, the financial depression continued in full force. From Rome in 1874 Elizabeth had written to her brothers that she was alarmed about the "commercial distress in America" and its possible effect on her income, which had become decisively important now that she was for a time unable to practice. To Henry she wrote secretly about her uneasiness at the way George and Sam were handling her affairs and her sisters'.

Beyond her natural concern, Elizabeth was aroused to indignation that summer by a letter from Sam "endeavoring" to make her financial affairs "intelligible" to her. "I do declare," she replied in a rage which caused her to make an amusing orthographic slip, "that the arrogance of the male sect is something astounding—though I've had fifty odd years experience of it, it constantly strikes me with fresh surprise!" [1]

Elizabeth's doubts, like the depression, went on for years, and letters reassuring her continued to travel across the Atlantic. By 1878, when the upturn was beginning, Sam was in difficult straits. Companies in which he had invested had failed, and he was attempting to sell his New Jersey properties, even his own house. In 1879 he did in fact sell his home in Somerville and move closer into the town of East Orange, where George and Emma lived. This was partly for financial reasons, but partly too so that he could more easily commute to the real-estate office he and George had opened in New York, and so that his adolescent daughters could more readily move among people their own age. Edith, now at Swarthmore, was less than grateful, and only wished she had the money to buy their familiar home. Even Nettie, who had at first been delighted, felt unhappy when it came time to move.

In the spring the *Woman's Journal* carried an announcement which was in effect an advertisement. Antoinette, "regularly admitted to the Unitarian ministry," was eager to find a permanent pulpit. "She is more richly prepared than are most teachers, to help in her chosen way from the pulpit." Nettie had continued to write. A series of articles had appeared in 1874 in the *Journal,* which were then collected in a book called *The Sexes Through Nature.* They argued for woman's capacities, her ability to work, think, learn.

Nettie did not at this time find a permanent pulpit; but in 1879 and 1880 she began to travel energetically about the country, lecturing and preaching in an effort to help Sam support their large family and repay their debts. She told Lucy unhappily that it seemed she and Sam might have to be separated for a year or two; [2] but it did not in fact come to such a pass.

In 1879 Emily and Marian were both troubled by George's desire to reduce the interest he paid on the money they had lent him. He could no longer afford to pay seven per cent when six was now the legal rate. Marian said that Sam, in spite of having four houses empty and the rest leased at nominal rents, regularly sent her the interest he owed her, but that George was less punctual.

Marian was eager to buy a house in Nice, where she had lived in rented apartments for several years. To Elizabeth she wrote long rambling letters about her plans, letters uncomfortably reminiscent of those confused communications she had sent to Cincinnati from the East more than twenty-five years ago, when she was with so little logic searching for a place to stay. These letters described, in detail and with diagrams, the houses she saw, their advantages and, even oftener, their disadvantages, her doubts about settling so far from Elizabeth, her financial problems. She felt sure she could raise olives and sell them. Elizabeth had offered to lend her money. Could she still do so? Throughout, the letters expressed a conviction of imminent death. Would the house she bought be of use to Elizabeth if Marian died soon, as she expected to? Could it easily be sold?

Marian needed the money she had lent to her brothers in America to invest, but was afraid to mention her schemes to them because they disapproved of her living in Europe and were constantly expecting her to return. She was annoyed at George because, having borrowed her money, he now spoke of having had the entire trouble and risk; but, Marian asked, hadn't he had all the profit too? [3] Even so, she would have offered to take the lower rate of interest if Emily had not kept dissuading her.

Emily had suggested to George that he borrow money elsewhere at six per cent and return her capital to her, but so far he had been unable to do so. Emily had been having her own financial problems. In 1876 a generous bequest had permitted the Infirmary to move to larger quarters on Livingston Place, with a pleasant view of Stuyvesant Square; and the medical college had spread through the Second Avenue buildings. But by 1878, a shortage of funds forced the trustees to cut college salaries, and there seemed to be a possibility that the school would have to close. Emily in any event felt a growing distaste for New York and her work there, but knew of no other way of earning a living. There was a new element in her complaint. Under her tutelage young doctors were growing up and taking over her work, and she began to feel she had completed her task. She told Elizabeth that "as Americans" these young people "seem to fit in to New York life more than we ever did. I feel as though all I now contributed was a certain weight of character and moral tone which while they may command respect in a few directions, do not add in the least to the popular success of the work." [4] But by the next school term she was cheered because both the college and infirmary were "prospering more." [5]

George continued to receive protests from the sisters he was trying to help. With the entire family's capital invested in real estate, Elizabeth several years later came upon Henry George's writings and, convinced by his single-tax arguments, grew concerned with the "question of landholding." In years gone by, the small Blackwells, living on money made by their father in sugar refining, had boycotted sugar because it was a product of slave labor. Now an aging Elizabeth, basically unchanged, asked George, who had made his living in real estate and invested his sisters' money in it, to consider giving it up.

Her brother answered moderately enough that ownership of land was part of the economic system as it existed and inseparable from it. Why, he asked, did she consider the "unearned increment" argument truer of real estate than of other investments? When Elizabeth announced her interest "in seeing cooperative farming developed" to replace private ownership of land, George answered that cooperation was no more than private ownership by a group instead of by individuals, a reform that reformed nothing. [6] Like Elizabeth, George had maintained the viewpoint of his youth, and Elizabeth failed to convince him, just as Emily in those long walks in Cincinnati had failed to swerve him from self-interest to the self-denial of reform. This unlikeness to the family pattern may partly have accounted for his niece Alice's scorn, for on one occasion she expressed amazement that he was interested in anything but eating, and on another stated that she believed him to have "no immortal soul—not even enough of one to be damned." [7] Yet his interest in worldly matters was fortunate, because George, nonreformer that he was, was the only one of the Blackwells to make a fortune, the only one in later years able substantially to help his sisters, though Henry and Sam never shirked any responsibility they were able to take.

In these years Henry returned to the enterprise which since childhood had lured him, his father's business, sugar refining. He took with him into his venture all the reformist energies that Lucy had so busily nurtured over the years. He would make sugar out of beets, out of sorghum; and the success of such an enterprise would destroy the sugar cane market and with it the still continuing slavery in the West Indies. His father too had nurtured such a dream. Henry's visit to Ainsworth Spofford in Washington included an interview with President Grant and a visit to the Patent Office, where he was attempting to patent a method of manufacturing glucose, a patent earlier refused. This time he was successful. He had developed his method at home, growing beets in the large garden of his Dorchester house, trying out their possibilities in the kitchen with kitchen pots and homemade machinery.

Like the ventures of his early years, this aroused the interest and advice of his sisters. Emily felt it necessary to tell Lucy how worried she was that Harry was working so hard and looking so tired. Marian fretted about the liability he had incurred in an industry which had been tried out in France under the best conditions and had failed. Elizabeth, on the other hand, was encouraging. In reply to his announcement that he was going to make a fortune and support them all, she told him that she believed his "manufacturing experiment had excellent reasons in its favor" and hopefully awaited the income he had promised.

Like the ventures of his early years, this too kept Henry for long periods away from home. After more than twenty years of marriage he still resented the necessity of separation, still wrote to Lucy, "I love you with my whole heart, soul, and spirit." He hoped "soon to return and never to leave home again" without Lucy or Alice or both.[8] Yet he continued to travel. He spent much time in Maine, where he organized and operated the Maine Beet Sugar Company. And in the summer of 1879, with the added inducement of buying sugar-refining machinery in Germany, he made the trip to Europe he had hoped ever since his marriage to make with Lucy, and for which Lucy, in a life occupied with speaking, writing, organizing for woman's rights, had found no time. When now at long last he went, it was Alice who accompanied him, not Lucy, who had a magazine to edit.

As soon as he returned, he was off for Maine again, full of enthusiasm. From there in October he sent home a telegram which in ten unpunctuated words wedded his two interests: BEET SUGAR MANUFACTURE A SUCCESS SLAVERY IN CUBA IS DOOMED. Both predictions were overoptimistic. That year, however, production was good, and by the spring of 1880 he announced a profit above his salary.

But he could not induce the farmers in either Maine or Canada to try a second crop on a sufficient scale to be lucrative. They had been tempted by state subsidies the first year, but were unwilling to venture a second time.

While affairs were prospering, Henry had taken Sam in business with him. They were both in Maine in the winter of 1880, and Emily was complaining that if "Sam's girls were worth anything, Florence or Edie ought to go up and keep house for them," but she supposed them incapable of it. Sam did not last long in the new position. Alice confided to Kitty that, against his partner's wishes, Papa had hired Uncle Sam for three months at a hundred dollars a month because he needed money so badly. He was "to get agents and make contracts for beets," but, perhaps through no fault of his, "with that large salary" [9] he accomplished almost nothing. Papa was sufficiently worried about the company's finances to put his assets in Mamma's name; and Alice, true Blackwell that she was, was troubled that this evasion of responsibility might be immoral. Lucy offered to sell one of her houses to help him. Yet Henry was still as much involved in the business in 1881, when he reorganized the company and shifted its center of operations from Maine to Schenectady, New York.

Henry's absence from the *Woman's Journal* and the suffrage association greatly increased Lucy's burdens. She was now in her sixties. A short, round-faced, round-bodied woman who wore a black dress and demure lace collar, she had a solid, healthy look, but was in fact subject to severe throat and chest infections, and to rheumatism which increased with the years.

Henry was away when the women of Massachusetts had their first opportunity to vote, only in school board elections it is true, yet first in New Hampshire then in Massachusetts, they were permitted this tiny symbol of equality with men. But when Lucy went to register she was told she could neither vote nor stand as candidate for a school board except as Mrs. Henry Blackwell. This name, with its personal anonymity, she would not adopt even for such a cause, and so the vote she had fought so long to gain, indeed had been one of the most important forces in gaining, was lost to her.

Besides her public life Lucy had a demanding private one, a

large house and garden and farm with chickens and a cow. Alice was now a student at Boston University, but she lived at home. From time to time, the household was also increased by members of the family who came to visit, or by one or another of Sam and Nettie's daughters who came to stay. Toward the end of 1877 Emily wrote commending Lucy for inviting Florence to live with her that winter. She did not know otherwise what Florence would have done, for "there is a curious slowness and let go about them, which I suppose results from the quiet rather stagnant life out on the Hillside." Yet Lucy's home, which was to provide so admirable a setting for Flo—the childhood name "Floy" had gradually disappeared—was presumably less beneficial to her own daughter, because Emily added the suggestion that instead of going to the university, Alice ought to spend a year in Europe for "wider experience of the world," presumably under Elizabeth's corrective influence.[10]

The following April Nettie wrote to Lucy that she was grateful for Lucy's efforts to train Florence, but was afraid Flo was not like the girls Lucy was used to; her chief interests were domestic and she would develop best after she was settled in a home of her own.[11] And a month later Florence was returning to New Jersey, and her mother was regretting that the experiment had not been more successful.[12] Yet Florence seems not to have been without interests or ideas; they were simply not those her relatives respected. She was studying elocution, seemingly successfully. And a year and a half later Alice told Kitty that Flo, who was again there for a visit, was seriously convinced she was "called" to become a Methodist minister, and had led a prayer meeting, speaking in a manner so like Aunt Nettie's that Alice found it funny. The girls had kept this episode a secret from Henry and Lucy, who would, for whatever reason, have been "disgusted."[13] Florence did in fact later become a lay preacher.

Meanwhile Lucy had tried again, taking eleven-year-old Agnes in the winter of 1878. Sam had gone to spend two weeks with Henry and Lucy, bringing Agnes with him, and had decided to leave her for the winter, presumably without consulting Nettie, who was much surprised. This experiment worked better. Agnes was helpful, liked school, was a good student and "a nice child." But when Grace, who throughout her life was nervous and sickly, was sent to England to stay with Elizabeth, the venture was a failure, and she returned home long before the scheduled year was over.

The family had by now been increased by two new members. In July 1876 Emma had given birth to a boy, named Howard Lane in memory of his father's favorite brother. He was the first male of the generation which had begun twenty years before when Florence was born.

At about the same time Ellen had taken a baby boy six months old, although she could barely afford to support Susie. Kitty had heard about him from Florence, who reported that Emily wouldn't have him in the house and Ellen wouldn't give him up; but Ellen and Emily had maintained an utter silence about him in their letters.[14] It was a year before Ellen herself told Kitty about little Paul Winthrop, whom she had taken "with his nurse from the Protestant asylum" and kept in her Long Island home during the summer. In the winter she had had to board him with people who were fond of him, because Emily would not have him in New York; but a friend who had seen little Pauli had been so taken with him that she had paid part of his winter's maintenance. Ellen was determined to bring him up if she possibly could.[15]

In view of this, the American family were more troubled than surprised when in 1877 Elizabeth, who had spent the winter of 1876 in Europe, and remained through 1877 in Austria and southern Europe because her health was again too bad to permit her to practice, wrote that she had adopted a son. This turned out to be a joke. The son was a twenty-four-year-old man she had met and grown fond of. It seems likely that he was the young artist who painted her portrait that year. He, in turn, was so charmed with her that he had decided to travel with her and Kitty. The combination of Elizabeth's fame and some quality of her personality seemed to attract young men in a way she had failed to do in her youthful and marriageable years, and from time to time one of these admirers was referred to, as often as not, in Kitty's letters to Alice.

The current Mr. Alfred Sachs was a special case. The relationship was long and close. Kitty said she had never seen Dr. Elizabeth so taken with anyone, and at first felt miserable because the relationship shut her out. He was a Jew, and this was apparently so unusual in Elizabeth's experience that she told Barbara Bodichon that her affection for Mr. Sachs would lead her thereafter to have a special interest in the "race." There was a further reason why this "son" was special to Kitty. At thirty she was deeply in love with the twenty-four-year-old man, a fact she concealed from her Doctor, and of which Elizabeth remained astonishingly unaware. The idea that Kitty was susceptible to such emotions seemed rarely to enter Elizabeth's head, and when, as on a later occasion, it momentarily occurred to her, it filled her with alarm.

Alice was Kitty's only confidante. Kitty told her rather pathetically that ladies, gentlemen, girls and babies fell in love with her, but not young men. What seemed so easy for other girls was impossible for her. She cried at night, but in the day was too shy to try to charm any eligible male.

To both of these moral ladies the fact that Mr. Sachs was a "reprobate," that he had led so dissipated a life that it had ruined his health, seems to have had a certain allure. To Elizabeth it was an invitation to reform. In the process of converting him to the good life, she searched fruitlessly in the foreign lands where they traveled for a Testament to give him. Kitty happily offered hers, in which she had penciled "Roma 1873." They took it without question and instantly erased her marking, so that she felt shut out again. In spite of her defective hearing, Kitty overheard a conversation in which Mr. Sachs told Elizabeth that his father, who had his own methods of reforming his son, insisted that he must marry at once and for money. Young Mr. Sachs had obediently determined to find a suitable wife, and Kitty was steeling herself for news of his engagement.

He did not marry then. A year and a half later their "boy" had been carried into evil ways again and wanted to come to Dr. Elizabeth in Hastings to be rescued, but she did not encourage him. Because of his immorality she felt it wrong to introduce him to her friends. Kitty, who longed to help him, knew that if he came it would not be to turn to her but to her elderly guardian and rival. Six months later a formal card brought the dreaded news of his engagement.

CHAPTER TWENTY-ONE

Young Howard Lane Blackwell, sole male of a generation that stretched over twenty years, was heartily welcomed by the whole family with the possible exception of his father, who in bachelor fashion had always been alarmed by small children and who, in his dealings with the new baby, Emily told Marian, "eschews propinquity, and regards him as a most objectionable little bundle of bad habits, who must be tolerated, and even slaved for, but not approached." Yet even Alice admitted that a happy marriage had had a propitious effect on Uncle George. His sarcastic manner was funny now instead of hateful. "He is queer and always will be; but he is much nicer than he used to be." [1]

As was the custom in those days, Howard, whose mother was unable to nurse him, had a wet nurse. The wet nurse's own child, Emily said, had died. "I was sorry for the poor little baby, when I went once to see it and saw the poor little shrivelled thing fading away, and remembered the fat healthy child it was when I went to engage its mother, and contrasted little Howard, then a little puny thing whose life hung on a thread, with his present self—plump, strong and well conditioned—I felt as though I had bought the poor baby's life for him. Wet nursing is a cruel sort of thing, for it almost always means saving the nursling and the death of the abandoned child. But," she consoled herself, "Mrs. Clarke is rather an unfeeling woman, and was I think glad to be rid of the trouble and expense of the child." [2]

Indeed Howard's life had been purchased at the price of the other baby's; but it would be more than could be expected of any relatives to defy a prevalent custom and let their child die when a way lay open to save it. It had been taken for granted in the Civil War that rich men might hire poor men to take their place in battle. In a laissez-faire society it was not merely assumed, as it is today, that the poor would have less chance of survival than the well-to-do, but that the rich might more directly buy the lives of the poor if they felt inclined to do so.

This battle, perhaps for personal reasons, the Blackwells never fought. There were of course many others. No one, not even a Blackwell, can enlist in every war. But it is significant which battlegrounds they chose and which they discarded. The struggle between capital and labor, which Susan Anthony took up, rather in the manner of a Lady Bountiful, it is true, was never a matter of concern to that generation of Blackwells, though many years later Alice became involved in the left-wing movement and was in the forefront of the fight to vindicate Sacco and Vanzetti.

Her parents had a different view. In 1882 Lucy and Antoinette argued at a meeting that the working class ought to be educated, "to free them from the domination of unions, which claim the same wages for each man, so that he who can shovel five loads of dirt can only have the pay of the man who can shovel one load," a somewhat eccentric view of the function of unionism. In 1872 Henry had announced in the *Woman's Journal* that "The political rights of women will soon be established and then the relations of capital and labor will be considered and adjusted." The equality of women was the major issue, as it was in that year's presidential campaign between Greeley and Grant. It was the major issue again in their attitude toward immigration, in their fear that hordes of ignorant foreigners would bring with them the viewpoint of backward European areas where woman's position was far humbler than in the New World, in their indignation that ignorant men, as soon as they became citizens, could attain the right to vote denied to the most educated woman.

About the position of women they were everywhere and forever united. "We have been soldiers in different Army Corps of humanitary advance," Elizabeth wrote to Lucy in a birthday letter, "but I have always recognized that we are fellow soldiers." This, with more or less acerb reservations, they all recognized. Emily over a period of several years in the eighties wrote articles in her fine, clear, incisive style, dealing with women in industry. These appeared in the *Woman's Journal* either as original contributions or reprinted from other periodicals. They advocated women leaving domestic positions, which were essentially servile and unsuitable to any educated person. They discussed the dangers inherent in a situation in which women were considered demeaned when they worked, and therefore the fair prey of men. "Classes, like individuals, are apt to be taken at their own estimate. When women form . . . a higher estimate of themselves as a body, men will learn to respect them also."[3]

In a deep sense nobody moves with the times, and it is a curious irony that the most rebellious seem least able to adjust to a world they have helped to change. The fervent battles are the battles of youth, and since the Blackwells had grown up in the era of moral reform, the wars of moral reform were those they recognized and fought throughout their lives. Even the young people tended to follow where their elders led. Kitty felt it "almost a Sin" to admire the beautiful garden of the Monte Carlo casino when she considered "how the money to keep it was made."[4] Alice discussed at length with her college friends the burning question of immorality in the theatre, for "if the habit of theatre-going is as pernicious as Papa says, ought one to encourage it in others by going at all?" One of her friends argued that if Alice went to see *Julius Caesar,* others would go to less worthy plays and plead her example in their defense. "Now," said Alice with assurance, "the ballet-dancing isn't going to hurt me; but what effect would it be apt to have upon the young men in the audience?"[5] The *Woman's Journal* supported Anthony Comstock's campaign to suppress "vile literature," which corrupted the minds of the young and aroused their baser passions. It advocated the use by colleges of expurgated editions of Greek and Roman literature to save susceptible students from corruption. It approved the militant, hymn-singing, whisky-spilling temperance movement, but condemned the railway workers striking against reduced wages, because the bitter strike led to rioting and bloodshed.

In the *Woman's Journal* the crusading family now in effect had its own medium of communication. The paper not only spread Lucy's and Henry's and Antoinette's news and views of woman suffrage, but enlisted as well in the battles of the medical sisters. These were usually inaugurated by Elizabeth, who as the years went by seemed to maintain an undiminished vigor in moral combat. In spite of the fact that at fifty she had found herself unable to "command the vigor of twenty years ago," aware of growing old and watching the process "with curious interest," in her middle fifties she was determined to fight the "organized forces which are now employed in the *direct promotion* of immorality by equally *direct* promotion of morality," to devote "what ever of strength remains . . . in promoting the 'organization of chastity.' "[6]

She had reason to be aware of declining strength, for by now her frequently recurrent illness forced her to admit that she could no longer live and practice in London, where above all other places she desired to make her home. The passing of the years was dramatized in 1877 when her friend Barbara, six years younger than she, was taken gravely ill and left with a partial paralysis that increased as time went on and left her for the rest of her life a semi-invalid. In 1878, however, Barbara was well enough to make a sad trip to Algeria to be with her husband. Dr. Bodichon, sixteen years her senior, was an old man now and very sick.

In the autumn of 1877 Elizabeth left Kitty in Nice, where Marian had settled with a seeming permanence unusual for her, and went to England to visit her old friend. Before and after this trip she spent her time in Nice writing *Counsel to Parents on the Moral Education of their Children,* which she told Barbara was "so frank spoken and in advance of ordinary received opinions" that she did not believe it would find a publisher in England.[7] The book was an extension of the ideas Elizabeth had expressed in her lectures to the Quaker ladies in New York almost twenty-five years earlier, and had amplified in *Laws of Life* and in her lectures over the years. Yet her writings were still so far in advance of their time, so frank in their statement of inadmissible thoughts on sex, though this frankness was not intended to make men free but to make them moral, that she had in fact to print the book privately before, after much controversy, it was most respectably issued by Hatchard and Company. In the United States, through Ellen's efforts as salesman and editor, an edition appeared under Brentano Brothers' imprint. Elizabeth expressed gratitude for Ellen's devoted efforts and hoped her younger sister would attain "some pecuniary advantage" from the publication. If Ellen retained any interest in the book, she probably did enjoy a reward. The public was less censorious than the publishers. By 1883 the American publication had reached a fourth edition.

Elizabeth's essential idea, the obligation of parents to deal frankly with sex in conversation with their children, to instruct them in a single standard of chastity for boys and girls, had been carried further as a result of her concern with the regulation of vice. It was a generally accepted concept, as her sister Emily put it, that respectable men should be immoral and respectable women moral. Elizabeth set out to counter the current belief that virtue atrophied young men's sexual powers. To bring up boys to be licentious, to condone their consorting with prostitutes, was to destroy society. To teach them the same self-restraint that was taught their sisters was to create a better world for both men and women. Knowledge of sex and of the possibility of its virtuous restraint and virtuous expression was the greatest barrier against vice; "every sexual indulgence is unmitigated evil." It was part of this theory which caused her to refuse to receive Mr. Sachs when he asked to come to England, for she believed that immorality was spread like disease, and considered Mr. Sachs, of whom she was so fond, as a carrier. It is strange that she seems not to have feared Kitty's contact with him. Perhaps Kitty was, in her view, because of her physical defects of sight and hearing, not susceptible to sexual attraction or capable of arousing it, or perhaps, having been brought up in the ways of virtue by Elizabeth herself, she was immune to corruption.

In her book Elizabeth told why virtuous women must be protected if society was to survive. "Women, as well as men, create society. Their share is a silent one. . . . All the splendid din of external life is wanting in the quiet realm of distinctive woman's work; therefore it is often overlooked, misunderstood, or despised. Nevertheless it is of vital importance. It preserves the only germ of society which is capable of permanent growth—the germ of unselfish human love and innate righteousness. . . . It is, for this reason, that no polygamous or licentious customs, which destroy the woman's nature, and dry up the deepest source of human sympathy, can possibly produce a durable or a noble and happy nation."

Into her council crept another of Elizabeth's favorite theses, that what was unnatural was bad. Circumcision was an "unnatural rite" taken over from licentious heathen nations, and performed in the hope of saving men from the effects of their vices. It was "based upon the erroneous principle that boys . . . are so badly fashioned by the Creative Power that they must be reformed by the surgeon." As a "Christian physiologist," she considered it an "ugly mutilation" involving "serious danger, both to physical and moral health." [8]

Vaccination was another unnatural rite. She consented to vaccinate her patients only at their insistence. She had once vaccinated a baby who, probably because of some special susceptibility, had died, and the shock of causing such a death had overwhelmed Elizabeth, who considered it the result of her having had too little faith in "the beneficence of Nature's laws." The experience had awakened in her "a growing distrust as to the wisdom of all medical methods which introduce any degree of morbid matter into the blood of the human system." [9] Why all medicine was not an interference with Nature's laws, she never seemed to consider. In 1880 she was much troubled by her lack of control over the National Health Society which she had inaugurated and nurtured, because it advocated vaccination, "a disputed point," instead of being content to promote "accepted sanitary truths." And until the end of her life she continued to oppose inoculation against disease "as an unfortunate . . . fallacy of medical prejudice."

When Elizabeth became interested in Henry George and the single tax, Ellen, inveterate purchaser of land and houses though she had been since girlhood, took up the crusade in the United States, and in the mid-eighties was writing articles on the merits of the "holding of land by communities instead of individuals."

She designed a plan for building and running such an enterprise, the Utopian community of her youth in modern form.

The family joined hands across the Atlantic too in the fight against vivisection. It is true that conditions in experimental laboratories in those days were often incredibly brutal. Animals were kept in unspeakable conditions, operated on without anesthetic—as humans had so recently been, though not at least for purposes of research—and allowed to die in misery. These conditions led humane people to shrink from the entire concept of using animals for experimental purposes. The Blackwells, like many others, did not oppose the abuses of vivisection, but the entire idea.

As in the battle about the regulation of prostitution, Elizabeth's views were combated in England by her disciple Elizabeth Garrett Anderson, who, verbally and vehemently in favor of vaccination and vivisection, commented that the language of those who opposed these practices could not "be said to have the lucidity proper to writing that deals with scientific matters." [10]

But Elizabeth had turned to medicine more for its reformist possibilities than as a science, and continued always to be more the Christian philosopher-healer than the scientist. In the fight against vivisection the *Woman's Journal* enthusiastically endorsed her stand. In 1881 Henry wrote an article in favor of the total prohibition of vivisection. The Infirmary Medical College resisted vivisection for some years after it was generally practiced; but as late as 1897, when the school had accepted it in a modified form, Emily complained that the *Woman's Journal,* without consulting her as to the facts, had printed a letter attacking an unnamed woman's medical college for requiring the delicate sex to take part in so degrading a process. A second letter writer stated categorically that scientific evidence showed that no good had come to medicine as a result of experiments with animals. Emily protested this assertion, and declared that the anonymous college attacked was in fact the Infirmary college. The technique used at the Infirmary was painless; only stray animals condemned by city ordinance to be drowned were used, and these only to the number of about twelve a year. It was the abuse of vivisection and not its use which was to be deplored.[11]

Six years earlier the battle of vivisection had raged across the

Atlantic between Elizabeth and Emily, with Elizabeth in the role of aggressor and Emily retreating behind the bulwark of an accomplished fact. By this time Nettie and Sam's daughters, Edith and Ethel, were both preparing to be physicians. Edith had studied at the Massachusetts Institute of Technology and was taking a year of internship at the Infirmary, though Emily thought her ill-fitted to be a doctor, too timid and nervous to practice medicine. At the Massachusetts Institute of Technology vivisection was an established part of medical education, and Ellen, who joined Elizabeth in her horror of vivisection and had been writing anti-vivisectionist articles, felt that Nettie's girls had already "enrolled themselves on the side of evil . . . the side of the devil." [12] From across the Atlantic, Anna announced her—as usual, extreme—distaste for Edith's involvement in "the hideous (and useless) monstrosity of animal vivisection, now so rapidly tending towards similar experimentation on human beings! Uh—what a branch of hell is this unhappy planet!" [13] But it was Edith herself who revealed to Elizabeth that the Infirmary too had fallen into evil ways, a fact Emily had been attempting to conceal.

Elizabeth wrote to Alice, also an antivivisectionist, to ask whether it was possible that Edith's reference to "operative surgery *in the Laboratory*" meant that the Infirmary was performing experimentation on animals. Elizabeth wanted the facts, without which she could not "*compel* an answer" or any expression of opinion from Emily.[14] Elizabeth considered her protégée Mary Putnam the worst enemy of her point of view because, apparently as a married woman and the wife of one of the most famous and forward-looking doctors in the United States, she was "a bond slave of the narrow male intellect." [15]

Finally, Elizabeth's insistence brought a reply from Emily. The students did not practice vivisection. Dr. Thompson did a very small amount, not in the least cruel, as illustrations to his lectures. It was impossible any longer to find a competent teacher who would agree not to illustrate by vivisection, but the Infirmary was still attempting to settle the matter amicably without losing the doctor's valuable services.

This failed to convince her sister. A year later Elizabeth was writing an attack on an official United States Government report which advocated the use of vivisection in medical teaching. So great was her outrage that, although she had not crossed the ocean in more than twenty years because of her fear of the virulent seasickness which always overcame her, she contemplated now, at the age of seventy-two, returning to the United States to combat "cruelty and lust, which have gained so great a footing in the grand New World."[16] Close to the end of the century she still stood out against so great a scientist as Pasteur because his research was "ethically unjustifiable" and therefore "intellectually fallacious." She even tried unsuccessfully to visit the Pasteur Institute, with the same impulse which, she said, would have led her to visit hell if she "could only preach to the spirits there imprisoned!"

Of them all, Emily alone was at first willing, if necessary, to accept vivisection and later to defend it. It is perhaps relevant that it was Emily who held this freer view, for it was she who, among the Blackwells of her generation, had most contact with a new intellectual climate. It was she who knew the young women of medicine, she who had told Elizabeth fifteen years before that the predecessors of these young women seemed to fit into New York life better than Emily and Elizabeth ever had. These younger women had in fact now taken over the Infirmary and moved it, and a perhaps reluctant Emily, forward with the times.

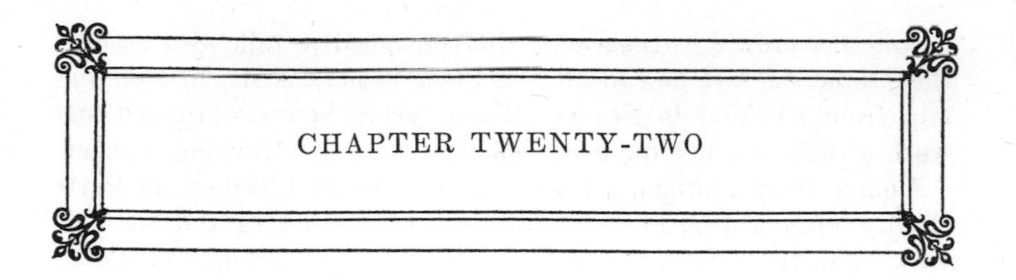

CHAPTER TWENTY-TWO

Anna, though she created less stir than her doctor sisters or her feminist sisters-in-law, was one of the most gifted of the Blackwells. Her talents had been recognized by no less an editor than Horace Greeley and no less a writer than Edgar Allan Poe, who called her "a real woman of letters." Her poetry had been applauded by the critics.

She might also lay claim to being the most eccentric of that far from conventional family. From her early years she had adopted every *ism* the winds blew her way in those gusty days; and with the years, particularly after her adored Howard's death, she became increasingly credulous. In the mid-seventies, ten years after he died, she was a more convinced spiritualist than ever. She continued to support herself by her newsletters from France, which in the eighteen-seventies went to eleven papers around the world, to India, Australia, South Africa, Canada; but she devoted her spare time to a labor of love—translating books about spiritualism and reincarnation. She asked Henry, in spite of his lack of sympathy for her belief, to help arrange publication of these treatises in the United States.

Unlike the other Blackwells, with the exception of Henry, Anna was outgoing and did not suffer from shyness, and unlike them, despite her growing strangeness, she continued to talk with ease to the people she met and to attract them to her, as she had on the trip from England to France twenty years before, although she wore a nightcap, not quite concealed, under her traveling bonnet.

Young Mary Putnam, introduced to Anna by Elizabeth in Paris shortly after Howard's death, found her interesting though odd. In spite of the oddity, in spite of Elizabeth's complaint that Anna, domineering and positive, constantly "snubbed and criticized" her, Mary was drawn to the older woman, and after Elizabeth's departure, continued to seek her out. Mary described Anna as "strong, naïve, unconscious and impulsive"; she also found her cordial and pleasant, but unable to "be with a person five minutes without criticizing them for something." [1] Even breathing was not safe from Anna's supervision, for once, while in the throes of a passionate conviction that inhaling through the mouth was dangerous, she tried to insist on Mary's breathing only through her nose. Yet Miss Putnam was sufficiently drawn to Anna's brightness of manner and mind to go on visiting her. Seventeen years later, still a medical authority, Anna was telling Henry that if he suffered from rheumatism, he must eat as many strawberries as possible. "It is now the great remedy for it and gout." [2]

In 1879 when Henry and Alice were to visit Europe, Anna, who had not seen her younger brother in over thirty years, arranged to meet him in England and take him back to the old places in and near Bristol which she remembered so well and which he, having last seen them as a boy of seven, had almost forgotten. Anna was naturally uneasy as she anticipated the reunion, for "a white-bearded Harry, with a daughter of twenty-two" was quite different from the brother who in her mind was fixed as the young man he had been when she last saw him. When she did catch sight of him, she cried out, "You don't mean to say that is Harry—It is impossible." She told him that he looked like Apollyon in their old *Pilgrim's Progress,* with his two horns of tufted grey hair.[3]

Anna was now sixty-three, white-haired, but still with the same bright though anxious look Henry recalled; she was as "graceful and well-dressed" as in the old days. And apparently, at least on this occasion, with no visible signs of eccentricity. Moreover her brother found her as full of fun and animation as ever.

Henry had come not only to seek a reunion with his sisters but to buy machinery for making beet sugar. For this purpose he went off to Germany, leaving Alice with Elizabeth and Kitty. He found time in England to go with Anna to Bristol and, in a long letter to Sam, he described the walk they took past the old familiar-unfamiliar streets and houses of their childhood. They went to the resorts where they had summered, to Weston-super-Mare, where they discovered the grandson of the "old bathing woman" and the beach where Marian had "once found a gold watchcase on the sand and made acquaintance with a little daughter of 'Lady L'Estrange' to the great jealousy of Anna and the other children." But Henry did not find time to visit Marian in her retreat in the South of France, and she was, or believed herself to be, too ill to make the trip north to see him.

Anna and Henry went to Bourton, where Anna recognized the house in which Uncle and Aunt Browne had lived. Anna thought of Uncle Browne as having led a much freer, more refined life than theirs, a genial, generous man, endowed by his niece in those early years with all the romance her own life lacked. Henry was startled to learn how bitterly Anna resented her childhood years, as well he might be, since her bitterness had never been made visible to her family in depression or brooding. Yet in spite of the view which she now revealed in detail, his own picture of their childhood was as fixed and irrevocable as hers, so that when he considered the present lonely lives of his "poor dear sisters in contrast with the social gaiety of those early days," he felt his heart would break. Yet none of his sisters, with the possible exception of Ellen, whose early memories were of America, and whose present life seemed to her drab and disappointing, could have been led to agree with him.

They spent "three days . . . wandering like ghosts over the scenes of early memories,"[4] and when Anna left Bristol without regret, Henry deplored her return to a lonely life in Paris without brothers or sisters to share it with her. After Henry went back to the United States, Anna complied with his request to write a letter of reminiscence about the Bristol days. This detailed account of "the old times before the flood which washed us off from our native land and set us loose from all our moorings" was written over a period of months, and grew to book length.

Unfortunately it was not only new ideas which Anna found irresistible. She was also the victim of every financial scheme that was proposed to her and of some which she sought out. She had been the first of the Blackwells to leave home to earn a living. She had helped to support the younger members of the family; and as she grew old, she became increasingly convinced that she would find an easy way to fortune, and support them again in their declining years. In the seventies she had invested the money Howard had left her in a project to build a bridge. By the mid-eighties this project had ended in heavy loss to her through the "shameful unfairness and dishonesty of the government," and she had nothing left but a part interest in the land where the bridge was to have been built.

During this time she also became interested in a product called *Enduit Universel,* a universal coating which, if applied to textiles, leather, paper, felt or almost anything else, would make the coated material sturdy, damp-proof, fireproof. She tried to interest her brothers, saying she could get a monopoly for the United States if they would undertake the agency there. But George complained that "Anna's glowing eulogies give no real idea of what it is, its uses or its application, nor its price." Henry, always less astute, expressed sufficient interest to lay down certain conditions under which he would consider handling the miraculous substance, but, no doubt luckily, the scheme fell through.

Henry, on his side, was sending samples of beet and sorghum sugar to Anna to test against the cane product. About Henry's obsession Anna was judicious enough. She told him she had no difficulty distinguishing beet from cane sugar because the cane was so far superior.[5] She advised him to stop being "a dear Goose" and trying to "frustrate the designs of Providence" by refusing to make sugar of sugar cane.[6] Why did he not simply import cane, she asked nearly two years later; interchange of products between countries was desirable.[7] She was sure he would lose his money if he continued to experiment; but, should he fail, she hoped to be able to help him.

Meanwhile it was he who was helping her. From the time he

returned home after his European trip, he frequently sent her gifts of money. Once she bought a guitar. Several times she used the funds to pay for winter visits to Nice, where Marian had been living since 1876. In 1881 she described Marian as living in a handsome apartment in the center of Nice, an apartment, however, where Anna found it impossible to stay because there was too much noise of convent bells and piano playing; besides, Marian needed draughts through the house, which utterly destroyed Anna. She included a protest directed at Henry. He had been addressing her as Madame; this pretense of matrimony was a silly affectation of Marian's which Anna did not condone.

In 1883 she also forwarded a complaint of Marian's that he should not address his letters to Nice, Italy. Nice had been ceded to the French, and the letters caused resentment among Marian's neighbors. This was Anna's last visit to her sister in the South of France. By the following summer Marian had left Nice, which she liked better than any place she had ever lived, and moved to Vernon, eighty kilometers from Paris. The explanation given for this move was that it would bring her nearer her sisters, particularly Anna. Indeed Elizabeth had long had the impression that Marian wished to be told she ought to live in England. This Elizabeth said she was unwilling to tell her, because of the climate as well as the cost of living, for neither Elizabeth nor Marian had much money; but in fact Elizabeth feared that her "missionary life" would be impeded by a dependent elder sister.

Whatever the truth of Marian's preferences, there was another and cogent reason for the move. With her son Leon old enough to be away at school, Frances Alofsen had for some time been separated from her undesirable husband, and was determined to get a divorce. Although Frances continued on the closest terms with her husband's family, she now turned to Marian, whom she considered a second mother. Frances was still so young, attractive, and charming that poor, moral Kitty, on hearing of her separation, expressed the hope that she would not settle in Nice, a horrid place for anyone who, like Frances, "quite innocently attracts men's eyes." There was a sounder reason for Frances not living in southern France, which was too far away for Leon to spend his vacations with her; and Marian, for whom the cold of central France had been unendurable for years, who had not had the strength to travel north to see Henry, now found it possible to move.

Anna was at Triel near Paris and fifty kilometers from Vernon. In the past ten years her life had become ever more closely bound to this little town, where the most long-lived and fantastic of her financial schemes was being carried out. Changes in world conditions and the advent of the cable with its rapid news communication had drastically reduced Anna's newspaper contacts; where there had been eleven, there now remained only two. If she lost her Montreal contact, as seemed likely, she would not have enough to live on. Her only remaining paper would be the Sydney *Morning Herald,* for which she had written and would continue to write for many years. By 1885 this was her sole remaining paper, at a fee of a hundred pounds a year.

But nothing of fortune or misfortune in those days concerned Anna like her preoccupation with Triel. The history of this concern had its beginnings almost two hundred years before, when in 1688 William and Mary were called from the Netherlands to save the English throne for the Church and for moderation, and Mary's father, James II, who had turned Catholic, fled to France with his Catholic wife and their infant son. According to an account written by the Curé de Triel in 1937 and still in the possession of Triel's mayor, "Jacques Stuart" was royally received by Louis XIV. "Le Roi Soleil treated him like a true monarch and put the ancient residence of the Kings of France at his disposal." This ancient residence was at St. Germain on the heights overlooking Paris. But, says Monsieur le Curé, "The last of the Stuarts, simple and modest, preferred the more intimate domicile situated at Triel to the luxurious chateau. He passed numerous moments of his exile in a property not far from the church where he may have hidden the considerable treasure which he is supposed to have carried away when he fled from England." This supposed treasure was assumed to consist of his personal fortune and of the royal jewels, including the crown, which had disappeared from England at about that time.

Triel is a typical town of central France. Its ancient church is built at the top of a steep hill overlooking the Seine, with the houses of the town clustered around it on the side of the hill and at its base. When Anna lived there, the property of the château where the deposed king and his family had been lodged stretched the quarter mile between the church and the house, and there are believed by today's residents to have been secret underground passages from the church down to the château. Since then, the accidental destruction of a dam higher up the Seine has diverted the river, so that it now flows between the church and the much reconstructed château with whose gardens and supposedly hidden treasure Anna was so long and intimately concerned.

What first drew her enthralled attention to the story of the hidden fortune is not clear, but at some time in the mid-seventies she became "as sure of the existence of the treasure" as though she already had her share of it in the Bank of England.[8] This conviction had come to her in the way she trusted most—by supernatural means; but how much the supernatural influence was aided by the suggestions of the current owner of the property, Madame Deville, it is hard to know.

The story had in it every element of melodrama likely to appeal to a credulous and passionate woman like Anna—including the tale that Lord Palmerston had come secretly to visit Madame Deville and had been seen digging in the château grounds—for Madame claimed to be no less a person than the rightful Queen of England. Her claim was supported by the extraordinary evidence of a Léontine Martin, a Frenchwoman who maintained that in England in 1852 a French gentleman had showed her a medallion portrait of a young woman he had been commissioned to find and for whom he had unsuccessfully searched through many countries over many years. He confided to her that the original of the portrait was the daughter of George IV and Queen Caroline, while the so-called-queen Victoria was of course only their niece. He told her too that the royal jewels and the crown of England to which this woman was the rightful heir were hidden on the banks of the Seine. If she ever saw the lady of the medallion, she must promise to let him know.

Mademoiselle Martin soon returned to France, where one day, to her amazement, in the studio of a Parisian sculptor, she saw a woman who looked exactly like the portrait and whom she immediately approached with the words, *"Madame, vous êtes la reine d'Angleterre!*" Madame Deville, for it was she, later told the young woman that she knew her origins but that, since her papers had been stolen, she thought it best to live quietly and incognito, giving her energies to concealing, not revealing, her history. She had, however, bought the property in Triel where she now lived, knowing that somewhere on the grounds was hidden the treasure which was rightfully hers.

According to a document prepared by the prefect of police of Triel at Anna's request for a Prince Orloff whom she was trying to interest in the recovery of the treasure, the "Demoiselle Deville" had moved to Triel in 1842, and had spent the intervening years tearing down buildings and digging up land. The prefect considered her to have "*les facultés intellectuelles un peu troublées à cause de sa manie de constructions,*" but although she had made herself poor in the work, her conduct had been irreproachable and she had always honored her commitments.

Despite the troubled intellectual faculties apparent to others who came in contact with the proprietress, Anna apparently moved without hesitation into a small house on the property. Elizabeth, visiting her there in 1882, described the house as "a very humble little cottage" with brick floors and small rooms, simply but attractively furnished.[9] Anna had long since put every cent she could lay her hands on, every cent she could borrow, every cent she could induce credulous acquaintances to invest, into the project of digging for the treasure. Her correspondence with an English couple, the Hodgsons, indicates that by late in 1879 they were already thoroughly disillusioned. They had by then, over a four-year period, lent Anna over two thousand pounds, and were beginning to believe that their friendly indulgence had done her more harm than good.

The Hodgsons begged her to let their lawyer, who was also trying to retrieve something from the bridge fiasco, come to France at their expense to investigate the situation at Triel, for by now Anna had discovered that Madame Deville and her friends, a couple named Bouilliez who had also led Anna to the universal coating, had deceived her about the status of the property. Anna had invested fifty thousand francs on the assurance that there were no mortgages, only to discover over a period of time that there were in fact two claims prior to hers. Undiscouraged, Anna continued to try to raise money for digging, on Madame Deville's promise that she would receive a third of the wealth to be uncovered, and in spite of her knowledge that any day the property could be sold without notice to her. As early as 1880 her English friends were trying to explain to her that the Triel estate, valued at five thousand eight hundred pounds, was already mortgaged for three thousand nine hundred and forty, and that any treasure which might once have been there had long since been removed. These arguments made "no impression whatever on [her] mind," [10] filled as it was with fairy tales and pots of gold at the end of the rainbow.

After learning about the mortgages, after being involved in a lawsuit, Anna was still in 1881 visiting ministries in Paris to ask their assistance, discovering new associates willing to take over the digging, and expecting to find the buried treasure and be "pecuniarly independent" [11] for the rest of her days. She expressed this optimism in the very letter in which she shrewdly accused Henry of being a "dear Goose" for continuing to follow the lure of beet sugar.

In 1882 she was still on friendly terms with the "Princess," and took Elizabeth to the big house to meet her. The "old swindler," Elizabeth said, was wearing a shabby dressing gown, though she had expected their visit. She was "a short fat thick featured elderly woman with gray hair," who "puffed and groaned" as she raised her bulk to greet them.[12]

In 1883 Anna was searching for someone to pay off the mortgages of which she said she had *only* learned in February 1878, five years before, the knowledge having been "wickedly and stupidly" kept from her. In 1884 she was still certain of the treasure and of "the reality of the Royal birth," and believed it would be insane of her now to sell her rights in the affair. And later that year, when Marian described Anna as destroyed by her ceaseless effort, so that, at sixty-eight, she looked aged and walked feebly like a broken old woman,[13] Anna was still bemoaning the fact that because she lacked a small amount of capital, she was to lose a property where there was a possibility of making millions. By 1885 she was again filled with hope because, improbably enough, she had found funds among the French nobility. A duchess and a marquis and marquise were giving her money to renew the digging, a tribute to her powers of persuasion and the inexhaustibility of folly.

But by the fall of that year even Anna had ceased to believe, not in the buried hoard for which she still expected to dig, but in Madame Deville, who had now by simple, if long-delayed, transition, become "Mrs. Devil." Anna planned to bring a criminal action to send her and the Bouilliez to jail as swindlers for trying to cheat her of the share she had bought in the treasure in 1877. The criminal action was a countersuit to civil proceedings Mrs. Devil had instituted against her. Anna was "wild with horror and terror" at the idea of having to testify, but must try to get back at least the money she had borrowed from Mrs. Hodgson, and keep herself from becoming a pauper, dependent on her family. She now believed that she had been led astray from the first by her informing spirits in "a piece of spirit revenge and misleading." [14]

In mid-1886, though the criminal suit had been started in the last months of 1885, matters had somehow incredibly been straightened out again and digging had recommenced. "But this horrible task," said Anna, "so strangely laid upon me, *must* be nearing its conclusion one way or the other!" [15] And the next month they were digging up supposedly Etruscan coins, glass, pottery, metal bits, but no jewels. Late that year the "old Devil" died, but even then Anna found someone to continue the digging.

The following year the Blackwells were much agitated because Anna was in debt to the extent of two thousand francs for two lawsuits decided against her, and worse still, had been borrowing money from Marian, who had promised to sell her French securities to help her sister. Anna was not only impoverished but mortified that her dreams of enriching the family had come to nothing. She still had her little house, and in 1889 Marian and Frances, who continued to live together, decided to move to Triel to be nearer her. Frances was away a good deal, leaving Marian lonely, and when she was there, liked sociability more than the older woman did. Yet in her moments of depression, she needed Marian's solacing presence and could not bear to leave her.

To Henry's pleas that his sisters should return to the United States, Anna had said two years before that she could not leave

France permanently because she would lose her only remaining paper. She had heard of an inventor and magnetizer who had made a belt which prevented seasickness; if she had known of this sooner, she told Henry, she would have come for a visit, but it was too late now. She, Marian and Elizabeth were determined never again to cross that "hideous ocean." In any case, she told him the next year, he would no longer want her. The past five years had aged her a quarter of a century. She was a "worn-out hopeless old woman, ill, sad, disgusted with the world and longing to be out of it."[16]

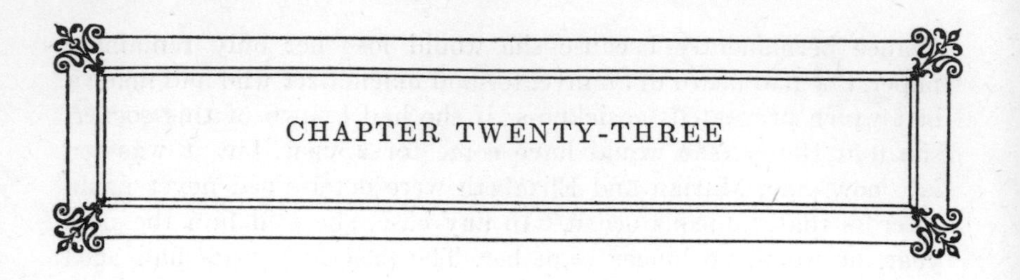

CHAPTER TWENTY-THREE

Whether Henry's impulse to have his sisters together was realistic is questionable. Elizabeth in England had managed to convey her disapproval of Anna in France so vehemently that for some time the relation between them was sorely strained. Indeed Elizabeth told Henry that Anna had so estranged her "affection by her proceedings" at Triel that she now felt bound to her eldest sister by family duty rather than personal fondness. Even so, their situation had none of the bitterness that was developing on the other side of the Atlantic between Emily and Ellen, who for years had lived in such close proximity. Whether this difficulty resulted from Ellen's impulse to take abandoned children endlessly into her heart and home, or whether that only exacerbated an inevitable conflict, it is hard to know.

The conflict certainly centered on the children. For Emily the final straw came when in 1876 Ellen took baby Pauli; and there was some justice in her dismay, for it seemed likely that Emily might ultimately become financially responsible for any child Ellen took. By 1878 the situation was tense. Emily was hoping to take the two older girls out of New York and to "make up"[1] a little income to take care of Ellen. Ellen, on her side, was complaining that Emily went off on vacations and left her saddled with the entire brood. A year and a half later, they were still managing to live together, but by then the accusations had grown shriller. Emily now believed both Cornelia (Neenie) and the younger girl, Susan, "quite beyond Ellen's power of management" when Emily had to be absent all day at the Infirmary. She also felt that Ellen found the housekeeping too difficult, and so failed to "make it a tolerable home." Emily had already refused to spend summers in the Lawrence house where, because it belonged to her, Ellen assumed "she ought to have the decisive voice in regard to household arrangements" [2]—which meant that Ellen insisted on keeping Paul there.

Under this pressure, both emotional and financial, Ellen decided to rent both the houses she now owned in the Rockaway area, and to go to Martha's Vineyard for the summer. Even with the houses rented, she was still in debt. She wrote and sketched and gave drawing lessons, and, like Anna, was constantly sure she was about to make a fortune, but, like Anna, she never did.

At almost the same moment when Emily was protesting about Ellen, Ellen was complaining that Emily owed her a hundred and fifty dollars in back rent on the Lawrence house. She sent Henry an elaborate accounting to prove Emily's indebtedness, and explained that though Emily had made a mistake in figuring, she now refused to discuss the matter. Alice said that both aunts confided in her mother, Ellen accusing Emily of being unkind and dictatorial, and that the two accounts were so conflicting that "if the two Aunt Es were not my aunts and both good women, I should say that there was a fib between them." [3] Alice expressed the family opinion when she said that Ellen had endless patience and kindness, but no judgment. "She is worthy of a crown in heaven; but meanwhile she will always be in hot water on earth." [4]

They all agreed Ellen ought to give up Pauli. Elizabeth went further. According to Alice, she wrote to Ellen, whose life without the children was empty, that she should give up not only Paul, but Neenie and Susie as well; even Emily did not want this, for she had "grown fond of Neenie, and reconciled to Susie, who she foresees may be useful in various ways." This dogmatism undeterred by secondary considerations was characteristic of Elizabeth, and is sometimes painful to observe, yet it was a ruthlessness which spared herself as little as others, and without which she could never have fought the seemingly insurmountable obstacles in the way of a woman's achieving a medical career.

She also tried, from far-off England, to enlist Henry's support in inducing Ellen to give up a boy "who has already acquired bad habits" and might bring disgrace on the family. Elizabeth believed Emily "constitutionally incapable of dealing with such a strong will as Ellen's"; [5] but in the event Emily seemed always to have the stronger will and Ellen the more ungovernable impulses.

That Ellen was not the ideal guardian for a group of children, there can be no doubt. Aside from her emotional problems, she had physical difficulties. As she grew older, she grew fatter, and, being short, was in her later years almost round. She was also increasingly deaf, and her only contact with the outside world was through a large ear trumpet. So equipped, she must have been a grotesque figure.

With her difficulties and the fact that she was barely able to provide for herself and Susie, her taking Pauli was a gesture quixotic in the extreme. Yet there is room to wonder whether Emily's additional ire, so much stronger than her reaction to the other children, may not have been because this child was a boy. Whatever the causes, the results must have been intolerable for young Paul, who from earliest childhood was constantly being "disposed of," and returned, only to be disposed of again. What was to have been a final disposal occurred early in 1881 when the boy was not yet quite five. He was sent to live on Long Island with a well-to-do family who wanted to adopt him and did give him their name. George's wife, Emma, herself now the mother of two sons, considered it "a forlorn life for a little child to go from place to place," and hoped "that this last" might prove a real home.[6] But fate was against him. Less than two years later his foster father died, and his foster mother, Mrs. Stedwell, no longer wanted a child in the house. Ellen, then living with the girls in Orange, New Jersey, took him there, whereupon Emily refused to supply her with housekeeping money while he remained. Ellen therefore delivered him again to Mrs. Stedwell, who refused to accept him; and when Ellen brought him back to Orange, there was such a scene with Emily that "the whole family, Nannie, Neenie, Aunt Ellen and Paul, dissolved in tears." [7]

In view of this history it is hardly surprising that when he was eight Ellen reported Paul's name being read out in school for "*de* merits." She coped with his recalcitrance by keeping him "under a continual fire of little penalties, and serious admonitions." He was less than eight when Ellen's suspicions of him were strengthened by his telling the maid that she had said he could have an apple when she had not. Ellen took the apple from him, at which he stuck out his tongue. She then put him in the cupboard. She considered his worst defect an "extreme petulance," his great virtue a sense of humor and love of fun.[8] He was generous too, and in the future would be "a giver rather than a receiver." [9] On one point she was determined. He was her adopted child and she would leave everything she possessed to educate him until he was eighteen. Sam and Nettie, who first saw Paul when he was four, had been astonished to find the monster of controversy a charming child. "He has a good open little face, appears truthful and docile, is a robust little chap." When Lucy and Henry came to know him a few years later, they too were much drawn to him.

If fate was unkind to the little boy, it was hardly kinder to Ellen, for in January 1883 her little blonde Susie, whom she adored, contracted scarlet fever and died. She was eleven years old. Ellen was heartbroken, and expressed herself, how loudly one cannot know, on the unfairness of its being angelic Susie rather than difficult Paul who had been taken from her. Later, when affairs had reached an astonishing complexity between her and Emily, she accused Emily of having caused Susie's death by coming to them directly from a house where there was scarlet fever.

It was not long after Susie's death when, in her sorrow, Ellen suffered a loss of a different kind. She and the children had been living in New Jersey for several years, and Emily, finding commuting too difficult, had arranged to have a room in New York with one of the young doctors on the Infirmary staff. With the passing of time Emily found her New York life increasingly attractive, as the New Jersey situation became correspondingly more irritating. Shortly after Susie's death she was contemplating taking

Nannie with her and leaving Cornelia with Ellen, though the two girls were close as sisters and had no wish to be separated.

Emily had originally roomed with Dr. Elizabeth Cushier, but by now Emily and Dr. Cushier, with her sister Sophie as housekeeper, had moved into Emily's house on Twentieth Street. Dr. Elizabeth Cushier was listed as a resident physician in the Infirmary report for 1874, and continued to rise in position on the staff. She was a tall, handsome, dark-haired woman who, unlike most of the doctors, troubled to have attractive, even dramatic, feminine clothes. "The Cushiers," Emily said, "keep house very well, and are very friendly and desirous to make things pleasant." She enjoyed again making her home "with grown people, and in a house . . . not arranged solely with reference to children." [10]

Yet there was more to it than that. When Dr. Cushier came to visit them in Massachusetts, Alice described Aunt Emily as going out to the gate "with a hop skip and jump of exultation . . . actually capering, in spite of her avoirdupois." Emily herself felt that she had a really comfortable home for the first time since she had left her mother's house. Almost the only people, she said, whose affection for her she considered strong and sincere were some of the young doctors who had studied under her supervision. For perhaps the first time in her life Emily felt she was loved. It was a heady tonic for a woman in her late fifties. Perhaps too, in this new Dr. Elizabeth, Emily found a surrogate for the sister whose path she had so hopefully followed, and in whose company she had been unable to make a life and a career.

This growing attachment made Ellen's situation more precarious than ever. She complicated it by the totally irrelevant idea that Dr. Cushier had designs on Emily's far from large fortune, and would induce her to will her money away from her relatives and adopted children. The Blackwells generally combined an extreme trustfulness in financial affairs with an equally extreme suspicion; and after Mr. Stedwell's death, Alice even accused Ellen of wishing to keep Pauli because she believed his foster father had provided for him.

Ellen had problems more real than these fantasies. In May 1884 she wrote to Henry that she had received a letter from Emily, "dissolving her connection with me, announcing her intention of taking away the children, 'dissociating her life from mine.'" This drastic move had evidently been precipitated by fear for the girls' welfare, for Ellen went on to say that Emily had put forth "unjust accusations against the poor children made simply on *hearsay,*" which from her knowledge of them she should have known to be untrue. "She makes no enquiry. The poor things are accused, judged, and sentenced, in a very summary way." Whatever the truth of Emily's suspicions, it was indeed a summary way to deal with a sister. Ellen rather pathetically added that she could no longer continue to be Emily's aide-de-camp, even if Emily desired it. She planned to make herself more independent. One of her methods was a project to board the children and members of the family for a weekly fee at her Vineyard house.[11]

The day after Christmas Ellen added another chapter to her tale. "Emily is making active preparation to carry Cornelia off to Wheaton, and Nannie to New York, with the idea of ending our connection and making the separation permanent. She is doing this without the slightest regard to my feelings or those of the girls. I think she is acting in an extremely arbitrary and cruel way. Her sole principle appears to be that 'might makes right'"; but it would have been closer to the mark to say that Emily's principle was, and always had been, that right makes might.

"All my 14½ years of devotion, as nursemaid seamstress, kindergarten teacher housekeeper counts for *nothing*. The children's bitter tears and entreaties count for nothing. Only seem to make her more set. I can't understand the influence at work." [12] The children, she added, were doing extremely well at a "capital school." And indeed even Emily admitted that the school was excellent.

Yet neither Emily nor Elizabeth was entirely ruthless. After events had worked out in the way Elizabeth felt they should, by the removal of the two girls from Ellen's care, she wrote her youngest sister a note of sympathy, "for the new arrangements in your domestic life must I am sure be very painful to you. And although I believe that the changes were inevitable, that belief in no way lessens my sympathy for the pain you must inevitably suffer." [13]

Emily, when it came to the point of taking the girls away, conceded for the first time that Ellen ought to be permitted to keep Paul, as a kind of consolation prize, it would seem, although this might be rather hard on Paul. It would be harder still on Paul if Cornelia too stayed with Ellen, for Cornelia carried tales which caused him to be treated "with chronic injustice."[14] Neenie at twelve had a habit of tattling, and at Martha's Vineyard was reported as teasing twenty-year-old Grace, who was nervous and childlike. When Grace tried feebly to retaliate, Neenie ran to Ellen and blamed everything on Grace.

Emily had always had a strong preference for well-behaved Nannie over Neenie. In this, as in her attempts to separate the two girls, she was encouraged by Dr. Cushier; and so it came about that, as Emily's plan took shape, Nannie lived more and more with her. Neenie was sent to school at Wheaton, then a seminary, and spent much time with Henry and Lucy, who lived in Boston, thirty miles away. Summers Ellen continued to go to the Vineyard, taking one or more of the children with her. When, in the summer of 1887, Dr. Cushier was invited on a European trip as medical advisor to a touring party, Emily with Nannie, Alice and Dr. Cushier's niece Lucie traveled over in the boat with her. Then Emily and her three young companions visited Elizabeth and afterward journeyed about Europe. Cornelia was left behind. Emily, though she had assumed responsibility for her, never treated her as Nannie's equal, though their foster cousin Flo found that Cornelia had "a good deal more to her than Nannie, only it is not brought out."[15] Yet the family, and Emily in particular, preferred Nannie, who was shy and ladylike, to Neenie, who was not.

As for Paul, he lived with Ellen, who became more and more incapable of providing a proper life for him. In the fall of 1886, when she was about to leave Martha's Vineyard, she arranged for Paul to stay there with farmer Herman Mayhew and to work for him. According to Alice, though Paul was very useful to him, Mr. Mayhew was mean to the boy, even refusing to buy him clothes. But when Ellen wished to find another place for him, Paul chose to stay with Mr. Mayhew, whom he loved, whom indeed he preferred to Ellen, perhaps because even the meanest of men seemed more desirable than the world of bickering females in which he had so far made his unhappy way. He may also have been influenced by a boyish fear of being laughed at, for Ellen by now created laughter. She carried her large ear trumpet, was very fat, and was followed everywhere by an equally fat dog named Fanny, on whom she lavished the love she had given her lost children. All three children, though they loved her, had now reached an age where it embarrassed them to be seen with her in public.

Many years before, after Lucy Stone had left Oberlin and her friend Nettie Brown had returned there to study theology, Nettie had confided to Lucy that, when she was a minister, she intended to adopt several children. Lucy, herself still unmarried, had replied, "Don't, don't, don't . . . take any children. . . . It will seem just like an old clucking hen who shows her setting propensity, without having any eggs, to the merriment of all the roosters, and the shame of all the hens . . . but the fact that God has made fathers as well as mothers necessary to the existence of children is conclusive evidence, to my mind, that the influence of both is necessary to their best development."[16] Certainly many of the problems involving Emily's and Ellen's adopted children resulted from their having no fathers. Yet the Blackwell women disapproved of each other's methods of bringing up children whether fathered or fatherless. And truly there were often oddities to be questioned. One such oddity revealed itself in the mid-eighties, when George and Emma had two sons and a daughter, and Lucy was writing Emma affectionate but chiding messages telling her she should give up the fad to which she currently adhered of feeding children only twice a day and babies perhaps three times.

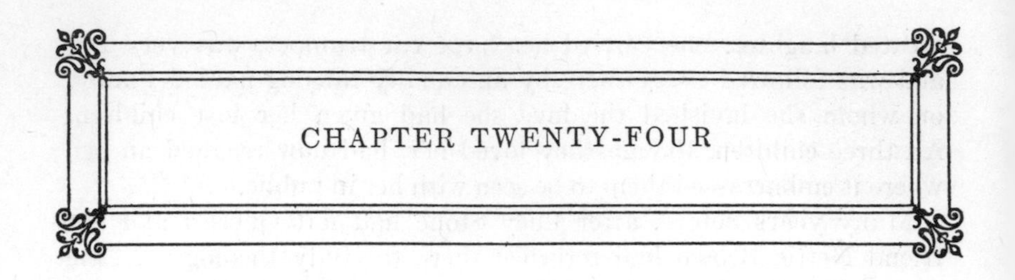

CHAPTER TWENTY-FOUR

In a sense the doctor sisters, and their sister-in-law Lucy as well, did more than disapprove of methods of upbringing. They disapproved of youth, for they had no patience with thoughtlessness or lack of discipline, the very essence of childhood.

In the summer and fall of 1881, there was an unusually large assemblage of Blackwells at Martha's Vineyard. It was before the breakup of Emily and Ellen's domestic arrangements, before Susie's death too. Ellen went to the island with her youthful brood, and in addition took Florence, who had not been well. Emily came several weeks later, to be followed by Kitty, who was spending six months visiting the American relatives, and was again winning every heart, children's and adults' alike. The family admitted that they talked to her with a freedom they never displayed toward each other, perhaps because Kitty lacked the censoriousness so common among the Blackwells. Even George, that cynical, sarcastic fellow, spoke of Kitty with an enthusiasm of which the family had never believed him capable.

During that summer Emily was thoroughly upset by Florence, who had fallen in love with Elliot Mayhew, a young neighbor, a year-round inhabitant of the island. Emily disapproved because, although he "bore a very good character" and was "a manly honest fellow of 29," his mother had rough manners and his sister a bad reputation. She was shocked too because Flo spent most of her time alone with him, which was far from respectable and set a bad example for the younger girls, in whom Flo confided, and who were fascinated by the development of her romance. Nettie and Sam, when appealed to, "declined to interfere, saying Flo was old enough to judge for herself," which brought Emily to the reluctant realization that "the girl was being destroyed by her life in Somerville, that her wishes and tastes were utterly on a different line and level from [Emily's], and that it was perhaps the one chance of her settling into a respectable, if common, marriage." On this basis she decided not to send Florence home, and merely tried to keep her within bounds. However, because of Flo's conduct, Emily began to consider taking Nannie and Cornelia to Europe for a few years. "I would rather see both of them dead, than have them grow up as some of our nieces and a good many American girls do, feeble, lazy, self indulgent and common." [1] She was determined never again to take any of Sam's girls away with her now that they were "old enough to flirt." [2]

Yet the outcome of this flirtation, so exasperating to Emily, was that the next year frivolous Flo married Elliot Mayhew and settled down to a far from frivolous life on the little island. Even the Blackwell men were so dubious of the outcome of this union that Flo's Uncle Harry suggested that he and George should each settle five hundred dollars on her, so that she could leave the island if life grew too tedious, and also because the money would increase her importance in the eyes of her new family.

The Mayhews owned a store and, at her cousin Alice's suggestion, Flo started a circulating library there, in order both to fill her time and to raise the island's cultural level. Eager to have a child and unable to have one, the flighty girl adopted a boy. In later years she and her husband helped to found the island hospital, and she fulfilled her secret ambition, so carefully guarded from her disapproving relatives, and became a lay preacher, an outcome which could hardly have shocked even Emily.

That summer of 1881 was unusual in Blackwell annals, for Kitty too had a flirtation. It was a small flirtation which caused a large flurry. Captain Asa Smith, who had been attentive when

Kitty was at the Vineyard before, renewed his attentions; and Ellen wrote to Elizabeth that Kitty, like Florence, had an island suitor. This so upset Elizabeth that she sent a telegram asking Emily for information. Emily responded promptly that Elizabeth "certainly need fear no Vineyard complications in [Kitty's] case. She was just girl enough to like to be rallied a little about her admirer, and there never was the smallest serious intention . . . or even attention beyond what wd naturally come from the very kindly feeling of himself and sister toward Kitty" [3]—a reply which might not have delighted some guardians of thirty-four-year-old spinsters, but seems to have alleviated Elizabeth's fears. She could have been reassured earlier, for Kitty confided to Alice that both she and Captain Asa were far too shy for anything to come of their attachment.

Kitty later discovered, to her indignation, that Ellen had described her interest in Captain Asa as a recurrence of a schoolgirl infatuation, and had reported that Kitty had been disappointed, but had borne up bravely. Elizabeth felt that Ellen had "vulgarly and impertinently" interfered with Kitty's "simple pleasant relations with the Vineyard people." She professed absolute trust in Kitty's "judgements and excellent instincts"—instincts which would perhaps keep her from marrying and leaving Elizabeth. Yet Alice later referred to the Captain as having hoped to marry Kitty. And Kitty, with a rare touch of irony, commented that though Emily had found Elliot socially inferior to Florence, she had considered Asa Smith quite suitable for Kitty.

Of the younger generation, Alice was most like her mother and her aunts. She was twenty-three that spring of 1881 when she was graduated from Boston University. She had for some time been helping to edit the *Woman's Journal,* had regularly written book reviews and articles for the paper, and was now to be a full-time editor. She was concerned with politics and had long assisted in the work of her parents' American Woman Suffrage Association. Of that virtuous young clan, she was most dedicated to virtue and most serious. Even her adored father's lightness of manner disturbed her. She wrote to Kitty critically, yet with a note of pride, that when her parents needed space in a crowded sleeping car, Papa had announced to the porter that they were the royal couple then traveling in the United States. "Wasn't that just like Papa? Very bright, but highly unprincipled." [4] As for herself, when she was visiting, and her hostess insisted she must let a young man who was with them pay her fare on the horsecars, Alice felt that her "self-respect was diminished by just the breadth of that car-ticket." [5]

Yet that romantic summer high-principled Alice too was suffering from an unhappy love affair. As long ago as 1877 a Mr. Black, a young man who was tutoring her in Greek, began to appear in her letters to Kitty. Though he was a Harvard student, she described him as different from the regular run of Harvard boys, who were a low type. She thought that "working for their living made boys more manly and knocked real character" [6] into them. Once, seeing Mr. Black at church, she walked in the opposite direction for fear he would think she had come to services to see him. On another occasion, he walked home with her, "but conducted himself pretty sensibly on the whole." Despite his virtues and his continued interest in Alice, Mamma and Papa took an odd view of him, and thought Alice a goose about him. They did not encourage his visiting her at home, though in spite of them he began to do so. He lived in Gardner, her aunt Sarah's home town, and in the summer of 1880 when Alice was vacationing there, he courted her, invited her driving with his sister, took her and her mother rowing, and entered into theological discussions with her in which, when she confessed her heresies, he turned out to be less orthodox than she. He infuriated her by maintaining that God was an unreal abstraction, an imperfect product of the human mind; and his letters were presumably a running dissertation on Spencer and Kant.

For about six years from the first mention of him, Mr. Black continued to appear in Alice's letters to Kitty, and always as Mr. Black. He never had a given name. In the summer of 1881 Elizabeth was describing Alice as being "in love where it is most undesirable she should be," which hardly seems to fit the respectable Mr. Black. Yet he was the only gentleman Alice mentioned in her correspondence with Kitty that summer, and she mentioned him often. She continued to speak of him after 1881, but as time went on her tone changed, and she had snubbed him or had not answered his letters, until in 1883, after a final rebuff, she reported that he had married his landlady, a handsome woman in her late forties.

But in 1881, when Kitty was visiting the United States, Alice was wandering from one summer resort to another trying to forget her unhappiness. Elizabeth, who later described Kitty and Alice's relation as "a real Jonathan and David attachment," [7] was much concerned for Kitty deprived of her friend. She wrote sympathetically enough of her hope that Kitty could get Alice away from "her cares and disappointments and 'love' scrapes . . . from . . . a most bitter rooting up of her life—a life in which a dangerous influence has mingled," and then really be able "to enter into communion with her." [8] But only two days later, presumably on learning that Alice was not joining Kitty, she was shocked that Alice had arranged to go elsewhere knowing "you were taking such a formidable journey on purpose to see the family. It shows how completely she is wrapped up in herself, and indeed I have yet to learn of one act of generous self sacrifice or self forgetfulness on Alice's part. But you can love her in spite of her faults, and I still hope that you may be able to arrange some time away from her most uneasy home when she will be alone with you. . . . I still think it was necessary that you should have gone to America this year—letters are one thing, and personal intercourse another, and events are rapidly stamping Alice's character in a way that makes it necessary you should know her as she is." [9] A sad motive surely for a three-thousand-mile journey.

Elizabeth's turning against Alice in defense of Kitty was one of the many signs of an attachment which had grown with the years. Whatever had been her emotions when she took the little orphan girl, her feelings now were of that dependence which commonly reverses the mother-daughter relationship as mothers, and daughters, grow older. At the same time her concern for Kitty's welfare was greater than it had ever been. She wrote to George that Kitty was to pay her board fully while in the United States, and to be under obligation to no one. She was to have plenty of funds to enjoy her trip, and not to spoil it by her overscrupulousness about money. She later wrote to Kitty, whom reports of Fenian uprisings had made fearful that the Irish would attack English steamers, that though the unrest was much exaggerated by the newspapers, and there was in fact no danger, Kitty might come on a French or German boat if that would make her feel safer. Even if they lost her return fare, no small matter in a household always pressed for funds, Elizabeth told Kitty that no expense was so important as her "comfort and thorough confidence." [10]

It was Kitty who decided that it would now be advisable to bring Flo's sister Grace back to England for a year. She was touched, as she always was by helplessness, by Grace's inability to cope with the more vigorous younger members of the family, by her lack of physical as well as mental stamina. Grace was to come to England to fulfill her ambition to study art, and was to be built up in physical strength by Dr. Elizabeth. But, in fact, Grace was bored and restless in the small seaside town where Elizabeth was now living, and Kitty and Elizabeth were constantly having to take her to London and Paris. As for her physical health, this was too bound up with her emotional instability to be capable of improvement. At the end of ten months the venture was given up as hopeless, and Grace was sent home.

It was Kitty whose preference was consulted when Elizabeth bought a home. In 1879 they had moved permanently from London to a rented house in Hastings on the English Channel, near the spot where William of Normandy fought the battle which made him master of England. It was a fine location for them, a lovely old town whose narrow hillside streets were, in the more ancient section, lined with wood-beamed white-plastered houses with overhanging upper floors. Some of the buildings dated back to the fifteenth century. On the steepest hills the sidewalks were built high above the road level, so that one entered the first floor of the houses from the street, while the basement entry opened on the roadway. The fact that the town was built on two sharp hills and on the cleft between them not only made it picturesque, but protected it from the cold blasts of England's winter winds. It also had a climate unusually sunny for that rainy country.

Here Elizabeth and Kitty finally settled into a red brick house, built on the side of a cliff high above the water. The house was approached on the land side by a steep hill up Exmouth Place, where from the street level a precipitous flight of stairs led down to a veranda overlooking the beach and sea far below. On the land side the upper windows looked out on green fields across which one could walk to the ruins of the ancient castle. On the water side the view would have satisfied the most demanding romantic. Besides the sea, where later they could watch the building of a breakwater, there was a beach where fishing boats lay at the water's edge, when they were not dotting the sea itself. On the beach was a row of high narrow huts, tarred over until they were black, where the fishermen hung their nets to dry. It was this "Rock House" which, in deference to Kitty's wishes, Elizabeth bought in 1883, and where she spent most of the rest of her life.

It was at Kitty's request too that Elizabeth here began in 1887 to write the informal memoirs which finally appeared in 1895 under the formidable title of *Pioneer Work in Opening the Medical Profession to Women.* The notes, addressed to Kitty, began with these significant words: "I should hardly care to [make this record of my past life] if I were not prompted by my affection for you; for as I draw near the borderland, the individual life seems so small, in comparison with the grand whole, that I should be well content, to let any useful work done, speak for itself, whilst the very imperfect worker were forgotten. . . . The little unknown child, whom I took to myself 33 years ago, at a very dreary time of my life, and whom I carried up to bed in my arms—has proved a real daughter to me; and this record shall be a legacy of my affection to her." [11]

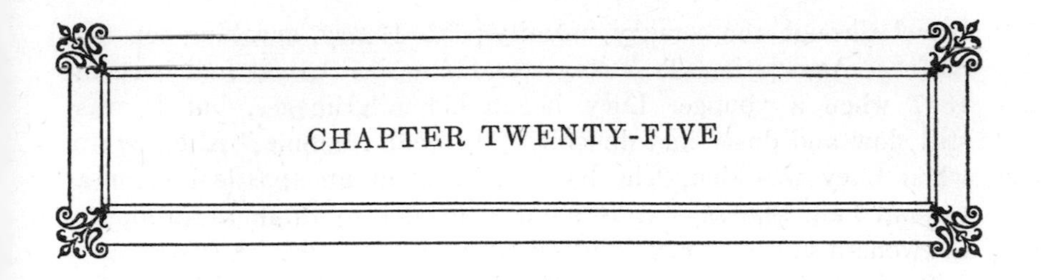

CHAPTER TWENTY-FIVE

If the Blackwells were intolerant of youth, neither did they succumb to age. It was the mature years, the years of discretion, of dedication to world betterment which they respected and to which they clung. Writing to Kitty in 1886 that she ought to induce Elizabeth to visit the American relatives, some of whom she had not seen since she left for England in 1869, Alice said, "She would find Uncle Sam just as saintly as ever, and Papa as fascinating and sinful, and Aunt Emily as sensible and dignified, and Aunt Ellen as kind-hearted and wrong-headed. Uncle G is the only one who has changed much, and he has changed for the better." [1] She could have added that, aware as they were of drawing "near the borderland," their commitment, their energy for reform was undiminished. Aging, white-haired, overweight they might be, but the vigor of their spirit seemed to suffer no decline.

Even illness did not long impede them. Lucy was so sick in 1880 that Alice left college for a time to go to Delaware with her. Lucy had for several years been plagued by a variety of ailments: increasing rheumatism, severe throat and chest infections and sudden attacks of faintness that made her feel she was "dissolving." Yet except in periods of acute illness she continued to edit the *Woman's Journal,* to write extensively for it, and to travel through the country, usually with Henry, speaking for the Suffrage Association. Traveling was far easier than it had been in 1847 when a younger Lucy began her pilgrimages, but it was still slow and dusty and difficult. "My dear Mamma," Alice wrote when Lucy was sick, "she has the heart of an apostle if ever a woman had. She says it is no use for her to think of dropping the woman suffrage work—she 'might just as well die.' "[2]

In the fall of 1882 Henry left his sugar-making experiments to go with Lucy to conventions in Wisconsin and in Nebraska, where a woman-suffrage amendment was to be put before the voters, and where, though the support was far greater than in former times, the result was again a defeat. They could by now leave the *Journal* in Alice's competent hands. In July 1883 Nettie, Lucy and Henry visited Oberlin. Sam was not with them. In 1880, with Nettie often away from home trying to augment the insufficient family income by preaching and lecturing, he had taken a temporary position with the Mexican Telegraph Company of New York, a position which turned out to be the most permanent he ever had. He therefore missed Nettie and Lucy's triumphant return to their college, where Nettie was enrolled by her fellow alumni as a graduate of the theological school, though the degree was still denied her, and Lucy, who in 1847 had not been permitted to read her own graduation essay, was invited to deliver a Fourth of July address.

If the younger graduates and students expected to see two hardened fighting females, they must have been amazed. Lucy was now round and comfortable in appearance, with a warm, motherly smile. She was dressed, as was her custom in these later years, in a dark dress, with a white, shawl-like lace collar, and on her head a demure lace cap. As for Nettie, Alice later described her as growing handsomer as she grew older. "She looks like a Dean, or a Bishop, or something. It is a very fine face."[3] And these two ladies were accompanied by Lucy's husband, a benevolent white-bearded gentleman who at fifty-eight looked like a sixty-five-year-old Santa Claus, and who, a few years later, when his daughter saw him in the morning "half-dressed and with his hair in disorder" and told him he looked picturesque, replied that things going to ruin were always called picturesque.[4]

In these years Henry continued, with a persistence that yielded to no defeat, to experiment with sugar-making; but in the mid-eighteen-eighties he also turned to the other money-making venture which had always enthralled the Blackwells. He bought property in Dorchester and began to build houses for sale. This enterprise was more realistic and more successful, if less idealistic, than beet sugar. As when Lucy first came into his life, his main interest was still, or so Alice believed, "a hope of making money." Yet after thirty years of marriage Lucy continued to be disgusted by each new financial venture, and Henry was still devoting his major energies to the battle for woman's rights. When he offered to run the *Woman's Journal* if Lucy would go south for the winter, Lucy refused, and Alice commented that if her mother had gone, Papa would have been lonesome and blue. But more than that, Alice went on, "He is very sociable and needs someone to talk to; and if she were not here he would talk to other people who ought not to be let into things." The suffrage movement had to be handled with tact, "whereas Papa's pugnacity is apt to be greater than his discretion." [5]

The Puritan morality, even more characteristic of the Stone-Blackwells than of the rest of that moral family, had abated no more than their energies. When the newspapers reported in 1880 that sixty-year-old George Eliot had married only two years after the death of George Lewes, with whom she had lived for so many years, Lucy refused to believe the news. It must be someone else, not her admired George Eliot.[6] Several years later Alice was disbelieving and Lucy shocked at reports of Garibaldi's morals and how he "came by Mme. Anita," [7] for they demanded of reformers the highest standards of personal virtue.

This persistent morality caused the *Woman's Journal* to come out against Grover Cleveland and in favor of James G. Blaine in the election of 1884, in spite of Cleveland's admirable record and Blaine's disreputable one. This was partly because Blaine was the Republican candidate, and to the old-line antislavery people the Republican Party was the party of freedom; it was also because Cleveland was accused—whether rightly or wrongly was never clear—of fathering an illegitimate child. This accusation he chose to ignore, causing the *Woman's Journal* to accuse him of undermining the American home and the "purity and safety" of the nation.

More lurid, though less public, was Alice's concern several years later for the virtue of her young cousin Howard. Howard was only ten when his younger brother, Laurie, who had been sickly for most of his short life, died of pneumonia at the age of six. George and Emma decided to take their two remaining children, Howard and his three-year-old sister, Anna, to Georgia for the winter. About this project Alice made the extraordinary comment, "I hope if they get a colored servant she won't corrupt Howard's morals." Alice found a safeguard in the fact that the boy told his mother everything. She also suspected that "the censorious streak which is very strong in [ten-year-old] Howard (as in most young Blackwells) . . . is a support to his morals." [8]

She came by her view of the power and prevalence of temptation naturally enough. Several years before, she had confided to Kitty, with instructions not to tell Aunt Elizabeth, that Papa had been upset by one of Elizabeth's manifestoes on the regulation of vice, because he felt it outlined "all the abominations of the continent, and the old world, and that he would not for the world have it circulate on this side of the water among young people, and especially boys, as it would be likely to put into their heads varieties of wickedness which otherwise they would never think of." [9] This response might well have astonished Elizabeth, who, in her researches into the darker phases of European customs, was fighting the battle of Christian Socialism and moral reform.

It could hardly have surprised her more than another reaction of Henry's, for late in 1885, when little Laurie was failing rapidly, Henry, to his daughter's indignation, expressed astonishment that George and Emma intended to leave the boy in the hands of "'women doctors instead of scientific doctors.' He has faith in Dr. Emily, I think," said Alice, "but outside of his own family, he seems to regard all women doctors with distrust. And he doesn't think much of doctors anyway." [10] Henry was relieved when a man was called in, but in spite of his ministrations little Laurie died some months later. Elizabeth had no inkling of her brother's doubts, nor, it is to be hoped, had his feminist wife, at whose side he had fought over the years in defense of the equality of women.

In far-off England Elizabeth was pursuing her various crusades with vigor. She lived in Hastings and journeyed regularly to London to attend meetings and deliver lectures. She was still known to the family as having some young man always in tow. Kitty in fact reported that there were sometimes as many as six, and in the mid-eighties, when Elizabeth was over sixty, a young barrister, Mr. Rowland Estcourt, for some time led the field.

Yet Elizabeth was aware of advancing years, and made more aware by the fate of her friends. Charles Kingsley, Lady Byron, Herman Bicknell, George Eliot, Dante Gabriel Rossetti, all were dead. Of the group that remained, Florence Nightingale, the same age as Elizabeth, was an invalid who had for years believed death to be imminent. She was one of the most powerful invalids in history. From her bed her influence spread over England. She wrote voluminous notes, memoranda, letters. Indeed in the mid-eighties her health was rather better than it had been for years. And her dream was realized. Hospitals were organized on sanitary principles; and the hospitals of England were filled with nurses taught in the Nightingale Training School. Ill, and sometimes so mentally beset as to be out of contact with reality, she was nevertheless a legend in her own lifetime. Her friend Benjamin Jowett told her that, after the Crimean War, England was full of baby girls named Florence. "Everyone has heard of you and has a sweet association with your name," the great classicist said.

In 1885 Florence's cousin Barbara Bodichon, who was seven years younger than Florence and Dr. Elizabeth, and who had been partially paralyzed for nearly eight years, lost her husband. Though Elizabeth had known the Bodichons through a long and loving marriage, she nevertheless, out of a spinsterhood far deeper than the mere lack of a wedding ring, wrote to Kitty, "Saw Barbara yesterday—I have never seen her look so shaken—I had no idea she would take her husband's death so much to heart—she looked like a feeble old woman!" She felt that Barbara's entourage were trying to make an invalid of her, like Florence Nightingale.

Elizabeth, if not looking for new worlds to conquer, was not turning away her eyes. On becoming a householder in Hastings, she was entitled to vote in municipal elections and was early petitioned by Liberals and Conservatives for her support; but since it seemed to her that both were motivated by party advantage, not social well-being, she refused to involve herself with either. Later, concerned with the heavy burden of taxation which she felt was driving the poor into pauperism, and with the diversion of "poor funds" to middle-class projects, she attended a meeting of the municipal council. To her astonishment she was the only ratepayer present. Worse, when she tried to interest substantial members of the community in city problems, they shrugged away responsibility. Finally when a new Corporation Bill was proposed which "re-enacted the obsolete regulation which regards vice as female" and attempted to turn Hastings into a "fashionable lodging-house town . . . instead of promoting permanent productive industry," the citizenry did become aroused enough to stop the passage of certain portions, but most of the bill went through in spite of protest.

Elizabeth, who had always been rather scornful of Lucy's and Nettie's concern with politics, now decided that women must join with poor taxpayers to fight municipal decay. She believed the national character to be at stake in its submission to official formalism. Ever the old-line Christian Socialist, she was convinced that citizens must "resolutely battle for the Theocratic Principle of human rights." As always when a cause drew her, Elizabeth sat down and wrote a firm, logical and simple statement of her aims, *On the Decay of Municipal Representative Government.*

Across the Atlantic, Emily, less verbal, less aggressive in public action, but always willing to follow where Elizabeth led, wrote a long article which appeared sectionally in two issues of the *Woman's Journal* reviewing Elizabeth's pamphlet and describing her thesis in detail. Emily argued that women in the United States ought to be given the vote in local elections. Municipal housekeeping was only an extension of domestic, and therefore a field in which women were already proficient. To keep the municipal vote from them was as unrealistic as to separate husband and wife in decisions about household and family.[11]

Meanwhile even Ellen had managed to lift herself from overwhelming personal defeats to a new vigor. All her life, though

Blackwell enough to be concerned with every aspect of reform, her deepest interest had been in art, in music, in the people she loved. Now she found a cause to which she could turn the devotion she had lavished on her lost children. In 1885 her contact with Neenie and Nannie was limited to their visiting her for a day or two at a time. Only Paul was still with her, and he, so battered about, was sullen and inexpressive.

She was still sure she could make a fortune in real-estate development. In 1886, besides her Long Island houses, in one of which she was living, and her two houses in New Jersey, both of which were rented, she was building a summer cottage in Rockaway.[12] Less than two months later, with the shell up, she had no money to continue, and grass was growing on the ground floor. When she had not even enough money to buy food for herself and Paul, Emily contributed two hundred and fifty dollars, and George the same amount, though he believed it would require a thousand dollars to complete the building.[13] Yet that year Ellen was able to sell her original Lawrence house for ten thousand dollars.

But her abundant emotion had turned to a new cause: Anna Ella Carroll. In the mid-eighties when Ellen began to dedicate herself to her rehabilitation, Miss Carroll was nearly seventy, sick, poor, neglected. This had not always been her story. She was the descendant of two of the richest and most famous families of Maryland. Brought up on a plantation, taught by an intelligent, well-educated father, who served as governor of his state, she was that rare specimen in those days, an intellectual woman. Much sought after, she nevertheless refused every opportunity to marry because, according to Ellen, she preferred to stay with her beloved father, whose "congenial presence seemed to be all-sufficient for her."

At the beginning of the Civil War, Miss Carroll freed her personal slaves; and she and her father supported the Northern cause. The citizens of Maryland were sharply divided. One of the first Massachusetts regiments, on its way to join the army, was attacked by a secessionist mob in Baltimore. But Governor Thomas Hicks was determined to keep Maryland in the Union. He sent Anna Ella to Washington as his emissary, and she further aided him by her able letters and articles in the press, which were effective in swinging popular support toward loyalty to the North.

A letter from Governor Hicks expressed his flowery gratitude: "When all was dark and dreadful for Maryland's future, when the waves of secession were beating furiously upon your frail executive . . . you . . . skillfully helped to work the ship, until, thank God, helmsmen and crew were safe in port." [14]

From the beginning of the war Miss Carroll was fascinated by military maps and troop maneuvers, and as plans were developed for opening the Mississippi by forcing a passage down it, she grew ever more certain that the strong Southern fortifications made such an enterprise impossible. She therefore traveled to St. Louis to learn the opinion of the river pilots, who agreed that the Mississippi could never be opened by gunboats. She then inquired about the navigability of the Cumberland and Tennessee Rivers, and learning that they were navigable, made a report to Assistant Secretary of War Thomas A. Scott at his request, suggesting the plan of moving the army up the Tennessee to take Forts Donelson and Henry. It was later repeatedly asserted by Secretary Scott and Senator Benjamin Wade that this plan was sent to the President, and that Mr. Lincoln then ordered the attack.

Miss Carroll had recommended that the thrust continue to Muscle Shoals, Alabama, and later contended that, had this strategy been followed, the war could have been ended in 1862. She also wrote to the Secretary of War telling him that Vicksburg could only be taken from the rear, not from the river, as had been attempted, a prophecy which also proved to be correct. In later testimony, Benjamin Wade, as a member of a Military Committee of the Senate, stated that both the President and Mr. Stanton had recognized Miss Carroll as the author of the plan which saved the Union, but, because of the jealousy of the military, Mr. Lincoln felt it inadvisable to make public during the war that a civilian, and worse, a woman, had originated the maneuvers. After the war Lincoln was dead, and Miss Carroll never received the credit which over the years Senator Wade and Secretary Scott persisted in claiming for her.

Miss Carroll's father lost his money and later died. From 1870 Miss Carroll attempted to persuade Congress to pay a bill of five thousand dollars for expenses she had incurred for pamphlets she had written and published during the war, on the basis of an informal arrangement with Secretary Scott that the War Department would reimburse her. One of the pamphlets, *The Power of the President to Suspend the Writ of Habeas Corpus,* was much lauded by Mr. Lincoln, and with others, including *The Relation of the Revolted Citizens to the United States,* was widely circulated with excellent propaganda results. The Military Committee repeatedly reported favorably on her claim. Congress repeatedly shelved the reports. By 1885, Anna Ella was poor and very ill. She had been stricken by paralysis, Ellen said, and for three years hovered between life and death before slowly regaining some vitality. Now she was living in Washington, and entirely supported by her sister Mary, who worked for the government.

The *Woman's Journal,* the woman's rights movement in general, had taken up her cause; and in 1891 Ellen, under her full name of Sarah Ellen Blackwell, published a book to bring Miss Carroll's plight before the public. Ellen, as she did with everything which captured her mind, gave her whole heart to the crusade. It became her habit, even when, besides her increasing weight and deafness, she was partially crippled by rheumatism, to spend six months of the year in a lonely boarding house in Washington, promoting Miss Carroll's cause.

In her absorption with Anna Ella, she one day entered into argument with Emily about General Grant, claiming that he was "not a man of any military genius." The discussion followed a familiar Blackwell pattern for, according to Alice, Aunt Emily "effected a diversion in Grant's favor" by pointing out the uprightness of his life. When one of his officers started to tell an "indelicate" story because there were no ladies present, Grant was said to have replied, "But please to remember that gentlemen *are.*" This high moral tone "somewhat mollified" Aunt Ellen, who said it was splendid, far the best thing she had ever heard of Grant.[15]

Perhaps Washington, where she had the companionship of the Misses Carroll, was not much lonelier for Ellen than New York, where in the late eighties even Paul was not with her, and she was living much of the time alone in a single room with her fat dog Fanny. It seems characteristic of the disorder of Ellen's life that one day Fanny gave birth to three puppies there in Ellen's one room. Ellen worked every day and evening at the Academy of

Art "partly to keep from being lonesome."[16] But even then fate was not through with her, and in 1889 her big house in Long Island burned to the ground with most of her possessions in it.

Anna Ella Carroll died in 1894, her claim still unsatisfied, her alleged service to her country unrecognized. As Ellen said of herself, every effort she ever made for the "right" seemed doomed to failure. It was. Ellen's failure, like Anna's, was inevitable. Such undeviating energy and conviction as the Blackwells' must be effectively leashed and directed throughout a lifetime, or they are doomed.

CHAPTER TWENTY-SIX

Henry and Lucy had no need to search for new causes. For them there were old worlds unconquered. Though sympathy for woman's rights was now widespread, the crusade Lucy had chosen in her early years was far from won. Legislatures in Western states continued to submit suffrage amendments to male voters. Men continued, though perhaps by narrower margins, to defeat them. Equality won in the territorial legislatures of Washington and Utah was lost when the courts declared the Washington law unconstitutional, and the national Congress, fighting Mormonism and multiple marriage, withdrew the vote from the women of Utah whether Mormon wives or not.

The suffrage movement had suffered from the long split between the two factions. The American and National Associations inevitably clashed, duplicating or contradicting each other's efforts, competing for always inadequate funds. Their ideological—and emotional—division was no less than it had been, and such necessary contacts as there were between the elder leaders were acrimonious and uncompromising.

Probably the bitterest pill for Lucy and her cohorts was the publication by Mrs. Stanton, Miss Anthony and one of their colleagues of a huge and detailed *History of Woman Suffrage.* This history, carried on by their successors, eventually comprised six volumes, each nearly a thousand pages long. The first volume appeared in 1881, the second in 1882. The second volume contained a biased account of the split between the factions, and in a single chapter of one hundred and seven pages disposed of the work of the American Association over a period of nearly twelve years. Even without this disproportion, the account would necessarily have been one-sided. History is not only a series of complex events; it is the record of those events as seen and believed by future generations, and it may be seized in books as surely as territory is occupied in battle. In writing their history, Mrs. Stanton and Miss Anthony took possession of the past of the movement, so that to this day they are known as its leaders, while Lucy Stone's name, at the time she lived of at least equal importance with theirs, is virtually unknown.

But in the second half of the eighteen-eighties a new generation was moving into the forward ranks of suffragists. These younger women, less aware of personal dissension and less bitter than their predecessors, were impatient of the ancient feuds that divided their ranks. For her part, Lucy, ill and feeling her years, was eager to put aside her burdens without shifting them onto Alice's shoulders.

Lucy continued to alternate between periods of serious illness and astonishing vigor. Alice was now in the forefront of activity. She had spread her efforts beyond the suffrage movement, and was an official of the Woman's Christian Temperance Union, in which she was associated with Anna Howard Shaw. Miss Shaw, like the older Blackwells, had been born in England and emigrated with her parents to the United States. Like Antoinette, but with so much less struggle, she had become a preacher. Ten years older than Alice, this round-bodied, round-faced, clear-eyed woman was her good friend. She was also an ardent temperance and suffrage worker. The link between temperance and woman suffrage, as between all reform movements in those days, was close. Susan Anthony had come to suffrage by way of temperance work.

But in the mid-seventies the temperance movement had been metamorphosed from an instrument of quiet persuasion to a psalm-singing crusade. Throughout the Middle West bands of women gathered in the streets, singing and praying and blocking the entrances to saloons. Sometimes, inflamed to greater militancy, they armed themselves with axes and smashed whiskey barrels. Many of the suffrage supporters, Lucy's close friend and coworker Mary Livermore among them, were leaders of the W.C.T.U.; and in the early eighties Lucy converted its president, Frances Willard, to woman suffrage. This link between the two reforms was disastrous to woman suffrage. It added yet another reason for unpopularity to the already far from popular cause. Though some men in the Middle West had been caught in the hysteria and joined the temperance forces, the majority had not learned to love the ladies who spilled their liquor and prayed publicly for their souls.

Henry saw this clearly. In 1889 when the territories of Montana, Washington and the Dakotas were about to become states, he made a prolonged tour for the purpose of persuading them to include woman suffrage in their new constitutions, and having failed, returned to South Dakota the following year to urge the Republican Party to include a woman suffrage plank in their platform, which they did not do. From the earlier trip he wrote home a partial explanation of his failure. In arraying women against men, he said, Miss Willard and her Association were "the most dangerous enemies" of woman suffrage. "The men are overwhelmingly for the saloons." Yet armed with this clear perception, on his return, as though honesty of purpose were more important than success, he helped to organize a group of antisaloon Republicans in Massachusetts.

Alice's activities in the Temperance Union and other reform organizations brought her into close contact with the younger leaders of the National Woman Suffrage Association, and among them they began to consider the virtues of reunion. The path was stony, the mistrust mutual, the tactlessness widespread. In the spring of 1887 Lucy, recovering from one of her many illnesses, went to stay with Emma and George, who with their children were wintering in Georgia. From Massachusetts Alice poured out her doubts of the other faction, and, surprisingly, it was her mother who had to reassure her. The next winter a meeting between Susan Anthony and Lucy took place at the *Woman's Journal* offices. Susan brought Rachel Foster, one of her young aides, with her. Miss Foster was an attractive, vigorous and wealthy young woman whom Alice already knew, in whom she had placed her always too easily won faith, and through whom she had suffered her always too easily induced disillusion. Alice served as her mother's second in what was indeed a duel for leadership of any future united organization, a duel in which Susan went so far as to suggest that the *Woman's Journal* ought to be abandoned in favor of a four-year-old newspaper published weekly in Nebraska by a leader of the National. After the meeting, the National continued a campaign to have Susan named president of the combined organization, an outcome Lucy could not accept.

In the spring an International Council of Women, organized by Susan, met in Washington to celebrate the fortieth anniversary of the Seneca Falls convention, the first woman's rights convention. Lucy Stone and the other heads of the American Association, Antoinette Brown Blackwell among them, were officially honored along with Mrs. Stanton and Susan Anthony; but in a speech, Mrs. Stanton could not resist attributing the beginnings of the movement to Susan Anthony and Lucretia Mott, though Susan had not joined the ranks until several years after the Seneca Falls meeting, and herself stated that she had been converted to the cause by Lucy. Alice said that Susan had called on Lucy to speak, but that even this seemingly friendly gesture had really been unkind, "one of those pieces of ostensible friendliness and real unfriendliness that are very riling to me,"[1] for Lucy had not been forewarned and was totally unprepared. And that summer Susan traveled through the Middle West visiting the American's local organizations in an attempt to capture them.

That the efforts toward amalgamation went on, that differences were wiped out and negotiations continued, was a miracle. Even Susan Anthony's somewhat idolatrous biographer Ida Husted Harper later stated that "no one person contributed so much toward the union of these two societies as Alice Stone Blackwell." By 1889 the majority of both societies were eager for union, and in February 1890 the first annual meeting of the National-American Woman Suffrage Association took place in Washington.

Lucy was again too ill to go. Her favorite brother, Bowman, had just died, and grief was added to sickness. Henry and Alice went, and to them Lucy wrote, pitying them in their battle with "the enemy." She had reason to be fearful. The backbiting and jockeying for position continued for years, until the old guard had died. And in spite of Lucy's efforts to keep all three leaders out of front positions, Elizabeth Stanton was elected president, Susan vice-president, and Lucy herself chairman of the executive committee. Susan had again managed to seize the spotlight.

During the difficult period of rapprochement Lucy had undertaken additional household burdens. Since 1885 when Cornelia, wrenched from Ellen's grasp, had entered Wheaton Seminary, she had spent much of her time in Lucy and Henry's home, and usually one and sometimes two of Nettie's daughters were also there. The gap between Cornelia and Emily, increased by Dr. Cushier's dislike of the girl, had widened beyond repair, and she was shunted about so as not to be at Emily's home and still not be left with Ellen. Yet in the summer of 1885, even though Cornelia was dependent on Lucy for at least a partial home, Emily told Lucy that she knew "well enough what Cornelia is, even under my control, to know she must have been a trial." The girl was "quite approaching maturity in some things, utterly childish in others." Emily said that Neenie wished to return in the fall to Wheaton and the company of young people there, and added, with the scorn of a Blackwell for a life of pleasure, that Cornelia's interests were purely social.[2] Yet a report from Wheaton the following year indicated that not only was Neenie doing well at school, but that she consistently chose desirable companions.

In the summer of 1886, Emily went with Nannie to visit Dr. Cushier and her niece Lucie in the Berkshires. Miss Sophie Cushier having married and deserted the New York household, Lucie had become their housekeeper. Neenic was not taken along. Instead Emily arranged for her to exchange visits with school friends. But the attempt to divide Neenie from Nannie had so completely failed that the two girls arranged to write daily journals for each other during their enforced separation. By the fall of 1887 Emily had decided that Cornelia should leave Wheaton, but she succumbed to the girl's pleas sufficiently to leave her there for at least one more term. However, a few months later Emily had prevailed, as she usually did in family plans, and Cornelia was sent to school in New Jersey near Sam and Nettie's home in the El Mora section of Elizabeth, where she could spend Sundays with their daughter Agnes, her close friend. The next summer she was again left out of plans which included Dr. Cushier, and stayed in New Jersey.

In 1887 and 1888 Lucy's household included two of Nettie's daughters, Edith and Ethel, both studying in Boston with the hope of becoming doctors like their famous aunts. Even this seriousness of purpose did not endear them to their critical relatives. In 1885 Edith, at the top of her class at Swarthmore, was taken ill and had to drop out. Alice, who did not like Dr. Cushier and could not see what made her "such a universal fascinator,"[3] reported that, though Edith was eager to return to school and determined to become a doctor, the powerful Dr. Cushier had convinced Emily that her niece was merely using illness as an excuse to abandon her medical ambitions.[4] She was wrong. Edith did not give up. By March 1888 she had been with the Stone-Blackwells for sixteen months, and her sister Ethel had been there for a school year. They were studying hard, too hard, according to Alice.

She told Kitty that her parents were far from happy with the two girls. They had loved Edith at first, for when she was happy, she was charming, but when she was dissatisfied, as she usually was, she was extremely disagreeable, "argumentative and pugnacious like the rest of us." Her faults, which became more obvious with time, and apparently with Lucy's increasing rebukes, were that she was unpunctual, which Lucy could not bear, and that, disliking housework, she not only shirked it herself, but induced her more willing sister not to help either. This was irritating to Lucy not only on a practical level, but because she was impatient of anyone whom she suspected of having "a contempt for manual labor." Edith fared no better with Henry, who considered her "lethargic and lazy." The very sound of her voice "drove him crazy" when he was tired. Yet they considered it their family duty to keep her on. It is not surprising that this attitude reflected itself in Edith's mood. Alice found her despondent and shy, with a sense—all too well-founded in that household—that no one liked her. When Alice, feeling sorry for the girl, made much of her, she blossomed.

Alice ended her report with a generalization none of the elder generation would have formulated. "It is odd that the Blackwells, while really attached to each other, should find it so hard to live together. I suppose we are an exceptionally angular family; and Edith is the most Blackwelly of Uncle Sam's daughters."[5]

Both Edith and Ethel studied at the Massachusetts Institute of Technology, where, to the disgust of the rest of the family, vivisection was practiced and used in teaching. In spite of Emily's suspicions, Edith was later graduated at the head of her class from Emily's own Woman's Medical College of the New York Infirmary, and accepted an assistantship in physiology there. The same spring, Ethel was graduated from college, and went on to study medicine at the Infirmary. Several years earlier, Agnes, the prettiest of Sam and Nettie's daughters, studying art at Cooper Union, had won the highest prize in life class. She later took a position as professor of art at a seminary in Texas. All these developments were duly recorded in the *Woman's Journal,* which naturally made no comment on how much better these girls had turned out than their relatives had anticipated. Only Grace, ill and mentally disturbed, did not develop.

The *Journal* also gave accounts of Alice's busy and useful life, as well as of her summers, which in the late eighties and early nineties were spent at a primitive camp in the Canadian woods. The camp was most respectably run by Mrs. Isabel Barrows, wife of a minister who edited the *Christian Register*. Here with an almost childlike abandon Alice entered into the "larks" and pleasures of camp life, so different from her staid and serious home. In the summer of 1890, so much had the younger suffragists forgotten the battles of their elders, she was joined for a short while by Anna Howard Shaw and Lucy Anthony, Susan's niece. What the *Journal* could not record was Alice's state of mind, which, in 1889, after her return from camp and the brief period of relaxation there, she herself explained to Kitty. "But I must manage to get a little more fun somehow. . . . Papa and Mamma are only too anxious to have me have amusements, but . . . most things which are recommended as amusing are simply bores. I can hardly keep awake at lectures, or at the Women's Club."[6] The sole idea that had occurred to her for brightening her life was to go every week or two to secondhand bookstores to see what she could find.

In 1893 when Alice was nearly thirty-six, a short respite from boredom came her way. That summer an attractive Armenian theologian, Johannes Chatschumian, was at the camp in Canada. Alice and he became friends, and together translated Armenian poetry into English. It was only after her mother's death that Alice could admit, even to herself perhaps, that she was in love with Johannes. But this romance too ended in disaster. In 1896 her Armenian friend was taken ill on a ship on his way to France. With Mrs. Barrows, Alice went at once to nurse him, only to learn on her arrival in France that he had died. As a legacy he left her a concern for the Armenian cause to which she devoted many years of her life.

Meanwhile, toward the end of the eighteen-eighties, Lucy and Henry had "adopted" a teen-aged girl whose mother, when she immigrated from Germany years before, had worked for Lucy, and who, dying, had turned to her former employer for help in providing for her two young daughters. Alice, again with an emotional childishness far beneath her years, deeply resented her parents' affection for the interloper, Beth Hagar, who was half member of the family, half maid, for Alice's cousin Howard remembers that she was treated like a daughter, but did not eat with the family. Yet after Lucy's death she stayed on with Henry and Alice; and even after Beth married, Alice remained her friend.

Lucy and Henry did not legally adopt Beth. None of the Blackwells went that far with the children they took in. Yet they continued to shelter waifs. George and Emma too took a child, little Emma Millette, aged three, who when they found her had a crushed hand about to be amputated. George prevented the operation, and for many months cared for the child's hand himself, nursing it back to health. The family, probably because of the confusion of having two Emmas in the house, changed the child's name to Frances. She lived with them until her wedding, which took place in their home.

Today Anna Belden, George and Emma's daughter, says that the Blackwells were and are "an awfully reserved lot" who rarely make friends with whom they feel entirely at home. Yet Henry at least was said to be jolly and outgoing, and both Elizabeth and Anna had the art of drawing people to them, whether or not they reciprocated the affection they inspired.

In the search for someone or something to love, the Blackwells not only adopted children; most of them as time went on adopted dogs. Ellen had her ample shadow, Fanny; in Europe Elizabeth and Marian had their dog companions; Kitty too had a passion for dogs, but hers had not yet grown to the point of idolatry. In 1885 when Frances Alofsen was about to leave for a visit to Holland, Kitty wrote to Alice that she hated to think of Marian left in France alone. " 'Tis doleful to think of Aunt M. all alone with Annie and Chadie. I am fond of dogs, but Aunt M. (since Chadie's arrival) is more than fond . . . now she takes more interest in dogs than humans (!!) She says so herself." [7]

Later Alice became convinced that her aunt Elizabeth and Kitty would not visit the United States because they could not leave their dogs. It was natural, she said, to love a pet, but not (as perhaps she saw Ellen do) to get up six times during a meal to let it in and out of a window. Nor, she went on sternly, for two adults to refuse to be away at the same time for fear the servant "will not feed the pampered beast on a clean plate. As a rational being and a biped, my soul recoils." [8] Then, caught by the recollection of Edith's and Ethel's relation to animals, she added that, after all, it was better to be a slave to a dog than to vivisect him.

Even when Alice was in her teens, before she had had time to contemplate marriage to any specific male, she had planned that when they were both old, she and Kitty would live together. Now she told Kitty that, when that time came, she was going to adopt two orphan babies. "I would no more adopt a dog, after the frightful examples I have seen in the case of three of my aunts, of an hereditary tendency toward excess in dogs, than I should dare to drink if I knew there was dipsomania in the family!"

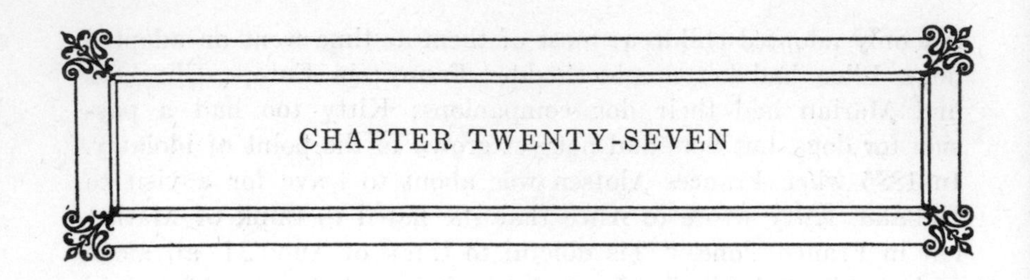

CHAPTER TWENTY-SEVEN

If their minds were fixed on the future, their emotions turned often, and with longing, to the past. Marian, Elizabeth and Kitty spent a holiday in and around Bristol, and though Marian had so hated her childhood that she refused to try to remember any part of it, she fell in love with the old haunts. "I really think," Elizabeth said, "that if not affectionately bound to Frances she would drift back and cast anchor here." [1]

By the fall of 1890 Marian and Anna had indeed drifted back across the Channel to England, in an effort to reconstitute a family group and to die, as they had been unwilling to live, together. They settled not in Bristol but in Hastings, in order to be near Elizabeth. Then, so as not to be too near, they found a house a good distance from her home. Moreover, they took both halves of a semidetached house, where they could live together yet apart. Anna named it the Doll's House because of its size, but probably also with sly reference to Ibsen's play recently performed for the first time in England. Such reference had its logic. The door which Ibsen's heroine slammed as she left her home forever signaled for women throughout the Western world the end of subservience to men. It was a sound long familiar to the Blackwell women. It was they and others like them who had started its reverberations.

The move to England was barely accomplished before Emily expressed her doubts. "I sometimes wonder whether after 20 years of French life Anna will not find English ways and climate aggravating, and on what will she expend her activity when her correspondence [with the Australian newspaper] ceases." [2] Yet when had Anna been contented with her lot, or Emily satisfied with someone else's plans? A few years later, George gave a realistic picture of his elder sisters' attitude. "It is a great pity that Marian and Anna withdraw themselves so much from simple enjoyments—It is not that they *cannot* enjoy what others do, but that they will not, and the persistent holding aloof makes them feel as though they *could* not take part." [3]

Shortly after the move to England, Elizabeth told Henry that Marian and Anna did not really like Hastings, which was too far from London and too quiet for their taste, and that for their sakes she had considered moving nearer London, but she never did so. Eternally enthralled by the figment of cooperation, she was still searching for "a Home Colony founded on true principles." [4] Anna continued to be depressed by her failure to find the Triel treasure, in the existence of which she still wholeheartedly believed, conceding only that she had been too late to find it. But at least she and Elizabeth had been able to compose the differences which divided them on the subject of Anna's monomania.

From Triel and later from Hastings Anna wrote to Henry about the sad state of her finances. She had only two sources of income left. One hundred pounds a year came from a settlement of Howard's estate, which would have been far greater had it not been for the "rascality of our government" in the affair of the bridge, one of the money-making schemes which had preceded her treasure hunt. There was also the income from her column in the Australian paper, which in 1890 raised her fee from one hundred to one hundred and twenty-five pounds a year. This, she said at once, gave her no pleasure, as they should have done it twenty-five years before.

It was shortly after this raise that she decided with Henry's help, for he was now sending her a regular stipend, to give up her writing and move to England, instead of working her "unhappy self to death" to pay for her "coming cremation," which she found herself anticipating with longing, as she did not believe that "*living* pays for the horror of *aging*." [5] From England, in an unsuccessful attempt to express gratitude, she told Henry that she hated to take money from him and ought to have remained in France to work, though doing so would surely have killed her. She varied this pessimism only to the doubtful extent permitted by her belief in spiritualism and reincarnation, on one occasion announcing that she hoped for better luck in life when next she returned "to this troublous and uncomfortable sphere." [6]

In the mid-eighteen-nineties, when travel had become so much quicker and easier, many American Blackwells crossed the ocean to visit the family home. Partly they came because the three eldest sisters were now approaching eighty, and who knew if they would see them again? Henry had for years been trying to persuade his sisters to visit the United States. Finally in 1894 Anna replied to one of his pleas that he must feel his age very little—he was after all almost ten years younger than she—if he could even imagine her taking such a trip. Why, it was all she could do to walk!

Next year George brought his son, Howard, about to enter Harvard, to visit his aunts. Sam and Nettie came to England too, for Sam, long employed by the Mexican and South American Telegraph Companies, and with his large family grown, was for the first time in his marriage easy about money. The four joined forces in Bristol, though Bristol represented a past life only to Sam, for George had been born after the family's emigration. The year after, it was Henry's turn to visit the old places. Alice was in England too—it was the year of her Armenian theologian's death—and when she left, Elizabeth lamented "seeing the last of [her] dear little face." Elizabeth's estimate of Alice was entirely revised from that of former times, and she expressed contentment in the knowledge that if she died, Alice would care for Kitty.

In 1895 Elizabeth's account of her early years, begun at Kitty's insistence seven years before, was published in England. In spite of its portentous title, *Pioneer Work in Opening the Medical Profession to Women* was an informal personal account written with simplicity and charm. It was widely and admiringly reviewed. Emily expressed her pleasure that Elizabeth had recorded details which might otherwise have been lost forever. But being Emily, she had an objection, and being Emily, she expressed it. "I should have been glad if you had adhered to what I understood was your original intention of leaving it to be published after our death. It always seems to me to be a mistake to publish during one's own lifetime . . . when it is necessary also to publish matter concerning other people, and thus invading their private life without their consent . . . and I regret your determination in your own case." [7]

Kitty, now in her middle forties, had also made an excursion into the past. She had never forgotten the little baby, Henry Paul Harvey, known as Paul, who, left in Dr. Elizabeth's care so many years before, had come to be Kitty's child, and whose connection with them "was most violently severed 20 years ago by M. and Mme. Drousart who first took charge of the charming little fellow." [8] Kitty, still longing for her lost boy, had instituted inquiries and discovered that after his early childhood in France, he had been sent at the age of eight to spend a lonely public-school life in England, had taken a first in literature at Oxford, and now, a tall, handsome fellow of twenty-four, had an excellent position in the War Office. Resurrected, he visited them often. "I do think," Kitty said, "I must have been starving for want of Paul all these years," and quoted him as looking back at his lonesome school life and saying, "All these years, and no one told me I had such friends!" And, though he was healthily unwilling to be so totally absorbed by Kitty as she was eager to absorb him, the relationship continued warm and close over the years.

It continued in spite of Elizabeth and Anna. Elizabeth was not drawn to Paul as Kitty was. "I think," Kitty said astutely, "she has always a natural disposition to be ready to doubt people's sincerity when they have such beautiful manners as Paul's." [9] Besides, Dr. Elizabeth had never cared for baby Paul as Kitty had, nor was she in general drawn to children. " 'Twas *I* who adopted her!" Kitty told Alice. Anna warned Kitty not to depend on Paul. As soon as he advanced in his career, he would have no use for her. Then, having spoken out about his mysterious origins, for he was apparently an illegitimate child of a respectable and wealthy family, Anna decided to ignore his existence. Even Frances Alofsen, who had at first flirted with him, turned against him and said Kitty was infatuated.

For once Kitty was not docile. Paul then and thereafter seemed to her to be her child.[10] Early in their renewed association, when the handsome young man became involved with a young friend of Elizabeth and Kitty, and foolishly let her believe his intentions more serious than they were, he confided to Kitty each detail of the painful breakup of the romance. Two years later he married Ethel Persse. "I hope that you will . . . spare for me a little of the affection you feel for *our* Paul," Ethel wrote to Kitty at the time of her engagement, "for he belongs to you as well as to me!"

When the couple had a daughter, Kitty was her godmother, and over the years little Susan came with her nurse to stay with Kitty and Elizabeth. Sometimes when her parents were away on government business, she remained for extended periods. From his strategic government posts in these last years of the nineteenth century, Paul wrote letters which reflect the history of England, then at the height of its imperialist phase. At first, as private secretary to the Marquess of Landsdowne, Secretary of War, he was involved with the after-effects of the ill-considered Jameson raid: the raid organized by the great colonial industrialist Cecil Rhodes, Prime Minister of South Africa's Cape Colony, who in 1895 sent a party of armed police under the leadership of Dr. Jameson to the Transvaal to dislodge the Dutch farmers known to history as the Boers. The raid was a failure, a failure moreover that brought down on England the reproaches of liberal forces inside and outside its borders. At the same time the Liberal Lord Landsdowne had "got to steer the Irish Land Bill through the Lords—no easy task, I fear." No possible task, for the bills relating to home rule for Ireland, while they passed the Commons, were consistently and vigorously defeated by the Lords.

Paul continued his upward march in government, interrupted at the end of the century by a lengthy illness which seems to have been tuberculosis. After his recovery, he was made Chief Commissioner for the Greek Debt, and in 1904–1905 spent a year in Athens. This assignment must have met with disfavor among the Blackwells, for after the three weeks' war in which Turkey defeated Greece and was ceded part of Thessaly and suzerainty over Crete, Ellen had expressed her grief, and probably her family's, in an exaggerated statement that Greece and Crete "are given back to that barbarous Turkish rule. It is very sad that England should have helped in the result."[11] But Paul was a civil servant, and later, in the spread of empire, was stationed in Africa and Asia, from which posts he kept up a frequent correspondence with Kitty. He was knighted in 1911.

Not only did he reach the heights of the British Civil Service, but in the best tradition of that service he returned to his first love, literature, and became the eminent compiler and editor of the *Oxford Companion to English Literature,* the *Oxford Companion to Classical Literature,* and other such dictionaries still in active use. Kitty's faith seems to have had more justification than Dr. Elizabeth's doubts.

The past was ending in less revocable ways for the older Blackwells. In 1891, two years before Kitty recovered her lost boy, Barbara Leigh Smith Bodichon, Elizabeth's closest friend, died after many years of illness. Her life had been a boon to the women of England, and every gain they had made in independence, equality, educational opportunity, was in some measure traceable to her energy and courage. Her portrait hangs today in Cambridge, in the Girton College she helped establish, one of the first great advances in England in higher education for women.

In 1893 there occurred the first break in the Blackwell family phalanx since Howard's death nearly thirty years before. On October 18, two months after her seventy-fifth birthday, Lucy Stone died, not of any of the diseases which over recent years had plagued her, but of cancer. As late as May of that year, Lucy had traveled with Alice to the Columbian Exposition in Chicago. The great change which had occurred in the status of women since the Centennial Exposition seventeen years before was symbolized by the inclusion of women in the many congresses held at the new exposition. It was even more dramatically stated in the fact that there was a special congress on woman suffrage. But by August, when the suffrage conference convened, Lucy was no longer able to travel, and it was Henry, as always her faithful representative, who went instead. At one of the congresses, Henry expressed his, and Lucy's, faith in a serene future. "It is a glorious privilege to live, as we are living, in an age of progress. The sun is already above the horizon, the tide is rising. . . . The Twentieth Century will bring a womanhood redeemed, regenerated and disenthralled by the irresistible genius of universal emancipation."

Lucy faced death calmly and with a belief in a future life which had increased in her later years. As Kitty wrote to Alice, "your mother, Aunt Elizabeth, and people like them, have the advantage of ordinary mortals—their work is . . . so utterly unselfish, no wonder they can look to the end in this world, with such serene courage."[12] The *Woman's Journal* reported Lucy's decline as it had her achievements. When she could no longer eat and had hardly strength to speak, her mind still dealt with the world and its improvement. "A flash of joy passed over her face when we told her that the Democratic State Convention in New York had adopted a woman suffrage plank; and she said; 'That ought to make the Massachusetts Republicans ashamed.' "[13] Her last intelligible words, whispered into her daughter's ear, were, "Make the world better."

Throughout her lifetime Lucy Stone had fulfilled this instruction to the best of her ability. Women throughout the world were freer because the little Massachusetts farm girl and others like her had fought to make them free. At her funeral eleven hundred people unexpectedly assembled, crowding far beyond its seating capacity the Church of the Disciples where the services were held. Newspapers throughout the country vied in praise, as in her youth they had competed in ridicule and vituperation.

Lucy Stone was "widely honored and lamented." Lamented by liberal thinkers, lamented after the long years of marriage by a husband who, in spite of giving over most of his life to help in her work, had always been tortured by the conviction that he had been unworthy of her. His first action only fifteen minutes after Lucy's death was, oddly enough, to give the news to the Associated Press, so that his sister Emily learned of it next morning when she picked up her paper.

After this gesture Henry seems to have sunk into desolation. Back in New York after the funeral, Emily wrote, trying to console him by telling him that no woman could have had a better husband; but he continued to blame himself, certain he had tried his wife in "a thousand ways." Nearly a year later Emily told Elizabeth that after thirty-eight years of "harmonious" marriage, Henry still brooded on his past failings. "Poor Harry is almost morbid in his regret for Lucy. It takes the form of self reproach for shortcomings and neglects. He loses sight of the fact that with all her good qualities, she was in many respects difficult and trying and quietly domineering, and that all their married life was full of trial, which was largely due to her peculiarities. He was one of the best husbands possible, and certainly modified his whole course . . . to adapt his life to hers, and yet now he dwells upon every dissonance that ever occurred as though he alone were to blame." [14]

When two years after Lucy's death the mood of misery was still on him, Henry's sisters ascribed his morbidity to his lack of faith in a future life. "To him," Emily said, "Lucy is simply annihilated, and he sees the same fate staring him in the face." Shortly before Lucy's death Henry had succinctly described his religious feelings: "I am a godless infidel—thank the Lord!" After her death, he said that Marian had misunderstood his view of a future life. He had no view. "I am not a *dis*believer, but simply an agnostic. Luckily what I believe or don't believe will not change the laws of the universe!" [15] But Marian, who like Anna was drawing closer to spiritualism and belief in reincarnation, tried to persuade her rationalist brother that Lucy too had believed in reincarnation. He could never reach her through a medium, Marian said, "but she will try to influence your thoughts if you don't repel her (by overeating and over absorption in worldly interests) and try to draw you near to her through your intellect and intuition especially in sleep and dreams." [16] Elizabeth had already described Anna as "so occupied with her occult studies, that she seems to look hazily down upon me from an immeasurable distance." Since moving to England, Anna had added to her oddities the "kink" of vegetarianism.

Elizabeth herself continued a skeptical interest in spiritualism. Unconvinced by her sisters, yet unwilling to deny the possibility of communication, she had devised a scientific test. She had written a special and characteristic message and hidden it. If, after she died, she could inform her friends where the message was and what it contained, she would have established the possibility of communication after death. She told her friend Thomas Huxley of the scheme, little thinking that he was soon to proceed her to the spirit kingdom.

A concern with spiritualism did not prevent the Blackwells from embracing a recent reform, one that would carry innovation to the grave and beyond: cremation. Anna had talked of being cremated when the process was still new in the modern Western world. Because Lucy had insisted that she must be cremated, her body had to be embalmed and kept for more than two months until the crematory being built in the Forest Hills Cemetery in Boston was completed, the nearest crematory before that having been in New York State. An innovator from her earliest years, in her lifetime the first Massachusetts woman to attain a bona fide college degree, she died as she had lived. She was the first person to be cremated in Massachusetts.

Henry wrote a detailed account to his sisters in England. Characteristically concerned with the moral nature of the performance, he told them, "The Massachusetts Cremation Society is officered by men of high personal and social character, and I was rather glad that Lucy would be the first person in Boston to be the subject of cremation." He went on in gruesome detail about the lighting of the fire, about his final view of Lucy's "dear form and face" two and a half months after she had died. He admitted an earlier "profound reluctance to have Lucy's body so disposed of," but this was counteracted by the sight of her body, in which "the process of decay had already begun." "It seemed appropriate too," he ended the long account, "that our Lucy" should be "in death as in life helping to make the world better."

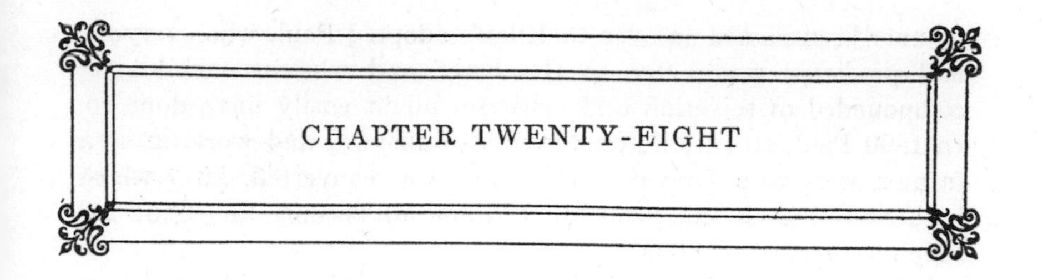

CHAPTER TWENTY-EIGHT

As their elders turned to the beginning of life and to its end, the younger generation, as was proper, faced the future. In 1890 just after Marian and Anna moved to England, Frances Alofsen came to Hastings with her son and stayed for some weeks. Kitty, seeing her for the first time in nineteen years, found her frank, truthful, defensive of the weak and full of higher standards than could have been expected from her education and experiences in life. Not unnaturally, for she was Elizabeth's first delivered child and Marian's semiadopted daughter, and so might lay claim to being a member of the clan with all its ideals. Without, however, its resistance to matrimony, for at the end of 1891 she married for the second time. Her husband was Henry Titterton, an Englishman. Elizabeth went to the "handsome" wedding, at which Frances's son, now in the English navy, and members of her first husband's family were also present. Elizabeth, glad "our homeless Frances is happily married," reported that the bride was so excited "she had not slept for three nights—but she declined Kitty's offer to rescue her and escape to America!" Her departing words to Elizabeth were a message to Marian, who was too ill to be there. "Tell Marian, I am very happy." [1]

The family tradition of virtue and reform had in some strange manner been passed on even to Ellen's adopted Paul, who everyone had predicted would "go to the bad," and who in a childhood compounded of rejection and criticism might easily have done so. In 1890 Paul, still living on Martha's Vineyard and working as a farmer, went to a revival meeting and was converted, after which he found time in intervals of farming to become an agent for religious books and tracts.

Ellen's other child, Cornelia, was rebelling in a different way, not only against society but against the Blackwells' stern standards. In the fall of 1890, three years before Lucy's death, "what-to-do-with-Cornelia," a perennial family game, had again been played out. Emily was "at her wits' end," and begged Lucy to take Neenie for two years while the girl studied to become a gymnasium teacher. Lucy confided to Nettie that she did not feel she "*could* have her. But she is a child badly born, badly brought up, with no habits of application or industry, and nobody wants her."[2] So Lucy, sick though she was, consented to take her.

Nettie's daughter Ethel, still studying in Boston, was at the Dorchester house too, as was fourteen-year-old Beth Hagar, whom Lucy and Henry had taken on a permanent basis. Ethel was "wild with delight" that Cornelia was to be there, and the three girls, in spite of the difference in their ages, were close friends. Ethel, quiet and level-headed, had a subduing effect on the ardent Cornelia, who behaved so well that Lucy forgot her dismay. Cornelia indeed had qualities with which the family never credited her. She was sympathetic and, according to Alice, would "devote herself to any extent for anyone who is ill or suffering."[3] Now she was so consistently helpful that Lucy in astonishment proclaimed her "as good a girl in the house as any girl need be." Even so, three giggling young girls were a trial to a woman who was increasingly weak and ill. Perhaps to set a good example for Cornelia, Alice and Henry went to church regularly on Sunday morning, and took her with them. "Papa," said Alice, "goes to sleep more or less, but seldom fails to commend the sermon."[4]

Both Ethel and Cornelia had admirers, and this required in those more cautious days that some member of the household sit up evenings until the young men left. Twenty-year-old Cornelia, who had a "striking and rather handsome face" and a flirtatious manner, was involved with two young men, of whom she much preferred Mr. Whall, a neighbor's son. She began to neglect her studies. Leaving the house promptly each morning to go to school, she often appeared there late or not at all.

Toward the end of January 1891, Emily came to Boston to read a paper. She had an interview with young Mr. Whall in which he showed himself less than enthusiastic about marrying Cornelia. Emily was left with the impression that he had supposed her richer than she was. He was the son of a poor but well-connected family, and had been brought up by rich relatives. His tastes were expensive, his reliability slight. The affair seemed to be at an end; and Emily expressed the hope that it would leave Neenie wiser though sadder. With "her headlong disposition" it was inevitable that she should have "a sharp lesson or two to teach her circumspection." [5]

Whatever the affair taught Cornelia it was not circumspection. In spite of his confessed lack of serious intent, Cornelia continued to meet Mr. Whall secretly. By summer she was pregnant, and he had decided after all to marry her. Known from infancy as a bad girl, just as Nannie had been known as a good one, it is hard to say whether it was prescience or the effect of such characterizations which defined their futures.

That Emily thought it prescience there is no doubt. She expressed herself as infinitely disgusted with both Cornelia and her husband. Among the advantages which Mr. Whall forfeited by his conduct, as far as the Blackwells were concerned, was a first name, for they never then or later referred to him as anything but Whall or W. or sometimes Mr. Whall. Yet Emily acted toward Neenie more generously than might have been expected, settling a small sum on her and giving her an allowance. She even consented to see her, but since her husband was not included in the invitation, Cornelia refused to come. Emily now, as though pregnancy were contagious, refused to allow Nannie and Neenie to associate with each other, to the dismay of both.

Ellen, who loved Neenie, rallied round, and in the summer of 1892 invited the Whalls and their sick baby to stay with her at Martha's Vineyard in a house next door to Flo and Elliot Mayhew's. Nettie's eldest daughter and her husband had just adopted a small boy, and, first in the Blackwell annals, had adopted him legally. The ensuing month was chaotic. Cornelia in earlier years had been accused of flirting with Elliot. Flo had defended her then, but now—with what justification it is impossible to know, though Lucy and Emily, usually so critical, did not believe Cornelia guilty—Flo suddenly credited the accusation. Such warfare broke out between the two households that Ellen, with her usual melodrama, told Emily she was moving to George's house because she could not continue to live "on the confines of hell."

The situation was saved when Whall was offered a job out West, and left with Neenie and their baby. Later they returned East, to the delight at least of Ellen, who was elated to have her "dear child" back again. She was now, in a sense, a dual grandmother, for in 1895, Cornelia had a second, and again a sickly, baby.

Ellen's passion for babies had not decreased with age. As late as 1893, encouraged perhaps by her niece Florence's adoption of a boy, she was determined to adopt another baby. The family hoped she would at least take a girl of eight or nine, but she was not to be diverted. Alice commented that Aunt Ellen, at sixty-five, was as cheerful, energetic and benevolent as ever, in spite of her infirmities and her overweight, but so consistently indiscreet that she kept herself and everyone else in a perpetual stew.

The family was politely though firmly opposed to this latest foible. Only George was cruelly unrestrained. He told Ellen that since she had one foot in the grave, was blind as a bat, unable to hear, and with almost no means, he would rather see a baby dead than adopted by her. Emily privately agreed that a merciful death would be better for a child than to be brought up by Ellen and go "to the bad" when it grew up—which in effect put the blame for Cornelia's lapse directly on Ellen's shoulders.

That Ellen, who was in fact much as George had described her, should have contemplated undertaking the responsibility of an infant shows both her loneliness and her lack of reality. She lived by herself most of the year now, either in Washington or in one of her houses in Lawrence, while the rent from the large Lawrence house and a small one in Orange supported her after a fashion. Summers she sometimes spent in Vermont with Aunt Eliza Major, the governess of their childhood and their uncle's widow, who after his death had settled again in the United States.

Living with her childhood governess must have increased Ellen's illusion of youth, which her infirmities and her image in the mirror failed to dissipate. Although in childhood she had had two younger brothers, she had been the baby girl of the household, a happy role which her mind had never over the years relinquished. On the eve of her sixty-sixth birthday she wrote to Elizabeth, "I wonder as I look in the glass to see the face and figure so rapidly aging. I feel now wherever I go that I am regarded as old. I who am one of the youngest of the family, and do not feel at all old in spirit, except that I seem no longer to care for personal advancement."

In Washington she went to the Corcoran Art Gallery to copy paintings, and sent her copies as presents to the family. "I left two for Harry and Alice, but Alice sent them to the suffrage bazaar and sold them at $5 apiece." [6] Still, Ellen was used to family rebuffs, and seemed with age to endure them with greater fortitude, for the Blackwells agreed that, inexplicable as it seemed, Ellen grew more cheerful with time; and in spite of an isolation made greater by her physical defects, her mind was as lively and her interest in the world around her as great as in her girlhood, the reward perhaps of her refusal to accept age.

More than any of the Blackwells of the next generation, Alice was walking in the footsteps of her elders. According to her aunt Emily, she was, since her mother's death, for the first time making an independent life, and "wonderfully developing her individuality." Emily saw in Alice a budding self-will which indicated how much she had unconsciously been dominated by her mother. One of the signs of release was her open interest in her Armenian theologian, for though Henry had always hoped his daughter would marry, Lucy, without taking a fixed stand, had consistently opposed each romantic interest Alice entertained. In the case of the seemingly irreproachable Mr. Black, Ellen later said "there was consternation" at the prospect of Alice's marrying.

Whatever change may have occurred in her personality, the change in Alice's way of life was negligible. Four years after her mother's death and the year after Johannes Chatschumian's, she wrote to Kitty, "Blackwells certainly tend to fads as the sparks fly upward, and my interest in everything Armenian lends variety to my otherwise rather monotonous life." [7] And seven months later she added this pathetic note: "I have started a 'pleasure book' to record day by day the pleasant things that happen to me, and make myself thankful." [8]

Her uncle George, less public-spirited than his kin, bemoaned Henry's and Alice's absorption in woman suffrage, to him a trifling social change which they believed would introduce the millennium. In the summer of 1896 when Alice and her father were in Europe, George commented, though not to her, that Alice ought not to hurry home. Both the *Woman's Journal* and the Armenians would get along as well without her. He went so far as to say that the vituperative and fault-finding tone of her articles did more harm than good. "She has been all her life in an atmosphere of antagonism and opposition to the community." [9] Lucy in death was still the dominant force in the household.

The year before this European trip, Lucy's husband, working for woman suffrage as ardently as in her lifetime, celebrated his seventieth birthday. A dinner, honoring his long dedication to woman's rights, was held at the Copley Square Hotel. In accepting the invitation, Henry objected that the occasion should properly have honored not him but "the dear and noble woman" who had been "the charm and inspiration" of his life. There were a hundred and fifty guests, his family, his friends, the leaders of reform in Massachusetts among them. John D. Long, former governor of Massachusetts, was master of ceremonies. What alteration time and his wife's death had effected in the "wild boy" whom Harriet Beecher Stowe had known, in the gay and joking father Alice sometimes found not quite decorous enough, is manifested in Governor Long's comments on Henry's own speech. "The only thing that I cannot credit is the claim he makes that he was ever a wild boy. . . . I don't believe the doctor was ever a boy at all. I think when he was born he wore a black frock coat, had a rose in his buttonhole, and a beard just slightly verging on gray." [10] Yet Alice could have supported her view of him by a letter he had written her not quite a year before. He had boarded the wrong train at Buffalo, only discovering his error "when the cars were going pretty fast. The colored porter shouted 'If you jump, it is at your own risk!' 'Whose else?' I responded, and took my flying leap." [11]

At the dinner, Mary Livermore, long associated with Henry and Lucy, and first editor of the *Woman's Journal,* made a tender speech praising Henry's work and his modesty. One sentence might have served as epitaph for all the Blackwells. "If anybody supposes," Mrs. Livermore said, "it is a pleasant thing to be a voice of one crying in the wilderness, I would like to have him or her try it in dead earnest for a couple of years and see what he thinks then."

Emily in her late sixties did not show the ravages of her struggle. "I do like Aunt Emily," Alice told Kitty, "so much solid worth and so little pretense—and not a bit of the conceit which spoils almost all people who have any ability above the average." [12] Emily continued to work busily as Professor of Obstetrics and Gynecology as well as Dean of the Medical College, and was listed as an attending physician at the hospital.

Emily had a quite different account to give of Dr. Marie Zakrzewska, colleague of their youthful years, when she visited her in 1892. Dr. Zak had retired to York Harbor, Maine, and urged Emily to buy a house there too. Marie and her friend Miss Sprague had enough money to live out their lives there comfortably. Dr. Zak had now given up her practice, but even while she was still active, she had not, Emily felt, kept up with modern discoveries. Three years younger than Emily, she had paid the price of such relaxation. She seemed both physically and mentally older than she was. Her memory for details had failed; and like Ellen she had grown immensely stout.

By 1896, however, Emily had suffered for several winters from debilitating colds and coughs. In the winter of 1895 she was so ill that the next summer she admitted she did not think her strength would return. "The long continued, incessant spasmodic cough produced a certain degree of emphysema." [13] Yet in the fall she again taught four hours a week. She would have liked to resign as dean, she told Elizabeth, but was unable to find anyone to take her place. She ought to go to Italy or California for the winter, but could bear neither to go alone nor to take Nannie away from a new circle of friends.

Elizabeth had expressed concern that Emily had no family life. On this score Emily reassured the sister she had not seen in eight years. She was still living with Dr. Cushier, who was like a younger sister to her. Dr. Cushier's niece Lucie, who had kept house for them, had died. Emily put it rather oddly that life was now happier, "since poor Lucie whose last years cast a shadow upon it, was removed." [14] Another niece of Dr. Cushier's, Bessie Mercelis, herself a doctor, was living with them; and she and Nannie, who was a year and a half younger, were close friends. Emily and Dr. Cushier had indeed acquired a house in York Cliffs, Maine, where they now spent long summer vacations away from the family embroilments on Martha's Vineyard.

Sam and Nettie, with their unaccustomed security and Sam's steadily increasing salary to make life easier, continued their reformist activities. Sam spoke from time to time at meetings, though as always he gave less time and energy to causes than his brother Henry. He was now, as in his youth, writing poetry. His verses, like his speeches, had a highly moral tone, and resembled the style of the days when he began to write more than that of the eighteen-eighties and nineties when he continued to do so. The results were competent but pedestrian.

Antoinette continued to write, to preach and to speak at meetings and conventions. In the early nineties, her magnum opus appeared. It was called *The Philosophy of Individuality.* An attempt to rationalize religion on the basis of the new discoveries of science, it met with a sharp rebuke from Anna, who admired its remarkable talent, but differed with its conclusions. Anna called on her minister sister-in-law to seek "higher teachings"; the rationalist approach was incompatible with those lofty conclusions about the human spirit with which Nettie ended her book.[15]

Early in 1893 Sam and Nettie's daughter Ethel was boarding in New York and studying at the Infirmary Medical College. Emily found her "the brightest and on the whole the most promising" of Sam's girls. She continued to have serious doubts about Edith and her interest in medicine. Nevertheless, shortly thereafter, Edith went into private practice in New York with an older woman doctor. Four years later it was Ethel who was in Emily's black books. It was Ethel who would never practice, and whom nobody would ever trust if she did; she was "a bundle of cravings and unsatisfied desires, so helpless in practical life." [16]

In 1896, because all their children except Grace had deserted the family home in New Jersey, and because Sam at seventy-two was still commuting to work, Nettie and Sam bought a house on East Sixty-fourth Street near the entrance to Central Park, and moved to New York. One of the advantages of the move was that Edith now set up her office in the new home, an improvement, Emily noted, over the shabby quarters where she had lived and worked for several years. By 1897 the beautiful Agnes was married —she was thirty-one by then—and in the same year, Florence, the eldest and most frivolous daughter, decided to preach one week a month for the Crusaders, an organization which Alice described as "like the Salvation Army."

In 1895, when Howard entered Harvard, George and Emma too had moved their family, including the little adopted girl, from New Jersey to Cambridge, because they could not bear to have their son leave home. Their fourth child, a boy born after Laurie's death, had died in infancy, and Howard, as the only boy in a generation of girls, was cherished by the Blackwells. Emily commented perspicaciously that George and Emma's move would benefit everyone but Howard. Henry's lonesomeness would be alleviated by their living nearby, at least during the school term. Emma could more easily visit her sick mother in Gardner. Young Anna would go to a better school and have more companionship. But Howard, who needed to be independent, would continue to be bound.

Emma, now that her family was grown, followed, though far more mildly, in the footsteps of her aunt Lucy. She was a suffragist, though not a militant. She wrote for the *Woman's Journal*, and was president of the Woman's Club of Orange, to which in 1898 Alice reported her reading a paper on "The Woman of Today." Some of the differences between today's woman and yesterday's might have been illustrated by Emma's own activities. One of her occupations was conducting a missionary sewing class for little girls in the slums, an organized charitable enterprise that her relatives of a generation before—for Emma was in truth a generation removed from her sisters-in-law—would never have considered. More significantly, she could be a suffragist without unraveling the fabric of her life. She could lecture to a woman's club without being ridiculed or hosed with icy water, because now women customarily spoke in public, and because there were women's clubs for them to speak to. Her husband's sisters and sisters-in-law and others like them had cleared a path in the jungle.

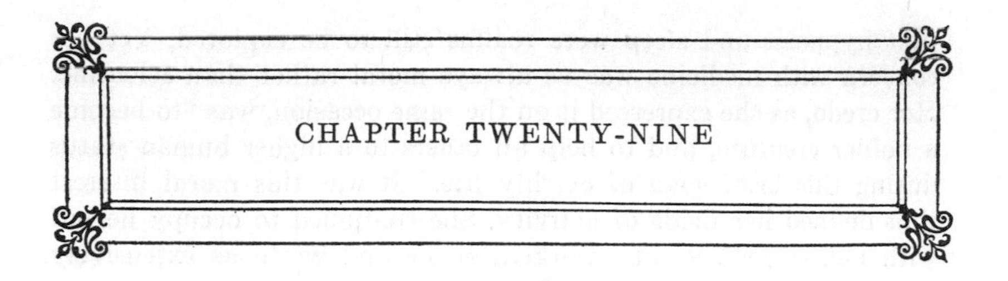

CHAPTER TWENTY-NINE

In 1894 Elizabeth gave up her private practice, because she found her "nervous force not equal to supply the magnetism that I have always given to my patients." It is curious to contemplate that she may have been speaking literally of the "animal magnetism" in which she had certainly believed in the early days of her practice, and not merely of the mystique of patient-doctor relationship.

She felt that, "Our ministrations to body and soul cannot be separated by a sharply-defined line." She was searching for a link between medicine and the whole human being, much as doctors are searching today. She had been doing so as long ago as 1848, when, in her first medical paper, she included fear, sorrow and anxiety as causes of famine fever among Irish immigrants. Inevitably, being a Blackwell, her conclusions were expressed in moral terms. In the state of today's knowledge, the terms are psychological, an interpretation which in the future may also be deemed no more than a phase.

In 1889 she addressed a class of young women studying medicine. Her demands for physiological and medical knowledge were precise. She drew the students' attention to the "new and valuable department of medical investigation, psycho-physiology," [1] and suggested that hypnosis and sleep were realms still to be explored. Yet her concern with medicine was as always moral rather than scientific. Her credo, as she expressed it on the same occasion, was "to become a nobler creature, and to help all others to a higher human status during this brief span of earthly life." It was this moral interest that defined her fields of activity. She continued to occupy herself with public welfare. She worked, spoke and wrote as extensively as ever on those subjects which evoked her reformist impulses.

The crusade against "licensed vice," which she had fought side by side with its leader, Mrs. Josephine Butler, had in a measure been won when the Contagious Diseases Act was repealed in 1886. Yet the fight against prostitution and venereal disease had to be maintained, and the constant threat of reenactment of licensing laws withstood.

In 1897 Elizabeth spoke before a meeting of women physicians. It must have gratified her that she had lived to see her battle so far won that such a meeting could be assembled. It came as no surprise, however. Ten years earlier she had commented that there were three thousand "registered lady-doctors" in the United States alone. In her speech, Elizabeth quoted from a report of the Royal College of Physicians. "About 13,000 soldiers return to England from India every year, and of these, in 1894, over 60 per cent had suffered from some form of venereal disease." And Elizabeth added, "Promiscuous intercourse inevitably tends to give rise to . . . venereal disease, no matter what precautions are taken," the results being disfigurement, loss of functions, often death. And with the simple grandeur of a Blackwell in battle, she stated her conclusions. "Thus, by the systematic perversion of the sexual instinct, the gradual destruction of so-called Christian civilization is taking place." [2] Morality came easily to the Blackwells.

From England too Elizabeth directed her American relatives in the fight. The idea of government regulation of prostitution had spread from Europe to the New World, and "town after town both in East and West," Elizabeth told Alice in 1893, "have organised female vice for the sake of male fornication." A fight must be made throughout the United States on a state and national level. The moral life of the nation was at stake. But, she warned, Alice must not allow her name or that of any young unmarried woman to "come *prominently* forward in the crusade." Why this stricture applied more to Alice than to Elizabeth herself can only be explained by the word "young," and perhaps also by "the sensitive and intense dislike of your father to hear this subject discussed, or even alluded to, by women." [3]

Yet Sam and Henry both entered the battle against licensing "houses of ill fame." In 1896, in a speech at a meeting on social purity, Sam said, "We must adopt as an axiom and must practice as an object lesson, an equally high moral standard for man as for woman." The next year Henry was rebuked by Elizabeth because, overcoming his personal prejudices, he had published in the *Woman's Journal* the speech she had made at the meeting of medical women. The speech on medical responsibility had been private, she pointed out, and to send out "the most delicate medical truths, naked and abrupt into our . . . prudishly dressed-up society, is to outrage and disgust the very people we are trying to convert." It was necessary to act discreetly "in this difficult warfare." In fact, having enlisted Henry's adherence, she attempted to free herself of it. In much the same tone his sisters had used when he first left home to go to Kemper College, she told him that in spite of his "brilliant ability and generous heart," there was still "an element of judgment lacking without which you may do harm, where you most desire to do good." [4]

She told Henry she had had only two hundred copies of her speech printed. Five years later, however, she included it in a two-volume collection of her essays and speeches, entitled *Essays in Medical Sociology*. The first volume contained her works on sexual morality, the second dealt with those other reforms with which over the years she had concerned herself.

Prominent among these battles was the fight against vivisection. She was still battling not only vivisection but its results, going so far as to reject the conclusions of such scientists as Koch and Pasteur because they were arrived at by the loathed method of animal experimentation. The differences between the lower orders and man, she argued, were so great that any conclusions drawn from such experiments were useless. This fallacy "produces the failure of M. Pasteur to prevent hydrophobia in man." She looked upon Monsieur Pasteur as no more than a man "whose skill and zeal in a false method of research may justly command intellectual recognition."[5]

She considered that the experimenters and those under their influence deteriorated morally as a result of their violations of decency. "Our treatment of a monkey or a prince contains an element of moral attitude which does not exist in our relation to inorganic Nature. . . . The divergence which now exists between some biological investigators and their critics rests upon the failure to recognize that moral error may engender intellectual error." There were many methods of arriving at knowledge, and every important medical discovery had been arrived at by other methods. Puerperal fever indeed had been conquered by "use of the comparative method, with absolutely no resort to experiment."[6]

The injury to the moral sense effected by vivisection caused physicians to turn to surgery rather than to "more natural methods of medical art" and to divert their attention from hygiene. Elizabeth's opinion had changed since the days of her youth, when she had hoped to be a surgeon. "I consider that the loss of a natural internal organ is a very grave mutilation of the human body, and the permanent effects upon the subjects . . . have never been carefully and honestly collected."[7]

The lowered moral sense led to an "exaggerated search for bacilli, as the chief cause of disease," a waste of scientific energy, since sanitation was the only satisfactory method of averting epidemics. It also encouraged inoculation. "The most serious fallacy arising from erroneous methods of biological research is the practice of vitiating human blood by the introduction of the diseased products of animals."[8] This dangerous method threatened to undermine national health. She was still opposed to vaccination, and certainly to making it compulsory, but because of her belief that fear predisposed to disease, she considered vaccination a kind of community sedative, and she vaccinated people when they asked her to do so.

Around her, her own family were falling victims to an incurable epidemic—that of advancing age. It was not only her elder sisters about whom she was troubled, but her younger as well. In 1896 she suggested to Henry that Emily ought to leave New York, where the weather was so bad for her chest, and spend winters in southern Europe. She hastened to add that she was not suggesting

Emily's permanent removal to Europe, which she did not in the least desire.[9]

Elizabeth already had her hands more than full with her two elder sisters. Anna's aberrations about money had increased with the years. She still believed she could make large sums—sometimes her estimates ranged as high as a million dollars—yet she was utterly confused about the small amount of money she did have. She tried to manage Marian's money, with the result that it rapidly disappeared. Elizabeth had to step in to protect Marian emotionally as well as financially, for Marian was ill, and Anna was interfering in every aspect of her life.

At the end of 1896 Marian suffered a stroke which affected her mind, so that, though at times she was rational, more often she was not. Frances Titterton, who loved Marian dearly, complained that for years Anna had treated Marian shabbily, accepting attention and giving none, and making her sister's life generally difficult. She suggested that Anna always gave her love more readily to strangers than to her family, a fact Frances deduced from the affection Anna had bestowed on her. She was glad Elizabeth was protecting Marian.

Elizabeth's efforts naturally ended in an embroilment with Anna. In the spring of 1897 Elizabeth had stated her intention of locking the door between Marian's and Anna's quarters in order to keep Anna out of Marian's half of the house. This gave rise to a scene in which Anna "grew scarlet," began to shake, and threatened to break down the door. It also brought a temporary end to the relations between Anna and her doctor sister. In June Anna wrote to Elizabeth, "On May 29, *you* remarked that under the circumstances you considered it would be better for you not to come into my house at present and *I replied* that I thought so too. . . . I am still of that opinion."[10] This far from affectionate letter she signed, "Yrs afftely."

Even before this battle, Elizabeth had told Henry that "Anna's extraordinary self love has been wounded by my unavoidably taking charge of Marian's expenses so that she can no longer confound her banking account with Marian's." She warned him to beware of Anna's confusion about money, for though he punctually sent his remittances, Anna had a fixed idea that the money did not come.

These aberrations of "our dear sister" really amounted to an unbalanced mind. Among other oddities Anna had a way of announcing to doctors and nurses that her rich family in America would take care of any expenses.[11]

Marian suffered for months; and, whatever the complexity of their relations, Anna wrote about her to Henry with compassion. She described Marian's "constant succession of painful fancies—almost like ugly dreams," [12] how she let out nervous cries because she believed she was "looking down into a deep, black hollow, into which she has a horrible fear of being swallowed up." [13]

To Ellen, Marian's illness brought back the days of her girlhood. She wrote a long letter about their early years together, a letter which Marian apparently understood, at least in part. With the mood of memory upon her, Ellen continued her reminiscences in correspondence with Elizabeth. She wondered if Marian remembered the room they had shared at the Vails' house in Walnut Hills, where the Vails' pet dog had lain between them on the bed until it became so hot Ellen couldn't endure it; how they "went together to the first Woman's Rights convention at Worcester, and met Mr. Channing, Lucretia Mott, Whittier, and other reformers and heard Lucy and Nettie speak for the first time"; and "the pleasant winter . . . in Boston, boarding first with dear, kind Miss Peabody," and later their stay at the North American Phalanx in Red Bank, New Jersey. Best of all, Ellen recalled the constant conversations, the friendly intimacy.[14]

Marian's long suffering continued until the end of August. Then she died. The sickly sister, who had not been expected to live past adolescence, had survived through more than seventy-nine years. In her will she left three thousand dollars to her beloved Frances, whose family had in the days of their prosperity been so generous to her. Frances's new husband, with whom she was happier than ever in her life, was ill, and they had little money. Her son, in Sumatra on naval duty, though he was devoted, had no money to offer her. The bequest was welcome. The rest of Marian's money, accumulated by the real-estate investments her brothers had made for her, was to be placed in trust, the income going to Anna for her lifetime, then to Ellen, and the capital ultimately to Sam or his daughters. The American branch of the family expressed indignation because Marian had bequeathed the money outright to Frances, instead of leaving it, at least for her lifetime, to husbandless Ellen.

Now the sad advance of time overtook the Blackwells one by one. Anna, the eldest, had survived Marian's long illness and her death, but these had had their effect. In July 1898, just after her eighty-second birthday, she told Henry that her eyes were going, "brain ditto, every little movement an effort." She walked now with a stick and someone's help besides.[15] Anna had found an eccentric doctor to give her the eccentric treatment she preferred. Doctor Elizabeth mistrusted him, but when she attempted to ask Anna about either her physical or her financial condition, Anna, like a stubborn child, closed her eyes and mouth and refused to respond.[16]

Elizabeth told Emily that Anna was very ill. Emily replied expressing her sorrow, but added that she had long ago given up writing to Anna. "I always feel that our lives have drifted so far apart that letters to her can not be of any great satisfaction."[17] Anna continued to be better and worse over another year and a half. In mid-December 1899 Elizabeth informed the American relatives that Anna was well and comfortable. On January 4, 1900, a cable announced her death, and a week later Elizabeth wrote to Henry that "our valued eldest sister died on January 4th, peacefully, but after a sharp attack of influenza and bronchitis." She had survived the eighteen-hundreds by only a few days. Now of the European sisters, only Elizabeth was left, and she was nearly seventy-nine.

She had never lost her girlhood habit of keeping a diary. Yet it was as though the initial impulse of intimate revelation was gone, and only the routine remained. Elizabeth's diaries were of two kinds, the first, ordinary small notebooks divided into dated spaces for daily entries. In these her records were in later years cursory in the extreme, the entries varying in number, but consisting usually of no more than a notation as to the weather and the day's occupation, such as a person might make who thought that in October she might wish to remember what she had done on a day in July.

On Wednesday August 30, 1899, she "Left cloak to be shortened—

Bought Highland tour tickets." The Highland tour, which included a stay at Kilmun on the shore of Holy Loch, was described in greater detail, but still without personal comment. The trip was her first experience of a spot she learned to love, to which she returned regularly for the remainder of her life. Kilmun is in the center of an area described by guidebooks as containing some of the most impressive mountain and loch scenery in Scotland. The mountainous region to the northwest has fine woods, with great thickets of rhododendrons.

Besides the daily diaries, Elizabeth had a series of notebooks in which from time to time she jotted down somewhat fuller notes, slightly more private communications. On February 3, 1900, she made an entry in this diary. "My birthday, 79 years old—physically I feel my advancing years—but spiritually it seems to me the outlook becomes increasingly wider and brighter as to the future."

CHAPTER THIRTY

The century was ending. A very different world was in the making. "It seemed quite uncanny to stand in the hall of our house in Dorchester," Alice said, "and hear Uncle George and Howard talking to us at Orange! The voices were faint but unmistakable."[1] The telephone was becoming a fact of family life. In 1900, the first National Automobile Show was held in Madison Square Garden. Most of the cars were electric, with rods instead of steering wheels. There was an attempt to use some electric automobiles—built in the image of hansom cabs, with the driver perched on high behind the passengers—to supplant horse-drawn vehicles as cabs for hire. Trolleys and cable cars were rapidly replacing the old-fashioned horse cars. In New York, there had for some years been elevated transit lines, and in 1900 work was begun on the subway.

The city to which the Blackwells had come from England nearly seventy years before was now a huge urban center. Narrow Manhattan had gushed its way uptown like cream in an over-stuffed tube. The Infirmary, built where in 1832 there had been only woods and fields, was now far downtown. The center of fashionable business had moved uptown, and was now centered around Thirty-fourth Street. The Waldorf Hotel at Fifth Avenue and Thirty-third Street had been completed in 1893. The Astoria built next to it in 1897 was sixteen stories high. At the lower tip of Manhattan skyscrapers of twenty stories and more lined the horizon.

In April 1897 Grant's Tomb had been completed. Emily described the celebration during which the sarcophagus was placed in the new building. The monument was situated at One Hundred and Twenty-second Street, overlooking the Hudson. The area around it was still quite empty. In the middle of the century, when the trend uptown had begun to be apparent, a park had been planned in the center of the island to give the future city breathing space. Work on Central Park was begun in 1857 as part of a city project to provide work for the unemployed during the depression then in progress. Now apartment buildings six and seven stories high were common among the rows of brownstone houses in residential sections on either side of the park, which stretched from Fifty-ninth up to One Hundred and Tenth Street. In 1892, Emily had told Elizabeth of another great difference in the city. It was wonderfully clean. The new "germ theories" had taken hold, and created great advances in the science of sanitation, and this in turn was eliminating epidemics.

Henry, impelled by the new century, wrote a letter to Elizabeth in which in effect he balanced the family's emotional books. His regret for those who were gone was never ending. Besides his feeling that he had failed Lucy, he still blamed himself because more than fifty years before he had urged Howard to leave his adopted country and return to England. He continued to believe that this decision had caused Howard's death.

As for Anna, Marian and Ellen, Henry was saddened by reflecting on the isolation of their lives, on their inability to "accept the society of their contemporaries and the connection of events." Ellen had made the most of her abilities, but Anna had largely wasted her brilliant talents, and Marian had been limited by her invalidism. Their problem had not been that they had never married, but that they had failed to create satisfying substitutes in a permanent activity or profession. Of the three remaining brothers Sam had done better than he, George better than either. This estimate of the brothers must of necessity have been economic. Yet it is significant that, since none of the family ever questioned the thoroughly unfinancial success of Elizabeth's and Emily's lives, Henry, because he was not rich, weighed himself on the side of the failures.

"I have somewhat modified my former radicalism," he went on, "seeing the foolish use that ignorance makes of opportunity."[2] This was partially true of him; yet he still supported such radical and idealistic causes as Henry George's single tax; and after a single-tax dinner in December 1900, Alice reported her father as having carried off the honors with a closing speech "that took the crowd." But in the serious and more immediate problem of free silver, Henry had supported the Republican Party against the Democrats and Populists in two presidential elections. To the Blackwells the Republican Party remained the party of liberalism and freedom. In fact, however, the issue of free silver was a class issue, with the Eastern capitalists favoring tight money and a gold standard, and the Western farmers, who had just survived or fallen in a great depression, clamoring for cheap money.

Henry's allegiance to "sound money" was won by other facets of the problem as well, for like most political questions this one was not clear-cut. In an article called "Silver Syndicate and Solid South" which he wrote in the fall of 1896, he suggested that a deal had been made between the Southern Democrats and the Western Republicans: the Southerners were to vote for free silver in exchange for Western votes against the so-called Force Bill, which would establish federal supervision at the polls in Southern states during national elections. Henry claimed quite rightly that the silver millionaires were campaigning for free silver more ardently and more successfully than the poor farmers; the South and West were in debt, and would benefit from a depreciated currency that would ruin the rest of the country.

Henry had been having grave financial problems of his own. It was difficult to keep the *Woman's Journal* going in these new and perilous times. It had been suggested that he convert the paper from a weekly to a monthly, but perhaps with a sense that Lucy would have frowned on such a move, he felt that it would be like giving up the suffrage fight. Emily described Henry at seventy-three as being physically well, but aging rapidly. "I was struck by the change in his walk—his marked stoop, and the evident general loss of strength. He is the same affectionate fellow." She continued to regret his "want of hopeful faith." [3]

Henry's physical needs were well provided for. In the Dorchester house, besides Alice and Beth Hagar, who more and more assumed the role of younger daughter, there was usually a housekeeper. In the summer of 1900, while both girls were away, Ellen, driven from the Vineyard by a severe attack of rheumatism, came to keep Henry company in a drier climate.

The entire family was joined in concern about Ellen. "Poor Ellen," Henry wrote to Alice, "really ought no longer to live alone. But who can and will make so great a sacrifice of home comfort as to make her a permanent member of the family?" Certainly not Henry, who, according to his daughter, was driven "nearly distracted" by his younger sister. Nevertheless to amuse her he would sit for hours reading to her through her ear trumpet. Ellen was never so happy, Henry thought, as when she was talking to someone; but during most of her life nowadays there was no one to talk to.

Yet Ellen, now in her seventies, continued independent in thought and vigorous in expression. In 1896 she had been an ardent supporter of McKinley because he was in favor of Cuban independence. The long and bloody rebellion of Cuba against Spanish oppression had become a matter of deep concern to many divergent groups of Americans: to the sugar interests with holdings in Cuba, to those who, in this period of imperialist expansion, feared that if Spain left the island a stronger power would move in, to those who had imperialist ambitions for the United States, and to those who, like Ellen, pitied the mistreated, rebellious Cubans. Ellen entered into verbal battle with Henry because he maintained "the fatal proposition" that the worst peace was better than the best war. She accused him of being "so warped out of his original nature and all his principles" [4] as to side with "the criminal oppressor Spain"; but shortly afterward she was asking indignantly how he could so misunderstand her as to believe she was pro-war. She believed the United States should offer to buy Cuba from Spain *"for the Cubans"* in order to avoid combat. To Henry's suggestion that republican leaders in Cuba might be venal, she replied that she considered them all intelligent and noble. There was no compromise in Ellen.

Then the S.S. *Maine,* standing by in Havana harbor to evacuate American citizens, was sunk—it was never clear how—and to the cry of "Remember the *Maine,*" war fever swept the country, and the United States declared war on Spain, in spite of the fact that at the last moment Spain had capitulated and agreed to Cuban reforms. A certain panic swept over the Eastern seaboard. Alice told Kitty that many people were "much afraid of being bombarded." [5] Emma was planning to move her family to Martha's Vineyard where there was no town large enough to be worth shelling.[6] Alice herself, who was busily working on a biography of her mother, thought of leaving Boston and going to stay with her aunt in Gardner.

The Infirmary played its small role in the war. It turned over its children's ward to "soldiers who had broken down" on their way through the city, until a hospital was set up in Long Island City, and the Red Cross induced Dr. Cushier's niece, Dr. Mercelis, and some of the other young doctors to volunteer as nurses and caretakers.[7] Women doctors were still not treated with the same respect as their male counterparts.

In 1900 Ellen alone of the Blackwells supported William Jennings Bryan in the presidential election, not on the silver issue, but because she believed he would have limited the war to the Caribbean, instead of carrying it to the Pacific and capturing the Philippines, as her formerly admired McKinley had done.

Ellen's personal life was harder than ever. "She grows more difficult to help as she grows older," Emily told Elizabeth. Her infirmities had increased. Her weak legs were less and less able to support her great weight. She ought not to live alone; but she could not adjust to the household of any of the family, nor could she keep "help." What were they to do about her as she grew older and feebler? [8]

However, in the early winter of 1900 Ellen was in particularly good spirits and financially sounder than usual. She had used her inheritance from Marian to refurbish her houses, and as a result they were all rented, and she even had a surplus of five or six hundred dollars in the bank. She spent that Christmas happily with Henry and Alice in Boston. Just after the new year, she stopped at Sam and Nettie's house on her way back to Lawrence. There she suffered a stroke, and lay for thirteen days in "complete helplessness and weariness, but not severe pain." On January 15, 1901, she died peacefully. She was a few days less than seventy-three. Exactly a week later, marking with a fine historic sense the end of an era and the beginning of a century, Queen Victoria died too.

Ellen was buried next to her mother and her adopted daughter Susie in Greenwood Cemetery. Henry, who in recent years had been driven to near distraction by her, wrote a brotherly and reminiscent obituary in the *Woman's Journal*. "A woman of warm affections, unwearied benevolence, and generous disposition, she devoted much of her scanty means to the aid of others, often at the sacrifice of her own comfort and convenience. Her life, equally rare and admirable, was a triumph of personal industry. . . . She did not leave on the face of the earth a single enemy." And he might have added, hardly more friends.

It was for Henry a year of mourning and obituaries. By mid-April Lucy's brother Frank and her sister Sarah, Emma's mother, had both died. They were the last of Lucy's generation.

At the time of Ellen's death, Emily was on her way to southern Europe to escape the New York winter, a trip which Ellen had unsuccessfully opposed because of the lack of indoor heating in Mediterranean countries. Emily was in Palermo late in January, and had not yet learned that Ellen had died. Elizabeth feared she would be much grieved, "for Emily and Ellen, just like Sam and Harry, was one of the pairs in which our family has been so curiously divided." [9]

But long years and many erosions had intervened, and Emily's response to Elizabeth's letter was less than heartbroken. "Your note enclosing telegram with the unexpected news of Ellen's death reached me yesterday. Certainly the departure of any member of the family comes with a painful shock, even though you may have known that it could not long have been postponed. Poor Ellen, she had a hard life, because her good qualities and her deficiencies were so compounded that it could not be otherwise, yet I think to the end she enjoyed life as much as any one of us." Emily said that she had long worried for fear Ellen would endure an extended period of incapacity when no proper provision could be made for her "in view of her extremely positive individuality and her eccentricities." [10] Emily went on to tell Elizabeth about her trip. It almost seemed that by taking herself off so expeditiously, Ellen had solved a problem.

But the Blackwells' concern, as well as Ellen's eccentricities, survived her. She had over the years repeatedly informed the family and Cornelia herself that the girl was her sole heir. Yet when the will was read, it was discovered that Ellen had changed it, so that not only had she not left Neenie everything, but had not even adequately provided for her. The reason was assumed to be Ellen's mistrust of Cornelia's husband, who she was afraid would get his hands on the money. Yet there is no satisfying explanation of her posthumous unkindness to a girl she alone had always loved and defended. Cornelia received nothing but a life interest in Ellen's East Orange house. The amount of her interest may be judged by Emily's suggestion that she be permitted to draw fifty dollars a month until her income began, so that she would not be in want. On Cornelia's death, the house was to go not to her children, but to Sam and Nettie's four younger daughters. The rest of Ellen's estate went to them at once. Even Sam and his daughters were unhappy that they had superseded Neenie. Ellen's other child, Paul, by now settled out West, received nothing. But Emily's Nannie was given outright three acres of Martha's Vineyard land.

Mr. Whall wasted no time in contesting the will, and, to Emily's alarm, intended to call Nannie as a witness, since Ellen had told Nannie she intended leaving everything to Neenie. Emily thought it might end by Ellen's being declared intestate, and that the "unfortunate circumstances" of Cornelia's marriage, which they had made such efforts to conceal, would be revealed. Whall claimed that Neenie was Ellen's adopted daughter, but of course the adoption had never been made legal. Emily's chief interest was to protect Nannie. About Cornelia she cared very little.

Nannie by now was also—and most respectably—married. Her husband, Elon Gail Huntington, like her adoptive mother, was a physician. When Ellen died they had been married for nearly two years. At the time of Nannie's marriage, Emily had written to Elizabeth that Nannie was an "affectionate little thing," who kept insisting that, wherever she might be, if Emily needed her, she would come. But Emily had encouraged the marriage, for she did not want Nannie to be "alone and lonely" when she was gone. And besides, "You know I have never relied on her as you do on Kitty. Dr. Cushier really occupies the younger sister's position toward me. Nannie has always been the child, and though she is now just 29, she has always been so much younger that I have always desired she should not feel responsible . . . toward me as I grew older." [11] Of all the adopted children, Nannie alone called her adoptive mother Mamma.

Nannie had indeed developed late. She was twenty-two when she joined a dancing class and went to her first dancing parties. And it was in 1896, when she was almost twenty-six, that Emily said she did not wish to winter in a warm climate alone, or to take Nannie from New York where for the first time she was beginning to have a circle of young friends.[12] However, even after Nannie's marriage, Emily was not entirely deprived of her companionship. Dr. Huntington was a naval officer on active duty, and for much of the early period of their marriage was away at sea. Even in the spring of 1902, when Nannie was about to have a baby, he was away, and his wife was with Emily. Nannie's son, Elon Gail, Jr., was born by forceps delivery at the Infirmary early in June. The next winter Emily was living with Dr. Cushier and Dr. Mercelis in East Orange, and Nannie, still without her husband, was boarding nearby.

"It is not cheerful to feel one's powers of work diminishing," Emily had written to Elizabeth as long ago as 1897. "I am far more afraid of living too long than of dying too soon." [13] She had had a severe cough again, and felt the winter had been wasted as far as work was concerned.

That spring provided a much greater threat to her work. In 1888, the Infirmary College had moved to a group of buildings on Fifteenth Street, next door to the Infirmary. Late in April 1897, at two-thirty one morning, smoke was seen pouring out of the elevator shaft at the college. The alarm was given. Within minutes the fire had spread disastrously. By great good fortune the thick outer walls between the buildings protected the hospital, and though plans for evacuating the patients were prepared, not one had to be moved. The *Times* of April 23 commented that "the splendid discipline of the institution aided the fire-chief and his men greatly."

Luckily the building was insured. College courses continued in makeshift quarters next door, and rebuilding began at once. Within a year a new, better-equipped building was in full operation. The new college was doomed to a short life. At the thirty-first annual commencement exercises on May 25, 1899, Emily delivered an address in which she announced that the school would be permanently closed at the end of that year. The Infirmary College had been created because most medical schools were associated with universities which did not admit women. Now Johns Hopkins admitted women, and Cornell University had opened a medical school in New York City where, as in its college, women were to be freely enrolled "in the same classes, under the same faculty, and with the same clinical opportunities as men," and with the better laboratory and clinical facilities made possible by a university connection. Cornell had offered to take any students who wished to transfer there when the Infirmary College closed. The college had outlived its function. In only one respect would there be a falling off; the Cornell school had no women professors. Five years later the *Woman's Journal* reported another difference. Cornell, in spite of its promises, was requiring women to spend their first two years of study at the medical school in Ithaca, though men students could take their entire course in New York City.

At the time the Infirmary College closed, Emily confided to Elizabeth that, with the fire and the opening of Cornell Medical School, their enrollment had dropped fifty per cent, and that they might be unable to survive. She regretted the disappointment of the young women teachers who had planned to make the Infirmary College their career; but she believed more could be accomplished by using the money and energy to enlarge and improve the hospital, which would continue to offer young women doctors special opportunities for clinical training.

The closing of the college completed, in 1900 Emily retired from active service. She was now listed in the Infirmary catalogue only as a consulting physician. She had in any case been confined indoors for several months each winter. Now she sold her house on Twentieth Street, and decided to spend the winters in a warm climate. But even this was not simple. "Dr. Cushier is not prepared to give up practice when it comes to the point, and I sh'd not feel free to terminate our present arrangements abruptly." Dr. Cushier was, after all, eleven years younger, and had a good practice and family responsibilities. So Emily decided to stay for a year as a tenant in the house she had just sold. She told Elizabeth she had a great deal still to live for and was not unhappy. "Dr. Cushier is sincerely attached to me, and would never wish to leave me." Emily wished also to make a home for Nannie until her husband was transferred to shore duty.

However, free of her obligations, and apparently financially secure, she began to make more frequent trips to Europe. She had been in Scotland with Elizabeth in the summer of 1899. Now in the winter of 1900–1901, Dr. Cushier decided to leave her commitments and go with Emily to southern Europe. It was during their absence that Ellen died.

They had barely returned in the spring when Emily was confronted with another sorrow. Sam was now very ill, and that summer had a major operation, followed in the fall by a second. Immediately after the second operation he suffered several strokes, which George was convinced were caused by the experimental "spinal narcosis" used without the family's consent.

Sam died in late October. What his loss meant to his wife can be imagined by a comment of Alice's the year before, when Nettie had gone to Martha's Vineyard some time before her husband could join her, and Sam was dreadfully lonely. "Such a pair of lovers I never saw, after more than 40 years of wedded life."[14] Yet, on another occasion, Nettie described her philosophy of death, which it is to be hoped came to her aid at this sad time. "But after all, it is only to me slipping through a door which opens to receive a new guest, and shuts again from the rest of us for the present."

Whatever disagreements the family may have had on other subjects, they had been in complete agreement about Sam. He had been for them the symbol of everything a man should be. Lucy, when asked who was the most saintly man she knew, had unhesitatingly named her brother-in-law. Now Elizabeth expressed the same feeling. "As I write, I can hardly realise that my next in age, my childhood's companion, the devoted father, the upright exemplary man—is gone from among us; and that in this life, I can never see him again!" [15]

Perhaps his most appropriate obituary was composed by Sam himself when, a year before he died, he wrote to Henry that he felt they had not lived wholly in vain, "nor wholly blind to the abiding and eternal verities. . . . The faith, hope and charity imbedded in the nature of man is Heaven's greatest gift and truest prophecy—our one assurance that 'the future will transcend the past, an endless betterment designed to last.' " His childhood faith had endured undefeated through a long lifetime.

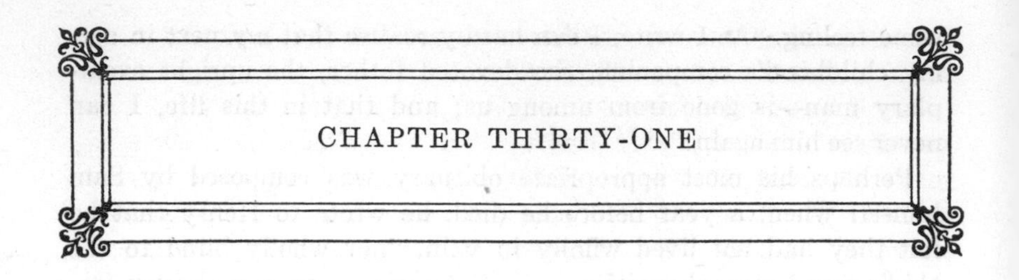

CHAPTER THIRTY-ONE

The shock of her father's death was too much for Grace. She was taken to the hospital, a victim of "nervous prostration." She had in fact passed beyond her former state of tension and eccentricity. Now periods of quiet and comparative normality began to alternate with deep depression and occasional violence. During her normal periods she stayed sometimes with Henry and Alice, sometimes with her sister Ethel and her husband, but most often with her mother. The family were constantly warning Nettie that Grace should be sent away, but it was a decision Nettie could not bear to make. It was years before she conceded that Grace was more relaxed and less subject to her "spells" in the quiet of Martha's Vineyard, and turned her over to a large extent to a local woman who loved and tended her for the rest of her life.

The family were also united in urging Nettie to leave her New Jersey house and live with one of her married daughters. She was figuratively and physically immovable; so before many months had passed, Agnes and her husband, Tom, temporarily moved in with her. Living with one or another of her children was an arrangement which persisted over most of the rest of Nettie's long life. Agnes's daughter, now Mrs. Charles Whidden, says that her grandmother had a close emotional and intellectual relationship with all her daughters, "but my mother was her favorite, and she made her home with us for a great many years." [1]

Edith, meanwhile, the only daughter besides Grace still unmarried, was in spite of her aunt Emily's dire predictions, continuing to make a career of medicine. She was doctor and teacher of physiology at the State Normal School in Greensboro, North Carolina, where late in 1902 she vaccinated fifty girls because of a smallpox scare. "How Aunt Elizabeth will disapprove!" [2] Alice commented.

Elizabeth was still living quietly with Kitty at Hastings, where Emily now visited her nearly every year. One of the results of this greater intimacy with Kitty was that in her letters to Elizabeth's adopted daughter, Emily at long last referred to family members not as Mr. and Mrs., but as Uncle and Aunt. It had taken Kitty fifty years to gain full membership in the clan. Even now she did not share the Blackwell name.

George was continuing, openly in presents and otherwise secretly, to supplement Elizabeth's income, for now that she had ceased to earn, she had barely enough to live on, to keep her house in repair, and to make her summer trips to Kilmun; and George was determined she should not touch her capital. Yet she continued as always to question the investment of her money; and George continued patiently to explain. In 1906, Elizabeth, who had always been as reluctant to accept money not due her as to be deprived of what she considered should be hers, permitted her rich brother to send her money so that she and Kitty could go to the United States. So small a sum was meaningless to George. He had continued to increase his real-estate holdings, and was now a wealthy man.

Though Kitty had over the years visited the American family, Elizabeth had never crossed the Atlantic since she went to live in England thirty-seven years before. Where she found the courage at eighty-five to brave the ocean and the virulent seasickness it always caused her, it is hard to know. Certainly she felt this was her farewell to the two brothers and the sister yet alive, and her only contact with the rapidly increasing family of great-nieces and great-nephews.

Emily and Dr. Cushier, though they spent the summers in York Cliffs and took winter trips to Europe or California, were still officially living in New Jersey with Dr. Mercelis. In 1904 Nannie, who was again pregnant, had settled with her son in a house ten minutes' walk away. They feared Elon would still have two or three years of sea duty. "The more I see of the service the more heartily I dislike and disapprove of the army and navy," Emily wrote to Elizabeth. And added with happy unawareness of the future, "I am very glad that there is so growing a feeling for the substitution of arbitration for wars." [3] Finally, not long before Elizabeth's visit, Dr. Huntington became ill, and was declared unfit for sea service. He was to be transferred to land duty and his family.

George and Emma also lived nearby in New Jersey for part of each year. In 1905, Emma had in fact been elected president of the New Jersey Woman Suffrage Association. Howard took his Ph.D. in physics at Harvard that spring, and his sister Anna spent a year at Smith.

Of the three remaining Blackwell women of her generation, Antoinette was now by far the most active. In 1905 she had at last consented to give up her home in East Orange, with what reluctance is apparent in a story Alice told in the *Woman's Journal* on Nettie's eightieth birthday, which took place that year. Only a year before, when Alice had found her aunt digging potatoes in her garden, Nettie had told her that "any woman who cannot go out into her own garden and dig potatoes does not know what pleasure is!" Nevertheless, after rearranging or disposing of the accumulation of nearly fifty years of marriage, she had moved to West One Hundred and Fifteenth Street in New York with her unmarried daughters, Edith and Grace.

She was still regularly attending suffrage conventions. In 1902 at the annual convention which she and Henry attended in Washington, D.C., she delivered an address in which she contrasted "the dying old chivalry, which made itself sole umpire of the benefits to be granted, and the increasing new chivalry, which consults the beneficiaries themselves as to their needs and desires." [4] In 1905 she traveled to Portland, Oregon, with Henry and Alice to attend the first national suffrage convention held on the West Coast. Carrie Chapman Catt was president of the National American Association. The old order was changing. Elizabeth Cady Stanton had died in 1902. Susan B. Anthony died in the spring of 1906. In introducing Nettie, Mrs. Catt said, "The combination of her sweet personality and her invincible soul has won friends for woman suffrage wherever she has gone." [5] After the convention Henry and Alice visited Seattle and Vancouver, but Nettie and some of the other old suffragists took a trip by steamer to Alaska. Two years before, Nettie had gone on a tour to the Holy Land, and had brought home a bottle of water from the Jordan with which by 1905 she had christened two new grandsons and a granddaughter in her proliferating family.

When Elizabeth arrived in the United States in the early summer of 1906, it was to find painfully few of the familiar old faces, but many bright new ones. She and Kitty stayed for nearly four months. They landed in Boston and spent most of their time visiting relatives in the country—York Cliffs, Martha's Vineyard, East Orange. Elizabeth was so frail and so shaken by the sea voyage, for she was as bad a sailor as ever, that the family kept her from visiting the Infirmary and the great city that housed it, though she longed to do so. It was, after all, the chief monument to her endeavor. But the real purpose of her visit was to bid what everyone knew must be final farewells for most of the older generation.

Yet the next family loss was not one of them. That summer at Martha's Vineyard, Agnes's son came down with typhoid fever, and Agnes's doctor sister, Edith, was called in to care for him. The child was saved, but Edith herself caught the disease, and died in the fall of 1906. So the girl, whose desire to be a physician and whose ability to be one Dr. Emily had so doubted, tragically proved her case.

The family's grief was lightened the following year by Howard's marriage and his sister Anna's engagement, though Emily commented that she did not see how George would be able to give up his beloved daughter. In 1908 Anna married Charles Belden, who a year after their marriage was appointed State Librarian of Massachusetts. Hannah's long-lasting and much-traveled wedding china came back across the Atlantic to Howard and his wife.

George, Emma, Anna and Henry had had an adventurous time in the early days of 1907, when on a Caribbean vacation they were caught in a severe earthquake in Kingston, Jamaica. George, who was in the street at the moment, was badly bruised and almost choked by dust. Henry, sitting in his room in the hotel, heard a "terrific rumbling roar," and was hurled to the floor. "The whole building seemed to go to pieces . . . the outer walls going out into the courtyard." He managed to escape, and in the corridor met Emma and Anna, who had been in the room opposite his. Characteristically Henry waited to grab his notebook before rushing downstairs. But they had been fortunate. Around them the city was in ruins, the number of dead and injured appalling.

The following year Nettie helped to dedicate the first Unitarian church in Elizabeth, New Jersey, built on land she had contributed, part of the property on which her own house stood. She must that year have been even more than ordinarily aware of how many who had been close to her were gone, for in 1908, almost sixty years after she had earned it, almost sixty years after the men who studied side by side with her had received their degrees, Antoinette traveled to Oberlin to receive an honorary degree of Doctor of Divinity. It was too late for Sam to know, too late for Lucy, who had thought that Nettie demeaned herself by returning to a college which had told her she could not hope for a degree.

Henry remained to celebrate her triumph. He continued to struggle to keep the *Woman's Journal* going, to make up its large yearly deficit, to keep alive this memorial to his dead wife. Yet his sense of guilt had never abated. Though he and Lucy had both considered theirs a happy marriage, he continued to brood upon his failures. To Alice at Monadnock Mountain he wrote of a trip they had taken there when she was a baby, and of how he had skipped down the mountainside with her on his shoulder, much to her mother's alarm. It is strange, he said, "that the few recollections of the trips of those early days are mostly connected with some silly escapade where I vexed my wife."[6] How true, he reflected, that the evil that "*we*" do lives after us. Yet underline "we" as he would, it was Lucy who had died, not he. How much in those days before the unconscious was a household word, did the "wild boy," the practical joker, the family wit, really blame his wife for those unhappy memories?

His years of guilt were nearly over. In the summer of 1909 he went with Alice to Seattle to speak at the annual woman suffrage convention. He had not missed a national convention in forty years. Now even his daughter was so advanced in age that she resigned as recording secretary of the association, an office she had held for twenty years. When Henry rose to speak, the audience stood to pay tribute to his years of service to the cause. He was in excellent health and spirits.

He returned from his Western trip still in apparent health, not feeling pressed or overworked, but with "unabated zest." At the beginning of September he became ill, and on the seventh day died quietly. "Papa passed away peacefully soon after noon today, after lying unconscious for some hours," Alice wrote to Kitty. "Uncle George and Emma are here, and everybody has been very kind. I cannot write more now." [7] She was, in spite of kindness, very much alone. Beth Hagar had been married in 1904 in a wedding at the Dorchester house, as befitted a daughter.

At memorial services held at the annual suffrage convention of 1910, words were quoted from Henry's first suffrage speech in Cleveland in 1853 when he had so recently met and fallen in love with Lucy Stone. "The interests of the sexes are inseparably connected, and in the elevation of the one lies the salvation of the other. Therefore, I claim a part in this last and grandest movement of the ages, for whatever concerns woman concerns the race." [8]

The tributes were many and warm. To the world, if not to himself, he had amply fulfilled his obligations to his wife and the cause for which she had fought. "He lived," his daughter said, "with protest on his lips, and resistance in his will, against everything that harmed or hindered humanity."

Elizabeth was still alive, or, rather, had not yet died. The summer after her American visit, in the inn at Kilmun, she fell down a flight of stairs. Her injuries were thought to be slight, but whether from physical damage or shock, she was never the same. Returned to Hastings, she lay in her bedroom or on the terrace overlooking the sea. By the time of Henry's death, she no longer spoke, and it was doubtful whether she understood what was said to her. She lay for months in this limbo, with Kitty in constant attendance. How long the time must have seemed to the younger woman is unimaginable, for Elizabeth was beyond companionship. She made the final step to death on May 31, 1910. She was eighty-one years old. The *Woman's Journal* noted that at the time of her death there were 7,399 women physicians and surgeons in the United States.

The obituary notices were laudatory. The London *Times,* which carried a two-and-a-half column account of Elizabeth's life and early struggles, decried the general opinion that Elizabeth was the first American woman doctor, for "England was the home not only of her birth but of her heart and her affection." The New York papers carried shorter but no less respectful notices.

Kitty, as though in thrall, remained at Rock House sorting Elizabeth's papers and disposing of her personal effects. She and Alice had always planned to live out the end of their lives together, but though Alice kept begging her to come to Boston, Kitty stayed on, with no one to hold her but a few close friends, Frances Titterton among them, and memories of her foster mother. She was still in Hastings in mid-1912.

Elizabeth had been buried in Kilmun, which she had so loved, and when Kitty finally sold the Hastings house, she moved not to Boston but to Kilmun, taking Elizabeth's books and other favorite objects with her, as though all that was left for her was to remain in Elizabeth's shadow. The family had contributed to the monument erected over the grave in the green mountain scenery of Scotland. The tomb was topped by an ornate Maltese cross, and under it were engraved Elizabeth's words: "It is only when we have learned to recognize that God's law for the human body is as sacred as—nay, is one with—God's law for the human soul, that we shall begin to understand the religion of health."

In March of 1912 when England was in the throes of a coal strike, in a time of general hardship and suffering, Kitty wrote to her suffragist cousin Alice, "To think that at such a time of distress those Suffragists take to window smashing! They must be clean gone mad! . . . Aunt Elizabeth always said 'Nothing is ever gained by bad manners!' " [9] It was in its way another epitaph.

Kitty did not tear herself loose until more than eleven years after Elizabeth's death. In the summer of 1921, when she was already aging, half-blind and half-deaf, she brought her dog, only remnant of her past life, and came to America to live with Alice. Alice had long since donated the Dorchester house as a home for convalescents, and was installed in an apartment in a Boston hotel. It was after her return to America that Kitty finally took for herself the name of Blackwell, so long withheld.

After Elizabeth's final visit, Emily lived on in York Cliffs in summer and New Jersey in winter. Dr. Huntington was transferred to New York in 1909, and he and Nannie bought a house near Emily's. Nannie now had three sons. In 1908 Emily had expressed her contentment to Elizabeth about their own professional child: "The Infirmary is thriving, it now has 100 beds, a large out practice and quite a staff of women doctors connected with it." And graciously, "Your work has borne fruit in many ways." [10]

Emily was well the summer after Elizabeth's death. Then in early September Alice reported to Kitty that Aunt Emily was ill, though not seriously. Six days later she added to the same letter that Emily had died. It was as if, in death as in life, she had followed her older, more daring sister. Strangely, she had died on September 7, the anniversary of her brother Henry's death.

Though she had spent most of her long life in New York, had been dean of the first woman's medical school there and head of the first woman's hospital, the notices of her death were no longer or fuller than those of her "English" sister six months earlier. They were seemingly based on a single release, and told the history of her rejection by one medical school after another, with no indication that this was because for a woman to try to enter a bona fide medical school was then—except among Blackwells—nearly unheard of. It is interesting that all the columns, though selective in other respects, contained the information that Sarah Ellen Blackwell, artist and author, had been Dr. Emily's sister.

Alice, who wrote the long and laudatory obituary in the *Woman's Journal,* found it necessary to include what may have been a partial explanation of Emily's failure to make a more sympathetic impression. "She had a warm and tender heart, though it was hidden under a reserved manner which made her rather awe-inspiring to strangers."

Less than a year later George too died, last of his generation of brothers and sisters. They left behind them many descendants, natural and adopted. In 1910 Alice had commented that there were fifty members of the family at Martha's Vineyard. Alice herself embraced every cause that arose during her long life. She was a partisan of the Russian Revolution, a friend of the Russian noblewoman turned rebel, Marie Breshkovsky, whose reminiscences she edited and published as *Little Grandmother of the Russian Revolution,* supporter of Sacco and Vanzetti, friend of Harry Bridges, whom in 1942 she addressed as Dear Comrade. The others were no more radical than their neighbors and friends. They had no need to be. They were secure because their elders had fought so long and so courageously.

Emma died in 1920, just before the final meeting of the National American Woman Suffrage Association, which was disbanded, its work accomplished. As heritage, it left the League of Woman Voters, formerly a section of the association, thereafter an independent organization. In the national election of November 2, 1920, women voted throughout the United States.

Among them was Antoinette Brown Blackwell. She was ninety-five years old. In 1911, a few days before her eighty-sixth birthday, she had taken part in a suffrage parade on New York's Fifth Avenue. In 1915 she had published her last book, *The Social Side of Mind and Action.* That year too she had preached her final sermon in All Souls' Church in Elizabeth. Now in 1920 she cast her vote, in spite of the fact that by then she was blind, and that a year earlier Alice had described her as subject to "illusions—happy ones, fortunately," which made her seem to be in "a pleasant dream," and although six months later it was thought that she might have to be hospitalized because of her mental state. Nevertheless, at the time of that first national election in which women were permitted to vote, she was well enough to go to the polls, and, with the help of an election officer, to mark her ballot.

Her long life ended the following year. The work she and her friends and colleagues had done had immeasurably extended the horizons of women. The elevation of politics, the international understanding, the ennobling of human life which they believed would come from women's freer participation in the world's work may seem today the bitterest of ironies. But they erred in expecting too much, not in achieving too little. No woman in our society will ever again be so limited in possibility as the women who lived before these early rebels fought their battle. Even the woman who chooses, as so many do today, to retreat to home and children and electrically equipped kitchen has been permitted a choice. Her role was not inevitably decreed for her because of her sex. And she can make her decision better trained and better educated than she would have been had these pioneers not made their choice before her.

A plaque on the wall of Elizabeth's Rock House in Hastings bears a short biography followed by lines adapted from Robert Browning, lines which might equally have applied to any of the Blackwells:

> One who never turned *her* back but marched breast forward,
> Never doubted clouds would break,
> Never dreamed, though right were worsted, wrong would triumph,
> Held we fall to rise, are baffled to fight better,
> Sleep to wake.

The great New York Infirmary is a living memorial. So expanded, rebuilt and modernized that if Emily and Elizabeth could see it they would not recognize it as their own, it is nonetheless their creation and their monument.

NOTES

Since the Blackwell name would have to be endlessly repeated in these notes, it has been omitted throughout. The great bulk of Blackwell manuscripts is in the Library of Congress. There is a large collection in the Library on the History of Women at Radcliffe College. Letters from Elizabeth and Emily to Barbara Bodichon are in the Columbia University Library. Abbreviated book titles refer to books listed in the bibliography.

CHAPTER I

1–5. Anna, Reminiscences written to Henry, Jan. 1880 and ff.
6. Henry to Samuel, Aug. 25, 1879
7–12. Anna, Reminiscences
13. Elizabeth, *Pioneer Work*
14. Elizabeth to Samuel, Aug. 15, 1885
15. Henry to Samuel, Aug. 25, 1879
16–17. Anna, Reminiscences
18–19. Henry to Samuel, Aug. 25, 1879

CHAPTER II

1. Hayes, *Political and Social History*
2. Wood, *Nineteenth Century Britain*
3. Elizabeth, *Pioneer Work*
4–5. Anna, Reminiscences, Jan. 1880 and ff.
6. Henry to Samuel, Aug. 25, 1879
7–9. Anna, Reminiscences
10–11. Henry, Reminiscences
12. Elizabeth, *Pioneer Work*

CHAPTER III

1. Samuel, Sr., Notes on Two Years Residence in New York
2. Greene, *A Glance at New York*
3. Henry, Reminiscences
4. Samuel, Sr., Notes
5. Greene, *A Glance at New York*
6–8. Henry, Reminiscences
9. Samuel, Sr., Notes

10. Samuel, Diaries
11. Elizabeth, Diaries, 1837–1839
12. Samuel, Sr., Notes
13. Henry, Reminiscences
14. Elizabeth, Diaries, 1837–1839
15. Samuel, Diaries
16–17. Elizabeth, Diaries

CHAPTER IV

1. Samuel to Mr. Gower
2. Elizabeth, Diaries
3. Samuel to Mr. Gower
4. Elizabeth, Diaries
5. Anna, "Elizabeth Blackwell"
6. Elizabeth, Diaries
7. Samuel to Mr. Gower
8. Trollope, *Domestic Manners*
9. Samuel, Diaries
10. *Woman's Journal,* Oct. 11, 1902
11. Elizabeth, Diaries
12. Henry to Cousin Samuel, Oct. 30, 1840
13. Marian to Henry, 1840
14. Hannah to Henry, undated
15. *Woman's Journal,* Jan. 22, 1887
16. Elizabeth to Henry, Mar. 18, 1841

CHAPTER V

1. Elizabeth, Diaries
2. Samuel, Diaries
3. Emerson, "Man the Reformer"
4. Frothingham, *Memoir of Channing*
5. Anna to Henry, Sept. 15, 1840
6–8. Samuel, Diaries

CHAPTER VI

1. Samuel, Diaries, 1842
2. Samuel, Diaries, 1847
3. Elizabeth to Marian, June 22, [1847]
4. Henry, Diaries, May 13, 1846
5. Elizabeth to Marian, Mar. 15, 1846
6. Elizabeth to Henry, Oct. 8, 1845

7. Elizabeth to Henry, Aug. 17, 1845
8. Samuel, Diaries, Aug. 21, 1845
9. Henry, Diaries, Jan. 16, 1846
10. Henry, Diaries, Feb. 1, 1846
11. Samuel, Diaries, Oct. 27, 1842
12. Samuel, Diaries, Aug. 9, 1845
13. Elizabeth to Marian, June 22, [1847]
14. Samuel, Diaries, Jan. 27, 1847

CHAPTER VII

1. Elizabeth to Hannah, from Henderson, undated
2. Elizabeth, *Pioneer Work*
3. Stanton, *History of Woman Suffrage*, Vol. I, p. 90
4. Samuel, Diaries, June 1845
5. Elizabeth to Marian, June 22, [1847]
6. Elizabeth, *Pioneer Work*, Appendix I
7. Brown, "Capability of Women"
8. Elizabeth, *Pioneer Work*, Appendix I
9. Anna, "Elizabeth Blackwell"
10. Elizabeth to Dr. Gertrude Walker, Apr. 21, 1900
11. Sanes, "Elizabeth Blackwell"
12. Hannah to Henry, Sept. 13, 1848
13. Johnston, *Elizabeth Blackwell and Her Alma Mater*
14–15. "Dr. Elizabeth Blackwell's Graduation"
16. Elizabeth, *Pioneer Work*

CHAPTER VIII

1. Samuel, Diaries, Feb. 17, 1847
2. Samuel, Diaries, July 25, 1847
3. Samuel, Diaries, Apr. 8, 1848
4. Henry to W. W. Wright, Aug. 3, 1848
5. Samuel, Diaries, Apr. 16, 1848
6. Samuel, Diaries, Jan. 24, 1849
7. Howard to Henry, July 14, 1848
8. Howard to Henry, Apr. 19, 1850 (Ac. of Med.)
9. Samuel, Diaries, Dec. 9, 1849
10. Elizabeth, *Pioneer Work*
11. Marian to family, undated
12. Ellen, Diaries, 1850
13. Marian to family, June 19, 1850
14. Marian to family, Aug. 4, 1850

15. Ellen, Diaries, Sept. 1850
16. *Woman's Journal,* May 11, 1895

CHAPTER IX

1. Elizabeth to Marian, June 5, 1849
2. Elizabeth, *Pioneer Work*
3. Elizabeth to Emily, June 5, 1850
4. Anna to family, Nov. 22, 1849
5. Elizabeth, *Pioneer Work*
6. Elizabeth to Emily, Nov. 20, 1855

7–8. Elizabeth, *Pioneer Work*

CHAPTER X

1. Emily, Diaries
2. Alice, *Woman's Journal,* Oct. 6, 1906
3. Elizabeth to Lady Byron, Aug. 5, 1852
4. Emily, Diaries
5. Henry, "Fourth of July," 1854
6. Elizabeth, *Pioneer Work*
7. Alice, *Woman's Journal,* Oct. 6, 1906
8. Meyer, ed., *Woman's Work in America*
9. Emily, Diaries, July 5, 1854
10. Elizabeth to Emily, Nov. 13, 1854
11. Elizabeth, *Pioneer Work*
12. Elizabeth to Emily, Oct. 1, 1854
13. Kitty, Reminiscences, dictated to Alice

CHAPTER XI

1. Henry, Reminiscences
2. Elizabeth to Marian, Dec. 24–26, [1850]
3. Henry, *Woman's Journal,* May 11, 1895
4. Henry, Diaries, July 2, 1846
5. Lucy Stone, Reminiscences
6. Lucy Stone to Antoinette Brown, undated
7. Elizabeth to Henry, Dec. 22, [1854]
8. Henry to Lucy Stone, July 2, 1853
9. Lucy Stone to Henry, July 27, 1853
10. Henry to Lucy Stone, Feb. 12, 1854
11. Henry to Lucy Stone, July 2, 1853
12. Alice, *Lucy Stone*
13. Henry to Lucy Stone, Mar. 18, 1855

14. Elizabeth to Emily, Sept. 15, [1854]
15. Elizabeth to Henry, Feb. 22, 1855
16. Ellen to Lucy Stone, Oct. 1, [1854]
17. Alice, *Lucy Stone*
18. Elizabeth to Henry, Feb. 22, 1855
19. Alice, *Lucy Stone*
20. William B. Brown, Memoirs
21. Antoinette, *Woman's Journal,* Mar. 4, 1879
22. Kerr, *Lady in the Pulpit*
23–24. Antoinette, Interview with Alice
25. Record of Ordination
26. Deen, *Great Women of the Christian Faith*
27. Samuel, Diaries, Nov. 8, 1853
28. Antoinette, Interview with Alice
29. Kerr, *Lady in the Pulpit*
30. Antoinette Brown to Samuel, Dec. 22, 1855
31. Ellen to Antoinette, Feb. 6, [1856]
32. Lucy Stone to Antoinette Brown, Jan. 20, 1856

CHAPTER XII

1. Henry to Augustus O. Moore, May 26, 1855
2. Samuel, Diaries, July 1855
3–4. Alice, *Lucy Stone*
5. Lucy Stone to Charles Burleigh, Mar. 10, 1856
6. Kerr, *Lady in the Pulpit*
7. Henry, Reminiscences, 1898
8. Henry to Lucy Stone, May 18, 1856
9. Lucy Stone to her mother, July 1, 1856
10. Kerr, *Lady in the Pulpit*
11. Samuel to Henry, July 7, 1856
12. Elizabeth to Emily, Nov. 13, 1854
13. Kitty, Reminiscences
14. Marian to Henry, July 22, [1856]
15. Elizabeth to Henry, [Nov. 3], 1856
16. Elizabeth to Emily, Nov. 13, 1854
17. Ellen to Lucy Stone, [1855]
18. Howard to Elizabeth, May 9, 1856
19–20. Samuel, Diaries, Feb. 2, 1851
21. Elizabeth to Henry, Nov. 29, [1846]
22. Emily to Henry, Mar. 23, 1855
23. Henry to Lucy Stone, Feb. 7, 1856

CHAPTER XIII

1. Hannah to Henry, Mar. 12, 1858
2. Elizabeth to Henry, Nov. 3, 1856
3. Henry to Lucy Stone, Sept. 8, 1857
4. Elizabeth to Mrs. William Elder, Oct. 16, [1857]
5. Elizabeth to Henry, Apr. 11, 1858
6. *New York Infirmary . . . 1854–1954*
7. Ellen to Lucy Stone, June 10, [1858]
8. Elizabeth, *Pioneer Work*
9. Kitty, Reminiscences
10. Elizabeth to Emily, Apr. 15, 1859
11. *British Medical Journal,* Nov. 22, 1958
12. Elizabeth, *Pioneer Work*
13. Elizabeth to Emily, Apr. 27, [1859]
14. Henry, Reminiscences
15. Susan Anthony to Antoinette, May 2, 1858
16. Samuel to Henry, Jan. 9, 1859
17. Elizabeth to Barbara Bodichon, Dec. 20, 1860

CHAPTER XIV

1. Howard to Samuel, Sept. 19, 1860
2. Marian to Henry, Oct. 8, 1860
3. Alice, *Woman's Journal,* Apr. 6, 1906
4. Elizabeth to Barbara Bodichon, Apr. 25, 1860
5. Emily to Barbara Bodichon, June 1–11, 1861
6. Elizabeth to Barbara Bodichon, June 5, 1861
7. *Woman's Journal,* July 10, 1897
8. Elizabeth to Barbara Bodichon, June 9, 1863
9. Elizabeth to Kitty, June 8, 1864

CHAPTER XV

1. Elizabeth to Barbara Bodichon, May 25, 1860
2. Elizabeth to Barbara Bodichon, Sept. 7, 1864
3. Hannah to Henry, Feb. 20, 1861
4. Hannah to Henry, July 1, 1861
5. Hannah to Henry, Mar. 5, 1861
6. Hannah to Lucy Stone, Dec. 11, 1861
7. Lucy Stone to Henry, Oct. 4, 1864
8. Lucy Stone to Susan Anthony, July 12, 1864

9–10. Antoinette to Samuel, undated

11. Emily, Diaries, Mar. 5, 1866

12. Anna to Elizabeth, Apr. 2, 1866
13. Henry to Kenyon, Feb. 11, 1864
14. Kenyon to Samuel and Henry, Mar. 4, 1864
15. Elizabeth to Marian, Oct. 5, 1866
16. Alice, Speech, Jan. 25, 1911
17. Elizabeth to Barbara Bodichon, Jan. 13, 1867
18. Henry to Alice, Mar. 31, 1867
19. Elizabeth to Henry, Oct. 16, 1867
20. Samuel to Henry, Aug. 19, 1868

CHAPTER XVI

1. Emily to Barbara Bodichon, Nov. 2–5, 1867
2. Emily to Barbara Bodichon, June 25, 1869
3. Elizabeth to Kitty, Jan. 29, 1870
4. Elizabeth to Kitty, Feb. 23, 1870
5. Elizabeth to Kitty, May 14, [1870]
6. Ellen to Henry, June 7, [1869]
7. Elizabeth to Barbara Bodichon, Aug. 25, [1869]
8. For detailed analysis of this split see Hays, *Morning Star*

CHAPTER XVII

1. Kitty to family, Nov. 7, 1871
2. Kitty to Emily, Oct. 19, 1870
3. Elizabeth to Henry, Nov. 15, [1870]
4. Elizabeth to Kitty, May 14, [1870]
5. Kitty to Antoinette, Oct. 10, 1870
6. Elizabeth to Henry and Lucy, May 29, [1874]
7. Elizabeth to Kitty, Nov. 21, [1869]
8. Henry to Elizabeth, May 3, 1870
9. Henry to Elizabeth and Kitty, Dec. 31, 1871
10. Alice to Kitty, Mar. 16, 1872
11. Ellen to George, July 28, 1871
12. Emily to Lucy Stone, Dec. 17, 1871
13. Alice to Kitty, May 24, 1872
14. Alice to Kitty, Dec. 27, 1872
15. Alice to Kitty, Mar. 13, 1872
16. Marian to Alice, Aug. 8, 1872

CHAPTER XVIII

1. Elizabeth, *Woman's Journal,* May 6, 1871
2. Elizabeth, *Pioneer Work*

3. *Woman's Journal,* Mar. 25, 1871
4. Alice to Kitty, Dec. 25–27, 1874

CHAPTER XIX

1. Baker, *Fighting for Life*
2. Ellen to Kitty, Jan. 18, 1873
3. Kitty to Alice, June 11, 19, 1874
4. Elizabeth to Henry, June 1, 1872
5. Elizabeth to Emily and Ellen, Jan. 5, 1874
6. Elizabeth to Alice, Mar. 26, 1872
7. Elizabeth to Kitty, May 15, [1874]
8. Elizabeth, *Pioneer Work*
9. Elizabeth to Samuel, Sept. 7, [1874]
10. Elizabeth to Antoinette, June 5, 1875
11. Elizabeth to Emily, July 18, [1875]
12. Elizabeth to Samuel, Oct. 8, [1875]
13. Kitty to Alice, Oct. 22, 1875
14. Alice to Kitty, Dec. 5, 1886
15. Grace to Kitty, Nov. 22, [1875]
16. Elizabeth to Kitty, Feb. 14, [1876]
17. Henry to Lucy Stone, Feb. 22, 1877

CHAPTER XX

1. Elizabeth to Samuel, Aug. 11, 1874
2. Antoinette to Lucy Stone, Dec. 9, 1879
3. Marian to Elizabeth, Aug. 30, [1879]
4. Emily to Elizabeth, Aug. 12, 1878
5. Emily to Elizabeth, Nov. 21, 1878
6. George to Elizabeth, July 17, [1882]
7. Alice to Kitty, Dec. 27, 1885
8. Henry to Lucy Stone, Feb. 27, 1877
9. Alice to Kitty, May 29, 1880
10. Emily to Lucy Stone, Nov. 10, 1877
11. Antoinette to Lucy Stone, Apr. 10, 1878
12. Antoinette to Lucy Stone, May 25, 1878
13. Alice to Kitty, Sept. 16, 1879
14. Kitty to Alice, Nov. 22, 1876
15. Ellen to Kitty, Aug. 11, 1877

CHAPTER XXI

1. Alice to Kitty, Mar. 28, 1880
2. Emily to Marian, Nov. 17, 1876

3. *Woman's Journal,* May 28, 1887
4. Kitty to Alice, Feb. 21, 1878
5. Alice to Kitty, Feb. 22, 1879
6. Elizabeth to Samuel, Mar. 17, 1878
7. Elizabeth to Barbara Bodichon, Feb. 13, [1878]
8. Robinson, "Elizabeth Blackwell"
9. Elizabeth, *Pioneer Work*
10. Manton, *Elizabeth Garrett Anderson*
11. *Woman's Journal,* May 22, 1897
12. Ellen to Alice, Jan. 3, 1891
13. Anna to Henry, July 16, 1891
14. Elizabeth to Alice, Apr. 10, 1891
15. Elizabeth to Alice, May 18, [1891]
16. Elizabeth to Alice, June 16, 1892

CHAPTER XXII

1. Putnam, ed., *Mary Putnam Jacobi*
2. Anna to Henry, June 13, 1884
3–4. Henry to Samuel, Aug. 25, 1879
5. Anna to Henry, Feb. 9, 1880
6. Anna to Henry, Apr. 12, 1881
7. Anna to Henry, Jan. 8, 1883
8. Anna to Henry, Feb. 29, 1880
9. Elizabeth to Henry, Aug. 20, [1882]
10. W. B. Hodgson to Anna, Jan. 11, 1880
11. Anna to Henry, Apr. 12, 1881
12. Elizabeth to Henry, Aug. 20, [1882]
13. Marian to Elizabeth, Sept. 21, 1884
14. Anna to Marian, Sept. 26, 1885
15–16. Anna to Henry, Aug. 16, 1886

CHAPTER XXIII

1. Emily to Elizabeth, Aug. 12, 1878
2. Emily to Lucy Stone, Feb. 10, 1880
3. Alice to Kitty, Apr. 18, 1880
4. Alice to Kitty, Sept. 5, 1883
5. Elizabeth to Henry, Sept. 24, [1881?]
6. Emma to Marian, Feb. 6, 1881
7. Alice to Kitty, Oct. 14, 1883
8. Ellen to Kitty, Feb. 9, 1884
9. Ellen to Alice, Dec. 24, 1883
10. Emily to Alice, Oct. 17, 1883

11. Ellen to Henry, May 31, 1884
12. Ellen to Henry, Dec. 26, 1884
13. Elizabeth to Ellen, Jan. 24, 1885
14. Alice to Kitty, Oct. 14, 1883
15. Alice to Kitty, Sept. 9, 1888
16. Lucy Stone to Antoinette Brown, [1849?]

CHAPTER XXIV

1. Emily to Elizabeth, Aug. 13, 1881
2–3. Emily to Elizabeth, Oct. 2, 1881
4. Alice to Kitty, Sept. 10, 1882
5. Alice to Kitty, Sept. 12, 1880
6. Alice to Kitty, Aug. 14, 1877
7. Elizabeth to Henry, Oct. 6, [1882]
8. Elizabeth to Kitty, June 29, [1881]
9. Elizabeth to Kitty, July 1, 1881
10. Elizabeth to Kitty, Oct. 22, [1881]
11. Elizabeth to Kitty, Jan. 2 ff., 1887

CHAPTER XXV

1. Alice to Kitty, May 16, 1886
2. Alice to Kitty, Apr. 18, 1880
3. Alice to Kitty, Oct. 28, 1888
4. Alice to Kitty, Jan. 26, 1890
5. Alice to Kitty, Feb. 26, 1882
6. Alice to Kitty, May 29, 1880
7. Alice to Kitty, Sept. 10, 1882
8. Alice to Kitty, Nov. 21, 1886
9. Alice to Kitty, Jan. 7, 1883
10. Alice to Kitty, Nov. 1, 1885
11. Emily, *Woman's Journal,* Sept. 26 and Oct. 10, 1885
12. Alice to Kitty, May 2, 1886
13. Alice to Kitty, June 20, 1886
14. Ellen, *A Military Genius*
15. Alice to Kitty, Aug. 23, 1885
16. Alice to Kitty, Oct. 14, 1888

CHAPTER XXVI

1. Alice to Kitty, Apr. 8, 1888
2. Emily to Lucy Stone, Aug. 6, 1885
3. Alice to Kitty, Aug. 12, 1887

4. Alice to Kitty, Apr. 19, 1885
5. Alice to Kitty, Mar. 11, 1888
6. Alice to Kitty, Sept. 22, 1889
7. Kitty to Alice, Sept. 1885
8. Alice to Kitty, Apr. 14, 1889

CHAPTER XXVII

1. Elizabeth to Samuel, Aug. 15, 1885
2. Emily to Elizabeth, May 10, 1891
3. George to Elizabeth, Jan. 4, 1897
4. Elizabeth to Henry, Feb. 14, 1890
5. Anna to Henry, May 29, 1889
6. Anna to Henry, Feb. 2, 1894
7. Emily to Elizabeth, May 22, 1895
8. Elizabeth to Alice, Sept. 16, 1893
9. Kitty to Alice, Jan. 13, 1894
10. Kitty to Alice, Dec. 7, 1893
11. Ellen to Elizabeth, May 16, 1897
12. Kitty to Alice, Nov. 3, 1893
13. *Woman's Journal,* Oct. 14, 1893
14. Emily to Elizabeth, Aug. 15, 1894
15. Henry to Alice, Aug. 21, 1894
16. Marian to Henry, Sept. 6, 1896

CHAPTER XXVIII

1. Elizabeth to Kitty, Nov. 25, 1891
2. Lucy Stone to Antoinette, Sept. 18, 1890
3. Alice to Elizabeth, Jan. 11, 1891
4. Alice to Kitty, Dec. 14, 1890
5. Emily to Alice, Feb. 3, 1891
6. Ellen to Elizabeth, Jan. 5, 1894
7. Alice to Kitty, Apr. 26, 1897
8. Alice to Kitty, Nov. 26, 1897
9. George to Elizabeth, July 10, 1896
10. *Woman's Journal,* May 11, 1895
11. Alice to Kitty, June 28, 1894
12. Alice to Kitty, Feb. 1, 1891
13. Emily to Elizabeth, Aug. 11, 1896
14. Emily to Elizabeth, Feb. 6, 1896
15. Anna to Antoinette, June 28, 1893
16. Emily to Elizabeth, Oct. 8–9, 1898

CHAPTER XXIX

1. Elizabeth, "Influence of Women," *Essays,* Vol. II
2. Elizabeth, "Medical Responsibility," *Essays,* Vol. I
3. Elizabeth to Alice, Dec. 7, 1893
4. Elizabeth to Henry, Aug. 12, 1897
5. Elizabeth, "Why Hygienic Congresses Fail," *Essays,* Vol. II
6. Elizabeth, "Scientific Method," *Essays,* Vol. II
7. Elizabeth to Alice, June 30, [1901?]
8. Elizabeth, "Scientific Method," *Essays,* Vol. II
9. Elizabeth to Henry, Apr. 11, 1896
10. Anna to Elizabeth, June 9, 1897
11. Elizabeth to Henry, May 6, 1897
12. Anna to Henry, Jan. 31, 1897
13. Anna to Henry, May 16, 1897
14. Ellen to Elizabeth, Mar. 28, 1897
15. Anna to Henry, July 5, 1898
16. Elizabeth to Henry, Sept. 8, 1898
17. Emily to Elizabeth, Oct. 8–9, 1898

CHAPTER XXX

1. Alice to Kitty, Apr. 26, 1901
2. Henry to Elizabeth, Apr. 18, [1901]
3. Emily to Elizabeth, Oct. 8–9, 1898
4. Ellen to Henry, Apr. 13, 1898
5. Alice to Kitty, Apr. 29, 1898
6. Alice to Kitty, Apr. 10, 1898
7. Emily to Elizabeth, Oct. 8–9, 1898
8. Emily to Elizabeth, July 3, 1899
9. Elizabeth to Henry, Jan. 29, 1901
10. Emily to Elizabeth, Jan. 24, 1901
11. Emily to Elizabeth, Dec. 13, 1899
12. Emily to Elizabeth, Aug. 11, 1896
13. Emily to Elizabeth, Jan. 8, 1897
14. Alice to Kitty, July 12, 1900
15. Elizabeth to Henry, Nov. 8, 1901

CHAPTER XXXI

1. Mrs. Charles Whidden to author, Mar. 24, 1965
2. Alice to Kitty, Dec. 12, 1902
3. Emily to Elizabeth, Dec. 18, 1904
4. *History of Woman Suffrage,* Vol. V, p. 33

5. *History of Woman Suffrage,* Vol. V, p. 139
6. Henry to Alice, Sept. 5, 1905
7. Alice to Kitty, Sept. 7, 1909
8. *History of Woman Suffrage,* Vol. V, p. 277
9. Kitty to Alice, Mar. 8, 1912
10. Emily to Elizabeth, Apr. 2, 1908

BIBLIOGRAPHY

MANUSCRIPTS AND SPECIAL COLLECTIONS

Academy of Medicine
Arthur and Elizabeth Schlesinger Library on the History of Women in America, Radcliffe College
Boston Public Library
Bristol, England, City Archives
Bristol, England, Public Library
British Museum
Butler Library, Columbia University
Columbia University Medical Library
Hastings, England, Public Library
La Mairie, Triel-sur-Seine
Library of Congress
Miriam Y. Holden Library
Missouri Historical Society
New-York Historical Society
New York Infirmary
St. Bartholomew's Hospital Archives, London
Wellcome Historical Medical Library, London

BOOKS

Alsop, Gulielma Fell, *History of the Woman's Medical College, Philadelphia, Pennsylvania.* Philadelphia: Lippincott, 1950.

Anthony, Susan B., and Harper, Ida Husted, eds., *History of Woman Suffrage,* Vol. IV. Rochester: Susan B. Anthony, 1902.

Baker, E. Josephine, *Fighting for Life.* New York: Macmillan, 1939.

Ballantine, W. G., ed., *The Oberlin Jubilee.* Oberlin: Goodrich, 1883.

Barrows, Isabel C., *A Sunny Life, the Biography of Samuel June Barrows.* Boston: Little, Brown, 1914.

Beard, Mary R., *Woman as Force in History.* New York: Macmillan, 1946.

Benton, Josiah H., Jr., *What Women Did for the War, and What the War Did for Women.* Boston: 1894.

Bestor, Arthur Eugene, Jr., *Backwoods Utopias.* University Park: University of Pennsylvania, 1950.

Blackwell, Alice Stone, *Lucy Stone, Pioneer of Woman's Rights.* Boston: Little, Brown, 1930.
Blackwell, Alice Stone, ed., *Armenian Poems.* Boston: Roberts, 1896.
—— *The Little Grandmother of the Russian Revolution.* Boston: Little, Brown, 1917.
Blackwell, Anna, "Elizabeth Blackwell," *English Woman's Journal,* April 1, 1858.
—— "The Philosophy of Existence" (pamphlet).
—— *Poems.* London: Chapman, 1853.
Blackwell, Antoinette Brown, *The Island Neighbors.* New York: Harper, 1871.
—— *The Making of the Universe.* Boston: Gorham, 1914.
—— *The Philosophy of Individuality.* New York: Putnam, 1893.
—— *The Physical Basis of Immortality.* New York: Putnam, 1876.
—— *Sea Drift.* New York: White, 1902.
—— "Sex Injustice" (pamphlet). New York: American Purity Alliance, *circa* 1900.
—— *The Sexes Throughout Nature.* New York: Putnam, 1875.
—— *Studies in General Science.* New York: Putnam, 1869
Blackwell, Elizabeth, *Counsel to Parents on the Moral Education of Their Children.* New York: Brentano, 1883.
—— *Essays in Medical Sociology.* London: Bell, 1902.
Vol. I: The Human Element in Sex. Medical Responsibility in Relation to the Contagious Diseases Acts. Rescue Work in Relation to Prostitution and Disease. Purchase of Women: The Great Economic Blunder. Moral Education of the Young in Relation to Sex.
Vol. II: The Influence of Women in the Profession of Medicine. Erroneous Method in Medical Education. Why Hygienic Congresses Fail. Scientific Method in Biology. Christian Socialism. On the Decay of Municipal Representative Government. Address Delivered at the Opening of the Women's Medical College. The Religion of Health.
—— *Laws of Life.* New York: Putnam, 1852.
—— "A Letter," *Boston Medical and Surgical Journal,* May 29, 1850.
—— *Pioneer Work in Opening the Medical Profession to Women.* New York: Longmans, 1895.
—— *Wrong and Right Methods of Dealing with Social Evil.* London: Williams, 1883.
Blackwell, Elizabeth and Emily, *Address on the Medical Education of Women.* New York: Baptist and Taylor, 1864.
—— "Medicine as a Profession for Women" (pamphlet). New York: Tinson, 1860.

Blackwell, Henry B., "Silver Syndicate and Solid South" (pamphlet). October 10, 1896.
Blackwell, Sarah Ellen, *A Military Genius: Life of Anna Ella Carroll.* Washington, D.C.: Judd and Detweiler, 1891.
Bode, Carl, *The American Lyceum.* New York: Oxford, 1956.
Bolton, Sarah Knowles, *Famous Leaders Among Women.* New York: Crowell, 1895.
Braikenridge Collections for Bristol History.
Bridges, Flora, "Antoinette Brown Blackwell," *Oberlin Alumni Magazine,* March 1909.
Brisbane, Albert, *A Concise Exposition of the Doctrine of Association.* New York: Redfield, 1843.
The Bristol Riots, by a Citizen. Bristol: Gutch and Martin, 1832.
Brittain, Vera, *Lady into Woman.* New York: Macmillan, 1953.
Brooks, Van Wyck, *The Flowering of New England.* New York: Dutton, 1936.
Brown, William Symington, "The Capability of Women to Practise the Healing Art" (pamphlet). Boston: Ripley, 1859.
Bruce, H. Addington, *Woman in the Making of America.* Boston: Little, Brown, 1913.
Burton, Hester, *Barbara Bodichon.* London: Murray, 1949.
Burton, Kathleen, *Paradise Planters: The Story of Brook Farm.* New York: Longmans, 1939.
Butler, A. S. G., *Portrait of Josephine Butler.* London: Faber, 1954.
Catton, Bruce, *Glory Road.* Garden City: Doubleday, 1952.
Chilcott's Descriptive History of Bristol. Bristol: Chilcott, n.d.
Child, Mrs. D. L., *The History of the Condition of Women,* 2 vols. Boston: John Allen, 1835.
Circular of the Medical Institution of Geneva College Spring Course 1850. Rochester: 1849.
Commons, John R., and others, *History of Labour in the United States.* New York: Macmillan, 1946.
Cone, Helen Gray, and Gilder, Jeannette L., eds., *Pen-Portraits of Literary Women.* New York: Cassell, 1887.
"Copy of a Letter from Elizabeth Blackwell," *Boston Medical and Surgical Journal,* May 29, 1850.
Cross, Barbara M., ed., *The Autobiography of Lyman Beecher,* 2 vols. Cambridge: Harvard, 1961.
Daggett, Windsor, *A Down-East Yankee from the District of Maine.* Portland: Huston, 1920.

Dall, Caroline, ed., *A Practical Illustration of "Woman's Right to Labor"; or a Letter from Marie E. Zakrzewska, M.D.* Boston: Walker, 1860.

Daniel, Annie Sturgis, "A Cautious Experiment," *Medical Woman's Journal,* 1939, 1940.

Dannett, Sylvia G. L., ed., *Noble Women of the North.* New York: Yoseloff, 1959.

Deen, Edith, *Great Women of the Christian Faith.* New York: Harper, 1959.

Dickens, Charles, *American Notes.* London: Chapman, 1900.

Dictionary of American Biography.

Dictionary of National Biography.

Disturnell, John, *A Guide to the City of New York.* New York: Tanner and Disturnell, 1840.

Ditzion, Sidney, *Marriage, Morals and Sex in America.* New York: Bookman, 1953.

Dopson, Laurence, "Pioneer Women Doctors of Hastings," *Sussex County Magazine,* September 1950.

"Dr. Elizabeth Blackwell's Graduation, An Eye-Witness Account," *New York History,* April 1962.

Dunbar, Janet, *The Early Victorian Woman.* London: Harrap, 1953.

Encyclopaedia Britannica.

Encyclopedia Americana.

Essays and Studies in Honor of Margaret Barclay Wilson. New York: Columbia, 1922.

Farmer, Lydia Hoyt, ed., *What America Owes to Women.* Chicago: Moulton, 1893.

Fedden, Marguerite, *Bristol Vignettes.* Bristol: Burleigh, n.d.

Filler, Louis, *The Crusade Against Slavery, 1830–1860.* New York: Harper, 1960.

Fleming, Thomas P., "Dr. Elizabeth Blackwell on Florence Nightingale," *Columbia Library Columns,* No. 1, 1956.

Fletcher, Robert Samuel, *A History of Oberlin College,* 2 vols. Oberlin: 1943.

Fletcher, Robert Samuel, and Wilkins, Ernest H., *Bulletin of Oberlin College.* Oberlin: 1937.

Frothingham, Octavius Brooks, *Memoir of William Henry Channing.* Boston: Houghton, 1886.

Fuller, William, *A Brief Discovery of the True Mother of the Pretended Prince of Wales.* London: 1696.

Furnes, Clifton Joseph, ed., *The Genteel Female.* New York: Knopf, 1931.

Gillie, Annis, "Elizabeth Blackwell and the Medical Register from 1858," *British Medical Journal,* November 22, 1958.
Greenbie, Marjorie Barstow, *Lincoln's Daughters of Mercy.* New York: Putnam, 1944.
Greene, Asa, *A Glance at New York.* New York: Greene, 1837.
Groves, Ernest R., *The American Woman.* New York: Greenberg, 1937.
Gunther, John, *Roosevelt in Retrospect.* New York: Harper, 1950.
Hale, Sarah Josepha, *Woman's Record.* New York: Harper, 1855.
Halévy, Elie, *England in 1815.* London: Benn, 1949.
—— *The Liberal Awakening.* New York: Smith, 1949.
—— *The Triumph of Reform, 1830–1841.* New York: Smith, 1950.
Hamer, Philip M., ed., *A Guide to Archives and Manuscripts in the United States.* New Haven: Yale, 1961.
Harper, Ida Husted, *The Life and Work of Susan B. Anthony,* Vols. 1–2. Indianapolis: Bobbs, 1898; Vol. 3, Hollenbeck, 1908.
——, ed., *History of Woman Suffrage,* Vols. V and VI. New York: National American Suffrage Association, 1922.
Harvey, Sir Paul, compiler, *The Oxford Companion to Classical Literature.* London: Oxford, 1904.
—— *The Oxford Companion to English Literature.* New York: Oxford, 1937.
Hawthorne, Nathaniel, *American Note-Books.* Boston: Houghton, 1900.
—— *The Blithedale Romance.* Boston: Ticknor, 1852.
Hayes, Carlton J. H., *A Political and Social History of Modern Europe,* 2 vols. New York: Macmillan, 1922.
Hays, Elinor Rice, *Morning Star: A Biography of Lucy Stone.* New York: Harcourt, 1961.
Higginson, Mary Thacher, *Thomas Wentworth Higginson.* Boston: Houghton, 1914.
Hofstadter, Richard, Miller, William, and Aaron, Daniel. *The American Republic,* 2 vols. Englewood Cliffs: Prentice-Hall, 1959.
Holmes, Oliver Wendell, *Currents and Counter-Currents in Medical Science.* Boston: Ticknor, 1861.
Holtby, Winifred, *Women and a Changing Civilisation.* New York: Longmans, 1935.
Hume, Ruth Fox, *Great Women of Medicine.* New York: Random House, 1964.
Hurd-Mead, Kate Campbell, *A History of Women in Medicine.* Middletown, Connecticut: Haddam, 1938.
In Memory of Dr. Elizabeth Blackwell and Dr. Emily Blackwell. New York: Academy of Medicine, Record of Meeting, January 25, 1911.

James, Henry, *The Bostonians.* London: Lehmann, 1952.
Jex-Blake, Sophia, *Medical Women.* Edinburgh: Oliphant, 1886.
Johnston, Malcolm Sanders, *Elizabeth Blackwell and Her Alma Mater.* Geneva, New York: Humphrey, 1947.
—— "The Elizabeth Blackwell Tradition and Other Problems" (pamphlet). Geneva, New York: 1948.
Kerensky, Alexander, "Catherine Breshkovsky," *Slavonic Review,* 1934–1935.
Kerr, Laura, *Lady in the Pulpit.* New York: Woman's Press, 1951.
Knapton, Ernest John, and Derry, Thomas Kingston, *Europe 1815–1914.* New York: Scribner, 1965.
Kouwenhoven, John A., *The Columbia Historical Portrait of New York.* New York: Doubleday, 1953.
Latimer, John, *The Annals of Bristol in the Nineteenth Century.* Bristol: Morgan, 1887.
Lipinska, Mélanie, *Histoire des Femmes Médecins.* Paris: Jacques, 1900.
Lovejoy, Esther Pohl, *Women Doctors of the World.* New York: Macmillan, 1957.
Major, Ralph H., *A History of Medicine.* Springfield, Illinois: Thomas, 1954.
Malassigné, Louis (Maire de Triel), "Triel-sur-Seine" (mimeographed).
Manton, Jo., *Elizabeth Garrett Anderson.* New York: Dutton, 1965.
Marryat, Frederick, *A Diary in America.* Edited by Sydney Jackman. New York: Knopf, 1962.
Mathew's Annual Bristol Directory for the Year 1825.
Maxwell, William Quentin, *Lincoln's Fifth Wheel: The Political History of the United States Sanitary Commission.* New York: Longmans, 1956.
Meyer, Annie Nathan, ed., *Woman's Work in America.* New York: Holt, 1891.
"Minutes of the Board of Governors of Saint Bartholomew's Hospital." Unpublished, 1850.
"Minutes of the Medical Council of Saint Bartholomew Hospital." Unpublished, 1850.
Morse, John Torrey, Jr., *Life and Letters of Oliver Wendell Holmes.* Boston: Houghton, 1896.
Mozans, H. J., *Woman in Science.* New York: Appleton, 1913.
National Cyclopedia of America Biography.
National Union Catalog of Manuscript Collections. Washington, D.C.: Library of Congress, 1959–1964.
Nevins, Allan, *The Emergence of Lincoln.* New York: Scribner, 1950.

Nevins, Allan, and Commager, Henry Steele, *A Short History of the United States*. New York: Random House, 1945.

The New York Infirmary: A Century of Devoted Service, 1854–1954. New York: N.Y. Infirmary, 1954.

New York Infirmary for Women and Children, Annual Reports, 1866–1912. (14 years missing.)

Nicholas, James Hastings, *History of Christianity 1650–1950*. New York: Ronald, 1956.

Norwood, William Frederick, *Medical Education in the United States Before the Civil War*. University Park: University of Pennsylvania, 1944.

Notice sur L'Ancienne Abbaye de Port-Royal (mimeographed). Paris.

O'Connor, Lillian, *Pioneer Women Orators*. New York: Columbia, 1954.

Our Famous Women: An Anthology. Hartford: Worthington, 1884.

Palmer, R. R., and Colton, Joel, *A History of the Modern World*. New York: Knopf, 1965.

Parrington, Vernon Louis, *Main Currents in American Thought*. New York: Harcourt, 1939.

Paxson, Frederic L., *The New Nation*. Boston: Houghton, 1927.

Penny, Virginia, *How Women Can Make Money*. Philadelphia: Potter, *circa* 1862.

Plain Truths; or a Collection of Scarce and Valuable Tracts. (Evidence on the legitimacy of James II's son.) Undated. (Contemporary.)

Pioneer Women: An Anthology. London: Sheldon, 1925.

Putnam, Ruth, ed., *Life and Letters of Mary Putnam Jacobi*. New York: Putnam, 1925.

Randall, J. G., *Lincoln the President*, Vol. II. New York: Dodd, 1945.

Rivail, Hippolyte, *The Spirits' Book*. Translated by Anna Blackwell. Boston: Colby, 1875.

Robinson, Victor, "Elizabeth Blackwell," *Medical Life*, July 1928.

—— *Story of Medicine*. New York: New Home Library, 1944.

Ross, Ishbel, *Child of Destiny: The Life Story of the First Woman Doctor*. New York: Harper, 1949.

Rourke, Constance Mayfield, *Trumpets of Jubilee*. New York: Harcourt, 1927.

Sand, George, *Jacques*. Translated by Anna Blackwell. New York: Redfield, 1847.

Sanes, Samuel, "Elizabeth Blackwell: Her First Medical Publication," *Bulletin of the History of Medicine*, June 1944.

Schlesinger, Arthur Meier, *The American as Reformer*. Cambridge: Harvard, 1950.

—— *New Viewpoints in American History*. New York: Macmillan, 1922.
"The Social Palace at Guise." Unsigned. *Harper's Magazine,* April 1872.
Somerton, W. H., "A Narrative of the Bristol Riots," *Bristol Mercury,* undated.
Spector, Benjamin, ed., *One Hour of Medical History,* Vol. II. Boston: Beacon, 1932.
Squire, Belle, *The Woman Movement in America*. Chicago: McClurg, 1911.
Stanton, Elizabeth Cady, Anthony, Susan B., and Gage, Matilda Joslyn, *History of Woman Suffrage,* Vols. I–III. Rochester: Susan B. Anthony, 1881–1886.
Stoddard, Henry Luther, *Horace Greeley*. New York: Putnam, 1946.
Strachey, Ray, *"The Cause."* London: Bell, 1928.
Swift, Lindsay, *Brook Farm*. New York: Macmillan, 1900.
Tocqueville, Alexis de, *Democracy in America*. New York: Knopf, 1945.
Trevelyan, G. M., *English Social History*. New York: Longmans, 1942.
Trollope, Mrs. Frances, *Domestic Manners of the Americans*. New York: Knopf, 1949.
Truax, Rhoda, *The Doctors Jacobi*. Boston: Little, Brown, 1952.
Tyler, Alice Felt, *Freedom's Ferment*. Minneapolis: University of Minnesota, 1944.
Van Doren, Mark, ed., *The Portable Emerson*. New York: Viking, 1946.
Vaughan, E., "The Early Days of Elizabeth Blackwell." *Fortnightly Review* (London), 1913.
Vertanes, Charles A., "Alice Stone Blackwell, a Symposium," *Magazine of Armenian Affairs,* Spring 1950.
Victory—How Women Won It. A Symposium. New York: Wilson, 1940.
Vivian, Herbert, "James II at Saint-Germain," *Littell's Living Age,* December 14, 1895.
Waite, Frederick C., "Two Early Letters of Elizabeth Blackwell," *Bulletin of the History of Medicine,* Vol. XXI, 1947.
Webber, Everett, *Escape to Utopia*. New York: Hastings, 1959.
Whitteridge, Gweneth, *A Brief History of the Hospital of Saint Bartholomew*. London: Governors of the Hospital, 1961.
Whittier, Isabel, "Elizabeth Blackwell" (pamphlet). Brunswick, Maine: 1961.
Wittenmeyer, Mrs. Annie, *History of the Woman's Temperance Crusade*. Philadelphia: Earle, 1882.
Wollstein, Martha, "The History of Women in Medicine," *Woman's Medical Journal,* April 1908.
Woman's Medical College of New York Infirmary, Annual Catalogue and Announcement, 1870–1899.

Wood, Anthony, *Nineteenth Century Britain, 1815–1914*. London: Longmans, 1960.
Woodham-Smith, Cecil, *Florence Nightingale*. New York: McGraw-Hill, 1951.
Zakrzewska, Marie E., *A Woman's Quest*. New York: Appleton, 1924.
Zehender, Carl Wilhelm von, "Ueber den Beruf der Frauen zum Studium und zur Praktischen Ausübung der Heilwissenschaft" (pamphlet). Rostock: 1875.

PERIODICALS
The Harbinger
The Independent
The Liberator
New York Daily Herald
New York Daily Times
New York Daily Tribune
Pall Mall Gazette
Punch
The Revolution
Sartain's Union Magazine of Literature and Art
The Woman's Column
The Woman's Journal, 1870–1912
Woodhull and Claflin's Weekly

INDEX